What is Authentic
Educational Reform?

What is Authentic Educational Reform?

Pushing Against the Compassionate Conservative Agenda

Edited by

Helen L. Johnson • Arthur Salz

LEA Lawrence Erlbaum Associates
Taylor & Francis Group

New York   London

#137325015

Lawrence Erlbaum Associates
Taylor & Francis Group
270 Madison Avenue
New York, NY 10016

Lawrence Erlbaum Associates
Taylor & Francis Group
2 Park Square
Milton Park, Abingdon
Oxon OX14 4RN

© 2008 by Taylor & Francis Group, LLC
Lawrence Erlbaum Associates is an imprint of Taylor & Francis Group, an Informa business

Printed in the United States of America on acid-free paper
10 9 8 7 6 5 4 3 2 1

International Standard Book Number-13: 978-0-8058-6049-8 (Hardcover)

Visit the Taylor & Francis Web site at
http://www.taylorandfrancis.com

Contents

Dedication

Because we are afraid of speculative ideas we do … an immense amount of dead, specialized work in the region of "facts." We forget that such facts are only data; that is, are only fragmentary, uncompleted meanings, and unless they are rounded into complete ideas—a free imagination of intellectual possibilities—they are as helpless as are all maimed things and as repellent as are needlessly thwarted ones.

John Dewey (1931)

This book is dedicated to everyone's grandchildren, who lead us to see beyond the facts and to understand the possibilities of imagination.

Preface

This volume is a response to the compassionate conservative agenda for educational reform that seeks to improve American education by foisting on schools the business model first imposed during the 20th century. Spearheaded by the No Child Left Behind (NCLB) legislation, educational initiatives across the country increasingly focus on testing and test scores, reading programs that reward parroting of words rather than comprehension, a narrow view of curriculum and teaching, and a general inclination to solve educational problems "on the cheap." Within this national context of devaluing of learning in favor of performance skills, the "reforms" initiated in the New York City public schools over the past several years are particularly illustrative. Successful teachers are now required to teach scripted lessons and follow lockstep approaches to teaching that have vitiated their creativity and turned them into conduits for instruction that often has little relation to the lives, abilities, or interests of their students. All this has taken place against the backdrop of the relentless testing of children, forcing many a talented teacher to abandon important curriculum and ignore teachable moments in order to "teach for the test."

Challenging the compassionate conservative agenda, this volume includes a critique of its assumptions, examination of the problems that have riddled its implementation in the public schools, and strategies for authentic educational reform. The volume offers a mix of perspectives, drawing from educational theorists and researchers, and also from classroom teachers and parents.

In a very real sense, defining authentic educational reform comes down to "the vision thing." Our view of the responsibilities and promise of the educational enterprise shapes the goals we set for reform, and the criteria we use to judge its success. This volume addresses essential questions to be asked in defining our educational vision, and thereby an agenda for reform:

- What is the role of schools in the lives of children and families?
- How does the allocation of resources both support and limit educational programs and individual achievement?
- What outcomes are important in evaluating the effectiveness of teachers and the academic achievement of students?
- Do high stakes tests encourage achievement or reinforce barriers for less successful learners?
- What does it mean to prepare "an informed citizenry"?
- How does this goal relate to current concerns with American competitiveness in the global marketplace?
- How can schools ensure "equitable opportunity" for a diverse population?
- Is it possible to "level the playing field" by including all children in the same programs with the same expectations?
- How do we move beyond stereotypes to implement culturally competent educational practices?

This book does several things as it pushes against the compassionate conservative agenda. Section I offers an examination of the social and political contexts of current educational reform initiatives. In Chapter 1, Joel Spring chides both political parties for accepting the notion, without any supporting evidence, that the establishment of curriculum standards and the use of extensive testing, which are at the heart of NCLB, would bring about real educational reform in our schools. He further exposes the law as a vehicle for a host of right-wing agenda items dealing with sex education, military recruitment in the schools, privatization of school services, school prayer, phonics-based reading instruction, and other issues dear to conservatives. In Chapter 2, Sonia Nieto and Helen Johnson describe the hard educational times we are presently facing and the mean-spirited and hostile discourse dealing with public education, and explain why the simplistic and fatuous solutions posed by NCLB have a superficial appeal to poor and immigrant parents. They then demonstrate how, in reality, the so-called reforms of NCLB are particularly hurtful to minority and immigrant youngsters.

Section II explores the negative impact compassionate conservatism has had on educational policies and practices. In Chapter 3, Florence Samson and Clive Belfield examine in considerable depth the serious threat that NCLB poses for the future of public education with the very real possibility for the take-over of "failing schools" by private, for-profit companies. The dire consequences of high-stakes testing on children, parents, teachers, administrators and the curriculum are detailed by Patrick Johnson in Chapter 4. Chapter 5 by Mikki Malow-Iroff, Michael Benhar, and Sonya Martin takes a close look at this so-called reform and the impact it has had on children with disabilities.

Section III examines the ways in which children and teachers have been affected by the conservative educational agenda. In Chapter 6, Richard Meyer tells the heartrending story of Kesha, a first grader moving into reading and writing in a wonderfully progressive environment and, in sharp contrast, the way another creative teacher has been thwarted by the imposition of a rigid phonics program. This autocratic stifling of teacher prerogatives has implications, Meyer reminds us, that transcend the school classroom and impinge directly on the future of democracy in our nation. In a similar vein, Chapter 7 offers a report by Marcia Baghban and Harriet Li of a conversation among several teachers and an activist parent detailing the consequences of the authoritarian approach taken by the administration in the New York City schools, problems that are prototypical in schools coast to coast. This is followed in Chapter 8 by a highly critical look by Myra Zarnowski, Liba Engel, and New York City public school teacher Amie Backner at the elimination of important curriculum offerings, as schools desperately try to raise scores in reading and mathematics.

Section III turns at this point to policies and approaches that hold out hope for some amelioration of the misguided conservative agenda that dominates education today. Since 1993, the Campaign for Fiscal Equity (CFE) has fought against the discriminatory funding by New York State of its urban schools. This battle, which recently shifted from the courts to the political arena, is recounted by Susan Kirch and Molly Hunter (CFE attorney) in Chapter 9. In Chapter 10, Lisa Scott and Angela Love examine the considerable benefits that can accrue from close community-school relations. Penny Hammrich and Michelle Myers provide a model of equity in science education in Chapter 11 through a report of their work in the Sisters in Science Equity Reform Project.

Section IV explores avenues to implementing authentic educational reform. In Chapter 12, William Ayers admonishes us to follow the advice of Bertolt Brecht, who urged that, even in the darkest of times, we must keep on singing, at least about the dark times. Despite the current educational climate, Ayers insists we really look at each child behind the test score and the label to deeply appreciate each youngster's remarkable potential, to work alongside the child, and in this way to bring about a revolution in education. In Chapter 13, Susan Ohanian, a former New York City "Teacher of the Year," demands that we challenge a system that treats its teachers as anything less than professional. Along with Ayers, Ohanian urges that we truly become allies of all children by not allowing those who know so little about kids or schools dictate educational policy to us. In like manner, Professor Helen Johnson brings this volume to a close by asking what perhaps is the most important educational question: Where is the child in this effort to reform education, and where should concerns about how children grow and learn be in discussions about educational reform? This volume offers more questions than answers, but taken together, the questions constitute a foundation for refocusing reform efforts in directions that will truly strengthen American public education for all children and their families.

It has been difficult to finish this book, because almost every day brings another news story about problems that have arisen with federal and local educational "reform" initiatives. States like Connecticut have begun to challenge federally mandated testing because of the funding it diverts from educational services. Massive scoring errors have raised questions about how to monitor the $2 billion educational testing industry. Middle-class parents have begun to voice concern about the impact of testing on their children's educational experience. Public awareness of the problems with current educational policies is growing but needs to be met with a vision of constructive alternatives. The current volume offers a response to this need, in hopes of fostering a more informed and thoughtful public conversation about what constitutes authentic educational reform for a democratic and truly compassionate society.

Acknowledgments

This volume grew out of a conference on authentic educational reform that was held at Queens College in the fall of 2004. We are grateful to the teachers, parents, college faculty, other educational professionals, and community leaders who participated in that conference, and whose comments guided the preparation of this book. Naomi Silverman, at Lawrence Erlbaum Associates, worked with us from the initial stages of conference planning through the completion of the volume. Her insights, guidance, and generous availability throughout this extended effort are deeply appreciated. Erica Kica and Joy Tatusko, also at LEA, provided important support with preparation of the volume. We also are grateful to Alberto Bursztyn, Gerald Coles, Prisca Martens, Susanna P. Flaum and Paula Wolfe for their helpful comments on the initial draft. Neither the conference nor the volume would have been possible without the support and efforts of Malaika Abdul-Waheed, Wanda Alexis, Eileen Bowen, Raeann Farrell, and Daisy Sanchez. Finally, we wish to acknowledge the contribution of schoolchildren in New York City, whose experiences provided a substantive base for the exploration of issues in this book. It is our hope that this book will benefit them and their families by pointing the way to meaningful educational reform.

HLJ and AS

Contributors

William Ayers
University of Illinois
Chicago, Illinois

Amie Backner
New York City Public Schools

Marcia Baghban
Queens College
New York City

Clive Belfield
Queens College
New York City

Michael Benhar
Suffolk Community College
Brentwood, New York

Liba Engel
Queens College
New York City

Penny Hammrich
Queens College
New York City

Molly A. Hunter
Campaign for Fiscal Equity
New York City

Helen L. Johnson
Queens College & CUNY Graduate
Center
New York City

Patrick B. Johnson
Dowling College
Oakdale, New York

Susan A. Kirch
Queens College
New York City

Harriet Li
Queens College
New York City

Angela Love
Queens College
New York City

Micheline Malow-Iroff
Manhattanville College
Purchase, New York

Sonya Martin
Queens College
New York City

Richard J. Meyer
University of New Mexico
Albuquerque, New Mexico

Michelle Myers
Queens College
New York City

Sonia Nieto
University of Massachusetts
Amherst, Massachusetts

Susan Ohanian
New York State Teacher of the Year
Charlotte, Vermont

Arthur Salz
Queens College
New York City

Florence Samson
Queens College
New York City

Lisa J. Scott
Queens College
New York City

Joel Spring
Queens College
New York City

Myra Zarnowski
Queens College
New York City

What is Authentic
Educational Reform?

ARTHUR SALZ

This book sets out to demonstrate that in the field of education the appellation "compassionate conservative" is a contradiction in terms, and that the No Child Left Behind (NCLB) legislation of 2001, the vehicle allegedly designed to bring about educational reform is, in fact, counterproductive to the well-being of children, teachers, and our American schools. The prism that best refracts the difference between proponents and critics of NCLB has been developed by cognitive linguist George Lakoff. His thesis is that all important personal and political issues are ultimately determined by one's model of the idealized family, either that of the Strict Father making all decisions and establishing and enforcing standards and, on the other hand, the Nurturing Parent, one who engenders mutual, respectful communication and shared decision making. In the Strict Father model, the male adult has "the authority to set overall family policy. He teaches children right from wrong by setting strict rules for their behavior and enforcing them through punishment. ... He also gains their cooperation by showing love and appreciation when they do follow the rules." In contrast, the Nurturing Parent believes that "children become responsible, self-disciplined, and self-reliant through being cared for and respected .... The obedience of children comes out of their love and respect for their parents, not out of the fear of punishment." Two starkly different ways of looking at the family and, as Lakoff poses it, the crucial difference in one's worldview:

> The conservative/liberal division is ultimately a division between strictness and nurturance as ideals at all levels—from the family to morality to religion and, ultimately, to politics. It is a division at the center of our democracy and our public lives, and yet there is no overt discussion of it in public discourse (Lakoff, 2002).

This paradigm turns out to be a most fruitful way to analyze the conservative attempts to improve education in the United States. Following the Strict Father model, educational standards have been promulgated from the top down, with virtually no classroom teacher input. Based on these standards, and again without consultation with classroom practitioners, programs have been foisted on teachers to achieve these goals. Because NCLB is fundamentally a punitive law, designed to punish schools that fail to make Annual Yearly Progress (AYP), the consequences of not meeting these standards are dire, including the loss of students and funding and, eventually, the takeover of the school by a for-profit corporation. Even Brent Staples of the *New York Times*, an early and ardent proponent of NCLB, now admits that

> No Child Left Behind was based on the premise that embarrassing test scores and government sanctions would simply force schools to improve educational outcomes for all children. What has become clear, however, is that school systems … have no idea how to generate changes in teaching that would allow students to learn more effectively (Staples, 2005).

This Strict Father model often exhibits itself in autocratic leadership behavior, and prototypically has been on clear display in New York City. Indeed, in September 2003, the City's newly conceived Department of Education had a unique opportunity to bring about authentic educational reform. A new mayor had wrestled control of the schools from the ineffective central Board of Education and the uneven-performing local boards. An administrative structure was developed that promised to be more responsive to the needs of principals, teachers, parents, and children. A progressive literacy curriculum, pioneered at Teachers College, Columbia University, was to be instituted citywide, and a well-respected Chicago University mathematics curriculum was to be put in place in grades kindergarten through fifth grade. Further, an emphasis was placed on staff development, with the assignment of coaches in literacy and math. Under the new plan, school principals were to be given assistance with clerical work so that each could play a role as educational leader in his or her building. It all looked very promising.

What has happened since 2003 is, unfortunately, the worst educational debacle in the recent history of the New York City schools. Teacher morale is at its lowest in the 50 years that I have worked with the schools, with thousands of teachers planning to retire as early as possible. Teachers have come to believe that the Department of Education, through its daily actions, demeans the work they do and fails to recognize their role as professionals. Walk into almost any school these days, and you'll find demoralized teachers, fed up with scripted curricula that have been imposed on them, the inordinate amount of time spent prepping students for high-stakes tests, their inability to work creatively with their children, and the lockstep approach to education that is now demanded of them. They object to the rigid way new curricula have been implemented, and many resent that coaches meant to be helpful are, in many cases, there to keep them on task moving ahead to the next topic rather than in assisting them in meeting the needs of their children.

Nowhere was this autocratic behavior more evident than in City Hall in March 2004 when, as reported in the *New York Times*, Mayor Bloomberg ousted three members of his own Panel for Educational Policy who opposed his policy on the retention of failing third graders, replaced them with yes-persons, and rammed through a plan that ignored overwhelming research opposing this policy (*New York Times*, 2004; Winerip, 2004a). As with NCLB, we see the Strict Father threatening 8-year-olds and their parents with the consequence of being left back as a method of motivation. Indeed, underlying NCLB and educational policy throughout the country these days is the view that all participants have been malingering. If only principals, teachers, children, and parents would work harder, positive educational goods would accrue. And the way to bring this about is to threaten them with serious consequences: a critical note placed in the file of a teacher who is not on the correct workbook page; the youngster's horror of being left back and viewed as stupid by his peers; or the parents who worry about their child's future. And all this is couched as tough love. But it does not work, neither in the family as made quite clear by Lakoff, nor as an educational policy, as one examines the most recent evidence of the failure of NCLB (Lakoff, 2002; *New York Times*, 2005).

But Jim Wallis, political, social, and religious activist, cautions us that protest is not enough; there must be a positive alternative presented. "Protest should not be merely the politics of complaint .... It should instead show the way for both personal and social transformation. That's what excites people and invites them to give their lives for something larger than themselves" (Wallis, 2005). So, for the many of us who are committed to giving our "lives for something larger than ourselves," let us for a moment consider what education might look like if the Nurturing Parent model replaced that of the Strict Father. How might matters be different concerning teachers, children, parents, curriculum, learning, and motivation? First, the guiding question that would have to be constantly asked by everyone within the educational hierarchy from the Secretary of Education down is, What do you, the teacher, need so as to be able to guide learning even more effectively? How can I, the chancellor, the superintendent, the principal, help you in your work with children? A principal might have to wait a moment for a teacher to pick himself or herself up off the floor—so stunned by this request, which should seem so obvious to any manager or person exercising common sense. But when a climate is created that fosters this approach, teachers will recover very quickly and come in with their lists. Smaller class size? This should be a goal of every school system; it is unconscionable that classes in wealthy suburbs have 16 to 18 children while in less affluent areas teachers are working with more than 30 children in a class. Yes, the evidence is clear that class size makes a difference (Winerip, 2004b). But what else? New curriculum ideas? Yes, there are wonderful programs out there: the Teachers College literacy program, the TERC mathematics program, and a host of other resources that might provide curriculum frameworks for teachers or groups of teachers. The principal, who should be a master teacher, must continue playing the role of educational leader in the building, but in an advisory and supporting capacity, and staff development, designed by teachers based on their needs, must be available in abundance. Math and literacy coaches? Absolutely, but as colleagues who are solely responsible to the teachers with whom they work, not the administration. Teachers may also request more books on a social studies topic, assistance with classroom management issues, more manipulative materials for math or science, help with a particular child, etc. The specific items are less important than the creation of a climate in which teachers feel like professionals who, like other professionals, can seek help and support when appropriate.

And within this new climate our grossly oversized schools must be decentralized into small families of teachers and children, preferably around like-minded educational philosophies and approaches. There certainly is a rash of research in support of small schools nationwide, and this explains why the Bill and Melinda Gates Foundation has invested $51 million in creating small high schools in New York (Institute for Education and Social Policy, 2001). So let us encourage teachers and administrators to form minischools within their mammoth buildings. This approach grows out of the fundamental management principles often collectively known as Theory Z:

- People work best towards goals that they have helped establish.
- Once people have bought into goals, you can trust them to perform.
- If people share a common set of values, they can develop workable project goals.

So bring small groups of teachers with similar educational values and beliefs together, give them a degree of autonomy, challenge them to do great things with kids, and we will find them working harder than ever, because they now have a vested interest in the enterprise. Pie in the sky? No, just look at the large number of small, public alternative schools pioneered by the MacArthur "genius" award recipient Deborah Meier in New York and Boston, or other similar schools throughout the country. Here, like-minded, committed teachers work cooperatively in settings in which every child is known by every teacher, and democratic decision making leads to a shared commitment to education (Meier, 1995,

2002). This is precisely what Susan Ohanian is proposing (chapter 13 of this volume): the creation of environments in which teachers are treated as valued and skilled professionals and, if provided the rich resources, support, and guidance of a progressive department of education, will bring about authentic educational reform. So, yes, we must nurture teachers so that they can more effectively nurture children.

But one more piece of the educational puzzle must be attended to. Neither the Department of Education in Washington nor local schools boards can continue to enjoy the luxury of viewing their task as dealing only with children ages 5 to 18. Too many youngsters arrive at school struggling cognitively, socially, or emotionally, and these children are, too often, doomed to become school failures despite heroic efforts. Both at the national and local levels educational authorities must begin to take a systemic view of education, by coordinating efforts with appropriate health and social service agencies to ensure proper prenatal care for all expectant mothers, and complete medical coverage for all children from birth onward. In addition, new parents, grandparents, or primary caregivers must have the opportunity to voluntarily acquire the skills of educational parenting, such as reading to their children, engaging them in valuable conversation, playing educational games and organizing activities, providing positive discipline, and making use of the rich cultural resources in every city and town. This is commonplace in many countries of the European Union, where as soon as a woman becomes pregnant a trained professional begins biweekly visits to the expectant mother, offering her counsel during and after her pregnancy, and complete medical coverage is provided. A comparable program in the United States, the very successful Nurse-Family Partnership, which might serve as a model for our country, serves only 20,000 out of 2.5 million low-income children under the age of 2 (Boo, 2006; Nurse-Family Partnership, 2006). It is also common in the Scandinavian and many other industrialized countries for a parent to remain home with the newborn for a year or more while the government provides a substantial percentage of that parent's previous salary. In addition, each child receives fiscal support until he or she reaches 18 years of age (Reid, 2004). Further, offerings such as the Home Instruction Program for Preschool Youngsters (HIPPY), pioneered in Israel with its immigrant and indigent populations, should be made available to all parents. In HIPPY, local, neighborhood people, trained by the university, work alongside parents, teaching them how to provide the most supportive emotional and educational environment for their youngsters (HIPPY, 2006). And every child must have the advantage of Headstart or an excellent preschool program. So, yes, families, parents, primary caregivers, and children must be nurtured.

And although all these efforts still will not completely level the educational playing field, this concern for equity, this focus on the learning experiences of each child from birth through the completion of formal schooling, must inform all educational policy. The Nurturing Parent model holds the key to authentic educational reform. Further, it ensures the development of citizens who will strenuously resist the imposition of authoritarian practices, people who will value the democratic process in the way John Dewey envisioned (Dewey, 1916). This book, as it pushes against the conservative agenda, explores the necessity for authentic educational reform.

REFERENCES

Boo, K. (2006, February 6). Swamp nurse. *The New Yorker.*
Dewey, J. (2006). *Democracy and education.* New York: The Macmillan Company.
http://www.hippy.org.il/html.
Institute for Educational and Social Policy. (2001). *Final Report of the Evaluation of New York Networks for School Renewal.* New York: New York University; Steinhardt School of Education.
Lakoff, G. (2002). *Moral politics: How liberals and conservatives think.* Chicago: University of Chicago Press.
Meier, D. (1995). *The power of their ideas.* Boston: Beacon Press.
Meier, D. (2002). *In schools we trust.* Boston, Beacon Press.
New York Times (2004, March 16).
New York Times (2005, October 30).
http://www.nursefamilypartnership. Org.
Reid, T.R. (2004). *The United States of Europe: The new superpower and the end of American supremacy.* London: The Penguin Press.
Staples, B. (2005, November 21). *New York Times.*
Wallis, J. (2005). *God's politics: Why the right gets it wrong and the left doesn't get it.* San Francisco: Harper.
Winerip, M. (2004a, March 17). *New York Times.*
Winerip, M. (2004b, May 26). *New York Times.*

I

COMPASSIONATE CONSERVATISM: CURRENT MYTHS OF EDUCATIONAL REFORM

The authors of the No Child Left Behind (NCLB) legislation, apart from indecently appropriating the slogan of the venerable Children's Defense Fund, have foisted on the American people a plan for educational reform that is fundamentally flawed and that, since its passage in 2001, has created an atmosphere of bitterness and recrimination between the Department of Education and educators, legislators, and the public throughout the country. Joel Spring pulls no punches in labeling the NCLB legislation as "political fraud," and he is very clear in implicating both political parties in this endeavor. Although NCLB is President George W. Bush's signature legislation, it had the overwhelming support of the Democrats in Congress. How did that come about? What were the historical antecedents, dating back to the publication of *A Nation at Risk* in 1983, which led to passage of NCLB? How did this legislation, whose centerpiece is the "accountability package," come to contain a raft of right-wing social/educational policies including privatization of the schools, abstinence-based sex education, and support for constitutionally protected prayer in public schools, as well as the Boy Scouts of America's antigay policy? And ultimately, did Congress have any evidence that a standards-based curriculum coupled with continuous testing of children would reform education and provide, as an intended goal, workers for the global economy? Spring explores these many questions, and what he uncovers reveals the political machinations that substitute for rational analysis of educational issues.

In this climate, Sonia Nieto and Helen Johnson find "a mean-spirited and hostile discourse concerning public education today, a discourse that shows little respect for teachers, for the children they teach, and for learning." What are the sources of this atmosphere? Who has created it and who has profited from it? What competing visions of education are being debated, and what are the implications of each? Why do many poor and immigrant parents initially support both the goals and the methods of the NCLB legislation, and why is it so important that education professionals understand the response of these parents? But is NCLB, in fact, having a salutary impact on children with the greatest needs? Nieto and Johnson make very clear from the research evidence that on the contrary, a standards-based curriculum coupled with high-stakes testing has had the most detrimental effect on the very children it purports to help. But there are ways for educators to cope in this hostile and counterproductive climate, and Nieto and Johnson conclude with a passionate credo of one Massachusetts teacher's defense of public education and its quest for equality and social justice.

1

No Child Left Behind
As Political Fraud

JOEL SPRING

Political fraud is the best description of the No Child Left Behind Act of 2001. The legislation was bipartisan, with both Democrats and Republicans claiming that curriculum standards tied to high-stakes testing would result in educating workers who would be able to compete for the best paying jobs in the global economy. Since the 1980s, Democrats and Republicans have pushed an agenda of high-stakes testing and standards as the cure for America's economic woes. Bipartisan support of No Child Left Behind was emphasized at the 2004 Democratic convention when Pennsylvania's Democratic Governor Edward Rendell told the panel on Creating Higher-Skill, Higher-Wage Jobs at the 2004 Democratic National Convention, "You know, when Teddy Kennedy [Democratic Senator Edward Kennedy of Massachusetts] stood with George Bush and announced No Child Left Behind, I supported it because I believe our kids do need to be tested once a year, but only if after we test them we have the dollars to remediate" (Democratic Leadership Council, 2004).

During the 2004 presidential debates, both candidates expressed their belief that improved educational opportunity was the key to preparing workers for the global workforce. In response to the question during the third debate by moderator Bob Schieffer: "Mr. President, what do you say to someone in this country who has lost his job to someone overseas who's being paid a fraction of what that job paid here in the United States?" President Bush responded:

> I'd say, Bob, I've got policies to continue to grow our economy and create the jobs of the 21st century. And here's some help for you to go get an education. Here's some help for you to go to a community college. We've expanded trade adjustment assistance. We want to help pay for you to gain the skills necessary to fill the jobs of the 21st century. You know, there's a lot of talk about how to keep the economy growing. We talk about fiscal matters. But perhaps the best way to keep jobs here in

America and to keep this economy growing is to make sure our education system works (Commission on Presidential Debates, October 13, 2004).

During the second debate, Democratic presidential candidate John Kerry was asked by audience participant Jane Barrow: "Senator Kerry, how can the U.S. be competitive in manufacturing given—in manufacturing, excuse me—given the wage necessary and comfortably accepted for American workers to maintain the standard of living that they expect?" Kerry responded:

> Jane, there are a lot of ways to be competitive. And unfortunately again I regret this administration has not seized them and embraced them … . I want to fully fund education, No Child Left Behind, special-needs education. And that's how we're going to be more competitive, by making sure our kids are graduating from school and college. China and India are graduating more graduates in technology and science than we are … . That's how you create jobs and become competitive (Commission on Presidential Debates, October 8, 2004).

Where is the proof that standards linked to high-stakes testing will improve the ability of American workers to compete in a global labor market? There are no longitudinal studies that prove this relationship. Could high-stakes testing, which often leads to teachers teaching to the test, reduce students' creativity and their willingness to take risks? Maybe a reliance on high-stakes tests reduces the ability of future workers to creatively adapt to new working conditions. The point, of course, is that we do not know the long-term effects of an educational system driven by standards tied to high-stakes testing.

Maybe an emphasis on high-stakes testing only results in improving the ability of students to take standardized tests. A 2003 study conducted by Stanford's Center for Research in Education Outcomes found that the average gain for fourth and eighth graders in mathematics was higher in states using high-stakes testing as compared to states not giving much weight to test scores. In this study, high-stakes testing meant that states imposed important consequences on students as a result of their test performance. Of course, the Stanford study only measures performance on tests and not the long-term consequences of an educational system centered on test performance. It could be that where standardized testing is used for promotion between grades or for high school graduation, students simply learn better test-taking skills (Amrein & Berliner, 2002).

Contrary to the Stanford study, a 2004 report by Henry Braun of the Educational Testing Service concluded that "comparisons slightly favor the low-stakes testing states." Braun's conclusions were based on a reanalysis of an earlier study by A. Amrein and D. Berliner that found that "there is no evidence that states that implemented high-stakes tests demonstrated improved student achievement on various external measures such as performance on the Scholastic Aptitude Test (SAT), American College Testing (ACT), Advanced Placement (AP), or National Assessment of Educational Progress (NAEP)." In other words, students in states with high-stakes testing did not perform any better on college entrance examinations than students in states with low-stakes testing (Braun, 2004).

Again, the Braun study uses tests to measure the impact of tests. In reality, there is no evidence that high-stakes testing will improve the ability of American workers to compete in the global labor market. Is the imposition of high-stakes testing and standards as required by No Child Left Behind a political fraud? Should politicians impose an educational reform for which there exists no evidence that it will improve the quality of American schools and the skills of American workers?

Why did both political parties unite around No Child Left Behind as the answer to American economic problems? First, it should be noted that not all Republicans were happy with the legislation. Democratic Leadership Council's Andrew J. Rotherham claims, "They [Republicans] grudgingly acquiesced to the education bill only because it was a top White House priority. Republican Tom DeLay (Representative, Texas) confessed to Rush Limbaugh that he 'voted for that awful education bill' only to support President Bush. 'I came here to eliminate the Department of Education so it was very hard for me to vote for something that expands [it]'" (Rotherham, 2002). Those Republicans who were wary of the massive federal intervention in local schools called for by No Child Left Behind found solace, as I discuss later in this essay, in many of the other items included in the 670-page legislation.

Republican support for standards and testing dates back to the senior Bush presidency from 1988 to 1992. Bush senior's education program was prompted by the 1983 report *A Nation at Risk* issued during Ronald Reagan's presidency. *A Nation at Risk* contained the unproven and often-repeated claim that the poor quality of schools was responsible for the difficulties U.S. corporations were experiencing in competing in international markets. The report opened with alarming language: "Our nation is at risk. Our once unchallenged preeminence in commerce, industry, science and technological innovation is being overtaken by competitors throughout the world." Dramatically claiming that the poor quality of U.S. schools threatened the future of the nation, the report stated: "If an unfriendly foreign power had attempted to impose on America the mediocre educational performance that exists today, we might well have viewed it as an act of war" (National Commission on Excellence in Education, 1983).

Bush senior's answer to improving America's competitiveness in the world's economy was Goals 2000, which was officially announced at the President's Education Summit with Governors at the University of Virginia on September 27, 1989.

The governors were formally represented by the National Governors' Association, which was chaired by Republican Governor, and later Secretary of Education, Lamar Alexander. Moreover, very importantly for later Democratic support of testing and standards, the vice chairman was Governor and future President Bill Clinton of Arkansas. Emphasizing the themes of the global economy, academic standards, and testing, the joint statement issued in 1989 by the President and the National Governors' Association reiterated what was becoming an unquestioned assumption: "As a nation we must have an educated work force, second to none, in order to succeed in an increasingly competitive world economy" (The President's Education Summit with Governors, 1991a). Linking the global economy to national academic standards, the joint statement declared: "We believe that the time has come, for the first time in U.S. history, to establish clear national performance goals, goals that will make us internationally competitive" (The President's Education Summit with Governors, 1991a). The heart of the implementation strategy was an "Accountability Package," which would appear in an altered form as part of No Child Left Behind. The first part of the accountability package, and dear to the hearts of neoconservatives, was the creation of world-class standards by a national education goals panel that would "incorporate both knowledge and skills, to ensure that, when they leave school, young Americans are prepared for further study and the work force" (The President's Education Summit with Governors, 1991b). The second step was writing American achievement tests based on the world-class standards created by the national education goals panel. These voluntary tests were "to foster good teaching and learning as well as to monitor student progress" (The President's Education Summit with Governors, 1991b). No proof was offered that "world-class standards" and "American achievement tests" would make America more competitive.

Although Bush senior failed to implement the standards and testing part of Goals 2000, President Bill Clinton continued to press for testing and standards as the key to improving America's position in the world economy. Clinton included these educational proposals as part of the New Democratic Movement. The term "New Democrats" was coined by the Democratic Leadership Council, which Clinton chaired from 1991 to 1992. Formed in 1985 as an unofficial party organization, the council developed plans to move the Democratic Party to the center of the political spectrum. The council formed a think tank, the Progressive Policy Institute (PPI), to support scholars formulating the new centrist political position. Both groups continue to be important in formulating Democratic Party policies.

The New Democrats' educational program assumed that the plight of the modern worker in a global economy depends on rapidly changing job skills. This assumption resulted in an economic plan that relied on education policies. For instance, consider the following problems and answers discussed by New Democrats:

1. Unemployment—The answer: educational opportunities to learn job skills needed in the new global economy.
2. Workers trapped in low-income and dead-end jobs—The answer: educational opportunities to improve job skills.
3. People who are unemployed because of restructuring and downsizing—The answer: educational opportunities to gain new job skills for the information and global economy.
4. Increasing inequality in income and wealth—The answer: expanded educational opportunities for the middle class and poor.
5. Improving overall economy—The answer: reinventing U.S. public schools for the information age and educating workers and students in the skills needed to help the United States expand in the global economy. (Democratic Leadership Council and the Progressive Policy Institute, 1996)

The importance New Democrats gave to No Child Left Behind in fulfilling their educational and economic goals was exemplified by their reaction to the passage of the legislation. "How Bush Stole Education" was the title given by Andrew J. Rotherham to his article in the March 25, 2001, Democratic Leadership Council's *Blueprint Magazine*. Rotherham wrote, "When it was pointed out that Mr. Bush was appropriating many New Democratic education ideas, the Bush team cited it as evidence of their candidate's moderate credentials" (Rotherham, 2002). Rotherham went on to claim, "Mr. Bush's education agenda is largely a New Democratic one … . The new education bill, which is regarded widely as 'Bush's education initiative,' was largely written by Democratic Senators Joe Lieberman (Connecticut) and Evan Bayh (Indiana) along with other New Democrats" (Rotherham, 2002). Bemoaning the fact that No Child Left Behind was associated with President Bush and not the New Democrats, Rotherham asserted, "The president's coup undermines Democrats in crucial 2002 elections by perpetuating, to the delight of Republicans, a debilitating view of the Democratic Party as a tool of the teachers' unions" (Rotherham, 2002).

So what ideas did the New Democrats claim Bush and the Republicans had stolen? The Progressive Policy Institute claimed the ideas of holding schools, districts, and states accountable for achieving educational proficiency and "establishing school report cards to hold schools, districts and states accountable to parents and the public" (Progressive Policy Institute, 2001). The New Democrats argued that Bush stole the idea that school districts and states should be required to improve failing schools; this had been part of Al Gore's agenda during the 2000 election. Also, the institute claimed the ideas of "giving children in failing schools the right to transfer to another public school" and support of public charter schools. The Institute's press release on No Child Left Behind states:

PPI has been at the forefront of advancing the charter school concept to improve public education, spur innovation, expand parental choice and move our schools from a factory model public monopoly to a public education system premised on standards, choice and publicly accountable schools. Public school choice and charter schools give parents options and provide alternatives for students trapped in low-performing schools, while also preserving accountability (Progressive Policy Institute, 2001).

In other words, the New Democratic Coalition claimed responsibility for those parts of the legislation dealing with accountability, aid to low-performing schools, and public school choice. The council listed the following as New Democratic ideas in No Child Left Behind:

- Increased accountability and focus on results
- Establishes a comprehensive accountability system that requires schools and school districts to show results for all students, and annual progress for low-performing racial and ethnic groups
- Stronger professional development standards and training for teachers
- Required state and school district report cards
- Increased commitment to public school choice (House NDC, 2001)

If the New Democrats claimed the accountability, aid to low-performing schools, state school report cards, and charter-school sections of No Child Left Behind, then what were the exclusively Republican sections of the legislation? If the New Democrats were accurate about their contributions to the legislation, then Republican contributions were sections on privatization of school services, the use of faith-based organizations, phonics-based reading instruction, school prayer, English acquisition, traditional American history, and Boy Scout access to public schools. These items satisfied the desires of neoconservatives and religious-oriented conservatives in the Republican Party.

Some of the purely Republican concerns that found their way into No Child Left Behind are resulting in major changes in public schooling. For instance, consider the issue of privatization of school services. Privatization has been on the neoconservative agenda for many years. The assumption of neoconservatives is that private enterprise operating in a free market can produce better goods and services than enterprises operated by the government, including public schools (Spring, 2002). Allowing the hiring of for-profit companies to provide school services appears throughout the legislation.

In some cases, the language of the legislation bars local school districts from providing certain kinds of services. In 2004, Chicago and Boston school systems were not allowed to provide their own free tutoring to students in low-performing schools. The U.S. Department of Education's interpretation of the law, according to an *Education Week* article, specifies that "districts that miss their state's academic benchmarks are barred from using federal money to provide those supplemental educational services and must leave the tutoring to others—mainly private companies" (Reid, 2004). Summarizing an interview with Nina Shokraii Rees, the deputy undersecretary in charge of the federal Department of Education's office of innovation and improvement, *Education Week* reported that she "stressed ... that the law's guidelines are unambiguous. School systems that don't make the grade can't run tutoring programs using federal money, she said" (Reid, 2004).

Some critics claim that No Child Left Behind will result in the privatization of public schools. Clive Belfield of the National Center for the Study of Privatization in Education has provided a useful guide to for-profit companies in education. He differentiates between companies that operate for-profit schools and also sell school services, such as Edison and National Heritage; companies that provide curriculum and materials to home schools, such as White Hat Management; and vendors of supplemental services, such as tutoring, summer school, music, and sports. Belfield identifies the major for-profit education companies as Sylvan Learning systems, Edison Schools, Princeton Review, Kaplan, Club Z!, In Home Tutoring Services, Brainfuse.com, Kumon North American, and EdSolutions Inc. (Belfield, 2004).

Also, under No Child Left Behind, for-profit companies are allowed to operate charter schools. Some of these companies offer services to homeschoolers. In 2004, six for-profit charter school companies formed the National Council of Education Providers to lobby for more money for charter schools and charter-friendly regulations. Also, the group wants to launch a public relations campaign supporting for-profit charter schools. Michael J. Connelly, the chief executive officer of Mosaica Education, a New York City–based company and a member of the new council, commented:

> "There are people who don't believe there is a role for private business in public education. And for those people, we are going to get the word out that we are not Beelzebubs. This is not a satanic plot to destroy public education." The six companies forming the National Council of Education are Mosaica, Chancellor Beacon Academies, Edison Schools Inc., National Heritage Academies, and White Hat Management. Combined, the six companies have 14,000 employees serving 140,000 students in 24 states (Belfield, 2004).

Also, high-stakes testing has been turned over to for-profit companies. In the past, grade promotion and school graduation were dependent on grades given by teachers who wrote and scored their own tests. Now, the teacher is being replaced by a mammoth for-profit testing industry. *Education Week's* Lynn Olson reports, "The No Child Left Behind Act has spawned new opportunities—and challenges—

for an increasingly diverse testing industry. With all of the federal law's testing requirements, the Government Accountability Office estimates that states will have to spend between $1.9 billion and $5.3 billion in the next 6 years, depending on the types of tests used" (Olson, 2004). According to Olson's article, the primary contractors for preparing and scoring state tests are CTB/McGraw-Hill, followed by Harcourt Assessment and Pearson Educational Measurement. In addition, these companies are now selling services that prepare students to take their tests (Olson, 2004).

School prayer was another favorite Republican concern that found its way into No Child Left Behind. Until the 1990s, the Republican Party, and its chief religious supporter, the Christian Coalition, advocated a school prayer amendment to the U.S. Constitution. In 1994, after failing to achieve a school prayer amendment, the Christian Coalition called for a change in strategy. Rather than campaigning for school prayer, the decision was made to support an amendment for religious freedom. Ralph Reed, at the time head of the Christian Coalition, argued that an emphasis on religious freedom as opposed to the narrower issue of school prayer would appeal to a broader religious audience. The religious freedom amendment would guarantee the right of religious expression to all people in all public settings (Reed, 1996, pp. 117–118).

In addition, the Christian Coalition believed that a religious freedom amendment would protect the rights of students to express their religious beliefs in the classroom. For instance, a student would have the right to support creationism over evolutionary theory in science classes.

In supporting the religious freedom amendment, Reed described the case of a Tennessee high school student, Brittney Settle, who was failed for turning in an essay on the life of Jesus Christ. Without citing the details of the case, Reed claimed that a federal court upheld the right of the school to flunk the student for her religious beliefs. In reaction to the case, Reed stated, "A religious freedom amendment would protect her, along with unbelieving students who are nervous about being compelled to participate in mandatory religious exercises in public schools" (Reed, 1996, pp. 117–118).

A religious freedom amendment was never achieved, but it did find its way into No Child Left Behind, which requires the following:

> The Secretary [U.S. Secretary of Education] shall provide and revise guidance, not later than September 1, 2002, and of every second year thereafter, to State educational agencies, local educational agencies, and the public on *constitutionally protected prayer* [author's emphasis] in public elementary schools and secondary schools, including making the guidance available on the Internet (No Child Left Behind Act of 2001, Public Law 107-110, 2002).

Dated February 7, 2003, a U.S. Department of Education guide reminds local education agencies that they must report that their schools have "no policy that prevents, or otherwise denies participation in, constitutionally protected prayer in public schools as set forth in this guidance." The guidelines state:

> Although the Constitution forbids public school officials from directing or favoring prayer, students do not "shed their constitutional rights to freedom of speech or expression at the schoolhouse gate," and the Supreme Court has made clear that "private religious speech, far from being a First Amendment orphan, is as fully protected under the Free Speech Clause as secular private expression." Moreover, not all religious speech that takes place in the public schools or at school-sponsored events is governmental speech. For example, "nothing in the Constitution … prohibits any public school student from voluntarily praying at any time before, during, or after the school day," and students may pray with fellow students during the school day on the same terms and conditions that they may engage in other conversation or speech. Likewise, local school authorities possess substantial discretion to impose rules of order and pedagogical restrictions on student activities, but they may not structure or administer such rules to discriminate against student prayer or religious speech (U.S. Department of Education, 2003).

Opposition to concerns about gay rights, another traditional Republican concern, appeared in No Child Left Behind as the Boy Scouts of America Equal Access Act. In the 1990s, the decision by the Boy Scouts to deny membership to gay adolescents was extremely contentious. In 2000, the U.S. Supreme Court ruled in *Boy Scouts of America v. Dale* that the Boy Scouts was a private association and had the right to set its own standards for membership and leadership. As a result, school districts across the country banned the Boy Scouts from using school facilities because they discriminated against gay adolescents. In the Scouts of America Equal Access Act of No Child Left Behind, public schools receiving funds under the legislation are prohibited from denying Boy Scouts use of school facilities. The legislation states,

> Notwithstanding any other provision of law, no public elementary school, public secondary school, local educational agency, or State educational agency that has a designated open forum or a limited public forum and that receives funds made available through the Department shall deny equal access or a fair opportunity to meet to, or discriminate against, any group officially affiliated with the Boy Scouts of America (No Child Left Behind Act of 2001, Public Law 107-110, 2002).

Abstinence-based sex education is another traditional concern of Republicans. The 2004 Republican Platform advocated abstinence education:

We support efforts to educate teens and parents about the health risks associated with early sexual activity and provide the tools needed to help teens make healthy choices. Abstinence from sexual activity is the only protection that is 100 percent effective against out-of-wedlock pregnancies and sexually transmitted diseases, including sexually transmitted HIV/AIDS. Therefore, we support doubling abstinence education funding. (Republican Platform Committee, 2004)

No Child Left Behind explicitly prohibits the distribution of federal funds to schools that "provide sex education or HIV prevention education in schools unless that instruction is age appropriate and includes the health benefits of abstinence." Also, schools are prohibited from operating "a program of contraceptive distribution" (No Child Left Behind Act of 2001, Public Law 107-110, 2002).

In summary, the Republican religious agenda was piggybacked on legislation that primarily emphasized accountability and standards. Also, it is important to note that the overall legislation was justified by the unproven claim that high-stakes testing and standards will improve schools or make American workers more competitive in the global labor market. This is political fraud!

REFERENCES

Amrein, A., & Berliner, D. (2002). *The impact of high-stakes tests on student academic performance: An analysis of NAEP results in states with high-stakes tests and ACT, SAT, and AP test results in states with high school graduation exams.* Educational Policy Studies Laboratory, Education Policy Research Unit. Retrieved September 29, 2004, from http://edpolicylab.org.

Belfield, C. (2004). *The business of education.* National Center for the Study of Privatization in Education. New York: Teachers College, Columbia University. Retrieved October 15, 2004, from http://ncspe.org.

Braun, H. (2004). Reconsidering the impact of high-stakes testing. *Education Policy Analysis Archives, 12*(1). Online publication retrieved September 23, 2004, from http://epaa.asu.edu/epaa/v12n1.

Commission on Presidential Debates. (2004, October 8). The Second Bush-Kerry Presidential Debate, Debate Transcript. Retrieved December 2, 2004, from http://www.debates.org/index.html.

Commission on Presidential Debates. (2004, October 13). The Third Bush-Kerry Presidential Debate, Debate Transcript. Retrieved December 2, 2004, from http://www.debates.org/index.html.

Democratic Leadership Council. (2004, July 28). *How a 21st Century Party Can Promote 21st Century Jobs. Panel II: Creating Higher–Skill, Higher–Wage Jobs.*

Democratic Leadership Council and the Progressive Policy Institute. (1996). *The new progressive declaration: A political philosophy for the information age.* Retrieved October 13, 2004, from http://www.ndol.org/print.cfm?contentid=839.

Democratic National Convention, Boston, Massachusetts. Retrieved October 23, 2004, from http://www.ndol.org/print.cfm?contentid=252833.

House NDC, Press Release, December 13, 2001, New Dems hail final approval of Education Bill. Retrieved September 23, 2004, from http://www.ndol.org/print.cfm?contentid=250063.

National Commission on Excellence in Education. (1983). *A nation at risk: The imperatives for educational reform.* Washington, DC: Department of Education.

No Child Left Behind Act of 2001, Public Law 107-110 (January 8, 2002). Retrieved September 15, 2003, from http://www.ed.gov/policy/elsec/leg/esea02/107-110.pdf.

Olson, L. (2004). NCLB law bestows bounty on test industry, *Education Week, 24*(14), 1, 18–19.

Progressive Policy Institute. Press Release, December 12, 2001, Education reform legislation reflects ideas proposed by PPI. Retrieved October 15, 2004, from http://www.ndol.org/print.cfm?contentid=250069.

Reed, R. (1996). *Active faith: How Christians are changing the soul of American politics.* New York: Free Press.

Reid, K.S. (2004). Districts spar with Ed. Dept. over tutoring: Chicago, Boston argue they should be allowed to help. *Education Week, 24*(10), 3.

Republican Platform Committee. (2004). *2004 Republican platform: A safer world and a more hopeful America.* Retrieved September 14, 2004, from http://msnbcmedia.msn.com/i/msnbc/Sections/News/Politics/Conventions/RNC-2004platform.pdf.

Rotherham, A.J. (2002). How Bush stole education. *Blueprint Magazine.* Retrieved October 13, 2004, from http://www.ndol.org/ndol_ci.cfm?contentid=250319&kaid=110&subid=900023.

Spring, J. (2002). *Political agendas for education: From the religious right to the Green Party* (2nd ed.). Mahwah, NJ: Lawrence Erlbaum Associates.

The President's Education Summit with Governors. (1991a). *America 2000: An education strategy.* Washington, DC: U.S. Government Printing Office.

The President's Education Summit with Governors. (1991b). *For today's students: Better and more accountable schools.* Washington, DC: U.S. Government Printing Office.

U.S. Department of Education. (2003). *Guidance on constitutionally protected prayer in public elementary and secondary schools.* Retrieved September 15, 2004, from http://www.ed.gov/policy/gen/guid/religionandschools/prayer_guidance.html.

2

The Sociopolitical Context of No Child Left Behind: Hard Times and Courageous Responses

SONIA NIETO AND HELEN L. JOHNSON

These are hard times for education. These are hard times for those of us who help prepare teachers for our nation's classrooms, for teachers who care about their students, for the students themselves, and for many families, especially those who have not benefited from public education. These include those raised in poverty, others who have come to this country as immigrants, and those who have suffered the consequences of racism and other institutional barriers. In what follows, we describe some of the ways in which these are hard times for education, times in which the rhetoric of democracy clashes with the rhetoric of No Child Left Behind (NCLB).

THE RHETORIC OF NCLB

There is a mean-spirited and hostile discourse concerning public education today, a discourse that shows little respect for teachers, for the children they teach, and for learning. The increasing emphasis on scripted curricula presumes that teachers cannot be trusted to make sound choices about how best to work with the children in their classrooms. The push toward standardized instruction reinforces the view of teachers as poorly educated and poorly prepared to do their jobs. Professional development experiences for teachers increasingly consist of training in the implementation of specific instructional activities; teachers are expected to be implementers rather than shapers of curriculum, technicians rather than professionals. At the same time as appreciation for teachers as professionals has eroded, respect for children as learners has also diminished. The emphasis on high-stakes testing assumes that children will not attend to learning without the threat of negative consequences for "low achievement."

These are hard times for education in the United States because public education has shamelessly appropriated the principles, the words, and the metaphors of the business world: The school is a "market," students and families are "consumers," and teachers are "producers." The federal No Child Left Behind legislation imposes this model on public education nationwide (see Spring, chapter 1 of this volume). Learning has been reduced to a series of discrete pieces of academic skill that can be fully described with quantitative terms, such as scores. There is no discussion of learning as a process of reasoning, problem solving, and creativity. There is no place in this model for the "release of imagination" described by Greene (2001, p. 30). In this discourse, "accountability" is the major buzzword, teacher tests are the answer to "quality control," and high-stakes tests are the final measure of student learning. As a result, public schools are challenged by countless privatization schemes (see Samson & Belfield, chapter 3 of this volume), including vouchers, tuition tax credits, so-called choice, and by charter schools, even though such alternatives may further disadvantage those who have the least advantages.

These are hard times for education in the United States because the marketization of education has been associated with an increasing focus on schooling as job training, and education as a vehicle to serve limited self-interests and consumerism. As a result, less attention than ever is being paid to education as a way to expand the human spirit and to create a better world. Students are being barraged with information but not allowed to explore the uses and applications of what they are learning. With learning defined solely in terms of units of information, without any consideration of the learner's capacity to use the information constructively, classrooms have become ostensibly objective, value-free reference rooms. The push for curriculum standards and standardized assessments is motivated by the need to bolster this view of classroom practices as equitable and inclusive. The difficulty with this approach, however, is that knowledge is always shaped by the process of learning, as well as by the participants, both teachers and learners, in the process. To assert objectivity and fairness or equity based on standardization denies the unique contributions and characteristics of the human beings involved in classroom processes.

Finally, these are hard times for American public education because the prevalent discourse defines learning as little more than rubrics, benchmarks, "best practices," and test scores. The emphasis on teaching "just the facts" aligns well with the push for national standards and high-stakes tests that ignore individual differences in students' resources and experiences. In this way, decontextualized models of learning restrict opportunities to develop students' engagement by drawing upon their funds of knowledge, and result instead in a proliferation of the "dead knowledge" that Whitehead (1929) described. Students are not encouraged to be active shapers of their learning; rather, they are guided to become compliant participants in the schooling process.

It is true that public schools have *never* really been the "great equalizer" envisioned by Horace Mann. However, in the present climate, there is not even a pretense that they should be. There has always been a lot wrong with how public education is implemented, but the language used to describe it has been one of hope and high ideals. This is not the case anymore. The shift to business terminology and procedures has led to a focus on "outcomes" rather than on "children's learning." The emphasis on accountability has led to a negative national discourse regarding education. Test scores are examined as "objective assessments" of student and school achievement. Instead of collaboration between groups that together could accomplish much good on behalf of American children, there has been an escalation of finger-pointing. Politicians blame teachers and schools of teacher education, while teachers blame parents and children.

COMPETING VISIONS OF EDUCATION

In spite of its limitations, the one thing that had been true of public education until now is that it largely was viewed as a beacon of hope by poor people, who saw it as the only option their children had. For many generations, public schools offered children of poverty-stricken and immigrant populations the opportunity to move into the mainstream of American society. Parents believed that schooling would make a positive difference in their children's lives and that public schools would provide their children with access to the activities and advantages of the American middle class. This faith in American public schools has eroded, however, as poor and immigrant parents have encountered teachers and administrators who dismiss their children's academic potential and needs, and who do less for their children because of their family backgrounds. The perception that schools do less for children considered outside the mainstream culture is part of the appeal of NCLB. Many immigrant and poor parents would like schools to show more concern for their children's academic achievement. The language of NCLB addresses these parents' concern by holding schools accountable in very specific, quantified ways.

Despite how challenging these times are for education, however, they are also hopeful times. There are two current—and competing—discourses concerning teaching and public education today. One is the "official" discourse embodied in NCLB language discussed earlier. This discourse focuses on accountability, standards, credentials, and testing, and it is accompanied by punitive measures for failing to live up to them. The other is the "discourse of possibility," that is, a way of thinking about teaching and learning that is embraced largely by teachers and families and others who view public education as an unfulfilled but nevertheless significant project in the quest for equality and social justice.

This "unofficial" discourse of possibility is visible in organizations such as Rethinking Schools and Teaching for Change, among others. In these groups, teachers, teacher educators, and community members have sought to strengthen public education by grappling openly and collaboratively with the complex issues involved in providing respectful and equitable educational experiences for all children in all communities. This discourse is also evident in the attempts by a growing number of teachers and administrators to reframe professional development so that it focuses on issues identified by teachers and families as worthy of attention, rather than on bureaucratic solutions to difficult problems. It is also reflected in the growing number of books and articles that focus on the positive and uplifting work of teachers and others who champion public education and that defy the current damaging climate in education (Freedman et al, 1999; Intrator, 2003; Irvine, 2003; Ladson-Billings, 2001; Nieto, 2005; Palmer, 1998; Rose, 1995).

Given these competing discourses, it is important to consider how different people might view NCLB and why. NCLB is a symptom of the times. But it is not simply a project of the radical right to hijack public education, although, of course, there may be elements of this in the legislation, as Spring (chapter 1 of this volume) so rightly points out. But it is not only the radical right that supports NCLB. Many economically disadvantaged families support NCLB and what it stands for, not because they do not believe in public education but because they do. And we need to understand this. These are families whose children have been shafted time and again by the public schools. Far too often, parents living in poverty or who have recently immigrated to this country have encountered public school teachers and administrators who have written off their children because of their very identities. Far too often, these parents' attempts to advocate on behalf of their children have been dismissed as "ignorant" or "uninformed" because they were presented in English that was less than perfect, or because they made school personnel uncomfortable. And it is not only parents who have experienced this disparity in expectations for children because of their non-mainstream backgrounds. Many teachers committed to providing meaningful educational opportunities for all their students find themselves labeled as "naïve idealists" or "Pollyanas" by their peers, who insist that unless children have the "proper" family background, schools can do little to improve their academic achievement. That is why a few of the best, most courageous, and most talented teachers actually support NCLB and high-stakes testing.

We need to understand the perspectives of the families whose children have always been left behind. Rather than simply lash out at high-stakes tests, we need to propose alternatives. It is difficult to argue with NCLB's stated goal of improving academic achievement for all children. But it is clear that NCLB is not doing what it proposed to do: level the playing field and raise standards for all children. On the contrary, NCLB has produced a chilling climate for teachers, students, and families, and this is especially true for those whom NCLB was supposed to help.

THE CLIMATE CREATED BY NCLB

Where can we see this chilling climate? Each edition of *Education Week* includes examples of the dilemmas confronting teachers, students, and families because of NCLB. In the state of Massachusetts alone, this climate is apparent at multiple levels. Consider the following data, most of which are drawn from a good friend and colleague, Anne Wheelock (Wheelock, 2000). These data indicate that since the Massachusetts Comprehensive Assessment System (MCAS) testing and graduation requirements took effect in Massachusetts, the following have been the consequences:

1. The high school attainment gap has grown wider. Compared to earlier years, on-time graduation rates for all groups declined for the class of 2003 (from 78% in 1994 to 72.4% in 2003). Then the rate bounced back to "normal" levels for white students in the class of 2004. But Latino and African American graduation rates for the post-MCAS classes of 2003 and 2004 remain the lowest in 10 years. Rates for African American students declined from a not-very-impressive 67.3% in 1994 to an even worse 58.9% in 2004; for Latinos, the numbers are even bleaker: Latinos' graduation rates dropped from a dismal 51.5% in 1994 to an even more depressing 45.7% in 2004. This means that more than half of all Latinos in Massachusetts are not graduating.
2. Grade retention rates for Latinos have worsened. Latino students make up about 9% of students enrolled in K-12 in Massachusetts, but they represent 23% of students not promoted every year. Overall, retention increased 6% from 1997–1998 and 13% from 1998–1999 (coinciding with the first and second years of MCAS testing).
3. Student exclusions have risen, and exclusion rates for Latino and African American students significantly exceed those for white and Asian students. In Massachusetts, student exclusion is defined as the removal of a student from participation in regular school activities for disciplinary purposes permanently, indefinitely, or for more than 10 school days. On September 22, 2003, the Massachusetts Department of Education released the state's annual report on student exclusions. Exclusion rates in Massachusetts rose 15% from 2000–2001. Exclusion rates for Latino students (4.6) and African American students (5.1) are more

than 5 times the rate for white students (0.9) and nearly 5 times the rate for Asian students (1.3).

4. Access to excellent education has been limited. There has been a steady and dramatic decline in African American and Latino enrollment at Boston Latin School (the premier public school in Boston). Between 1996–1997 and 2003–2004, enrollment of African American and Latino students at Boston Latin School dropped by nearly half. About 7 years ago, approximately 1 out of every 3 students at Boston Latin was African American or Latino. Last year, approximately 1 out of every 6 students at the school was African American or Latino.

5. Proportionately fewer Latino and African American students are included in MCAS testing. Grade 10 MCAS gains are often due to a smaller number of students taking the test. In a number of poor districts with high number of Latino and African American students, a lower rate of students taking the tests contributes to the widely touted gains. The least-resourced districts in the state are squeezing out higher pass rates at the expense of their most vulnerable students. This is true in Holyoke, Chelsea, and Springfield (where half the students originally in the class of 2006 did not make it to the tenth-grade testing). One out of four African American students and one out of three Latino students from the class of 2006 were not included in 2004 MCAS testing. This corresponds to findings reported by the *New York Times* regarding the pressure New York City schools exert on "low-performing students" to remove themselves from the testing pool.

TEACHING IN THE ERA OF NCLB

The "chilling climate" of NCLB is also very evident in the classrooms of teachers across the country, where the push is on to improve scores. This is especially true in poor districts with poor scores. As Zarnowski, Backner, and Engel point out (chapter 8 of this volume), any material or subject that is not going to be tested is neglected, or not covered at all. In this way, the educational experience of children in poor districts is impoverished not only by lack of resources, but by curricular choices that constrain learning. Wealthier districts with higher scores have less to worry about, although they too feel the pressure to "teach to the test."

Both experienced and novice teachers feel the effects of NCLB on their work. The relentless emphasis on test scores and academic achievement has changed the role of teachers in their classrooms. Some of the effects are quite overt, others more subtle. Some of these effects are described in the following text:

- Constraining the curriculum: Every teacher we speak with tells us how his or her curriculum has been negatively affected by the pressure to teach test-related material and strategies. Content is restricted to material covered by the tests, and areas that are not tested (often this includes science, social studies, and the arts) are not being taught.
- Less innovation, more towing the line: Teachers are not encouraged to develop creative classroom experiences, or to respond spontaneously to the teachable moments that arise within the classroom. Instead, teachers are praised and rewarded for adhering rigidly to the script and timeline of standardized curricula that have been aligned with the standardized tests.
- Less collegiality, more competition: The NCLB model of accountability is essentially punitive, emphasizing the negative consequences of poor performance. Teachers understandably feel vulnerable and threatened. These feelings do not encourage openness and sharing; they result in defensive and unilateral responses.

FAMILIES AND NCLB

The messages of NCLB to families regarding public education have been particularly destructive. The insidious undercurrent in this discourse is the failure to acknowledge the chronic and disproportionate underfunding of public schools for children in poor districts. Instead, NCLB affirms families' beliefs that public schools have not done all that they can or should on behalf of children outside the mainstream middle-class culture. But rather than leading families to hope for more and better from public schools, NCLB focuses attention on test scores that can have serious negative consequences for children. Increasingly, this leads families to believe that to safeguard their children's futures, they must seek alternatives to public education through charter and private schools. But as Samson and Belfield point out (chapter 3 of this volume), there is really very little evidence that these options will prove more beneficial.

The result? In the words of Anne Wheelock (2000), "In Massachusetts, education reform has become synonymous with improving MCAS scores. The use of MCAS score changes as the sole measure of school performance, in turn, distracts educators, parents, the public, and local policymakers from an examination of other indicators of school success."

MOVING TOWARD AUTHENTIC REFORM

What can people do and what have they been doing to counter the consequences of NCLB? The challenge for teachers, teacher educators, policymakers, and parents is to push for reform that does not reduce learning to numbers or educational progress to changes in test scores. How can we do this? Across the country, there are teachers who are implementing authentic education reform by

- Thinking creatively through the standards.
- Teaching how to take tests while opposing them.
- Teaching students what Lisa Delpit calls the "codes of power" about the tests by engaging students in considering such questions as: Why do students have to take these tests? For whose benefit are they given? Who benefits? Who loses? How? What can we do about this?

An eloquent example of the kinds of strategies that teachers have been using is offered by Bill Dunn, a high school teacher in a vocational high school in Massachusetts. Bill, more than many others, knows what it means to teach students who have been marginalized and dismissed, and he is angry about NCLB, MCAS, and other high-stakes ventures that further alienate students of color and students of all backgrounds who are economically disadvantaged. Bill wrote about this in an essay for *Why We Teach* (Nieto, 2005, pp. 180–182), and an excerpt from his essay follows:

Over the last ten years my state has very rigidly defined what it means to be an educated student in a Massachusetts public school. There are clear winners and clear losers. Unfortunately even the kids who pass the test in my school are considered losers because it usually takes them three or four tries to pass the test. Schools throughout the state have been forced to goose-step to the beat of mandated exams, and the result is continuous drill, and in urban schools that drill often goes on for three to four years. Gone are the interesting ideas and intellectual curiosity that made it a pleasure to teach. They have been replaced with the stress of doing the same thing over and over again. Eventually it will be evident that it's a lousy deal for society as well because uninterested kids on the street often cross the line from victim to victimizer.

The major source of stress [in teaching] over the past ten years has come from unexpected places, and the most insidious thing about the march to higher standards and "high stakes" testing is that those leading the charge purport to be doing it on behalf of the students in "underperforming" schools like mine. No Child Left Behind translates into horrendous dropout rates between freshman and senior year; and in schools like mine thirty to forty percent of the students who continue through senior year are still left behind through little fault of their own. The rhetoric of education reform is in itself appalling. Headlines such as "State Threatens Takeover of Underperforming Districts" should insult everyone, not just those students, parents and teachers in poor districts. If you're a fascist regime, you "take over" the states next to you. When you're a state and you "take over" schools, you're on the road to being a fascist regime. As I write, my school has just been threatened with a takeover, which means a visit from the "accountability and targeted assistance team." I am uncertain who comprises this group and what I am going to be held accountable for, but I am dead certain that they are not on *my* team. I am fairly certain that they have less classroom experience than I have. I am also fairly certain that they do not live in a community like mine, and that their children have not attended "underperforming" schools like my children have. I am also dead certain that they will not know the realities of living in a community like mine which ranks among the highest in poverty, teen pregnancy, and drug and alcohol abuse in the state. In fact, as a community, we are first in the state in just about all the bad things, and I am certain that they will not see me or my students. They will only see artificial scores which have little to do with anybody's accountability, intelligence or effort except those who made up the test in the first place. Finally I'm a bit queasy about the oxymoron "targeted assistance."

So why do I teach? I teach because someone has to tell my students that they are not the ones who are dumb. They need to know that only the blissfully ignorant and profoundly evil make up tests to prove that they and people like them are smart. I teach because my students need to know that poverty does not equal stupidity, and that surviving a bleak, dismal childhood makes you strong and tough and beautiful in ways that only survivors of similar environments can appreciate and understand. I teach because my students need to know that in their struggle to acquire a second language, they participate in one of the most difficult of human feats. My students also need to know that four days of reading in a second language under 'high-stakes' testing conditions would shut down even Einstein's brain. I teach because my students need to know that right and wrong are relative to one's culture, and that even these definitions become laughable over time. I teach because the people who make up these tests don't know these things, or worse, they do.

Bill Dunn will continue to teach because he recognizes the value and power of what he offers to his students. There are many teachers like Bill Dunn scattered throughout the schools in our country. They are passionate about their vision of public education despite the regulations that have been imposed by NCLB and all its state and local spin-offs. And in their classrooms, students are able to succeed because of who they are and what they bring to school, not despite it. Those of us who recognize the negative impact that NCLB has had on public education must also acknowledge the shortcomings that have led to the appeal of this legislation for many parents and policymakers who genuinely care about children. We must, in a strong and united voice, offer ways to truly support teachers in providing high-quality and equitable education for all children.

REFERENCES

Freedman, S.W., Simons, E.R., Kalnin, J.S., Casareno, A., & the M-CLASS Teams (Eds.) (1999). *Inside city schools: Investigating literacy in multicultural classrooms.* New York: Teachers College Press.

Greene, M. (2001). *Variations on a blue guitar.* New York: Teachers College Press.

Intrator, S. (2003). *Tuned in and fired up: How teaching can inspire real learning in the classroom.* New Haven, CT: Yale University Press.

Irvine, J.J. (2003). *Educating teachers for diversity: Seeing with a cultural eye.* New York: Teachers College Press.

Ladson-Billings, G. (2001). *Crossing over to Canaan: The journey of new teachers in diverse classrooms.* San Francisco, CA: Jossey-Bass.

Nieto, S. (Ed.) (2005). *Why we teach.* New York: Teachers College Press.

Palmer, P.J. (1998). *The courage to teach: Exploring the inner landscape of a teacher's life.* San Francisco: Jossey-Bass.

Rose, M. (1995). *Possible lives: The promise of public education in America.* New York: Penguin Books.

Wheelock, A. (2000, September). *MCAS Alert.* FairTest/Coalition for Authentic Reform in Education.

Whitehead, A.N. (1929). *The aims of education and other essays.* New York: Macmillan.

II

THE IMPACT OF COMPASSIONATE CONSERVATISM ON EDUCATIONAL POLICIES AND PRACTICES

Policies and practices may have both intended and unintended consequences, and it is not always easy to determine motivation. Nevertheless, there seems to be sufficient evidence to conclude that one of the purposes of the No Child Left Behind (NCLB) legislation was to bring about an increased amount of privatization of education in the United States. What components of the legislation allow for private schools to replace public ones? To what extent do corporations stand to profit from these takeovers, as well as by providing tutoring services and publication and grading of tests? In what way is the Adequate Yearly Progress (AYP) goal a device to ensure the failure of thousands of schools? And what propaganda methods utilized by the administration in support of NCLB were deemed illegal by the Government Accountability Office? After describing the various modes privatization might take, Florence Samson and Clive Belfield examine these tactics in great detail and raise the possibility of the demise of public education and the consequences for the future of democracy in our nation.

Because wide-scale, relentless testing of children is at the heart of accountability under NCLB, it is of considerable importance that Patrick Johnson draws a very clear distinction between standards-based instruction and authentic assessment, on the one hand, and its "evil twin," high-stakes testing, on the other. In the discussion of privatization, the focus of this testing is on the school and its viability. Johnson explores in considerable depth the impact high-stakes testing has on the two stakeholders most directly involved, children and teachers. What effect does this testing have on children? What theory of motivation undergirds this approach? Does fear of failure and punishment cause children to utilize more effective learning strategies? Are they motivated to struggle to remain in school, or are they more likely to drop out? In this climate of high-stakes testing, do teachers develop curriculum that is richer and more educationally valuable, or is there a narrowing of focus as the test approaches? Johnson not only probes these issues but analyzes both summative and formative evaluation in his important discussion of alternative assessment methods.

In considering the impact of NCLB legislation on children with disabilities, Micheline Malow-Iroff, Michael Benhar, and Sonya Martin first explore two pieces of legislation, Public Law 94-142 (1975) and Public Law 101-476, Individuals with Disabilities Education Act (1990). As they look at NCLB, the most recent legislation impacting children with disabilities, the writers ask whether the focus on individuation, so crucial in special education, can be maintained in a system that requires all children to undergo the same curriculum, take the same high-stakes tests, and meet the same AYP standards. Are there other options that would better serve the needs of youngsters with disabilities? NCLB raises many issues and challenges for educators of these children, and the writers present thoughtful suggestions that emerged from a workshop at a conference dealing with NCLB and its consequences for children with disabilities.

3

The Privatization of America's Schools

Florence Samson and Clive Belfield

INTRODUCTION

The privatization of America's schools has grown dramatically over the last decade, and it is poised to grow even further in the next decade (Henig, 1994; Levin and Belfield, 2004). Pushed to its limits, such privatization has the potential to fundamentally change America's education system, influencing what schools children attend, what and how they learn, and who pays for this schooling (Hoxby, 2003). Almost by default, it has become the primary educational reform that policymakers must focus on, either in the hope that it will improve the education system or in the fear that it will undermine the opportunities for all children to learn.

In this chapter, after commenting briefly on public education, we review how privatization has developed, report on the evidence, and then speculate as to its future influence. First, we describe and classify education privatization, and outline the many policy reforms that fall within this description. Second, we briefly review the research evidence on privatization, recognizing that many reforms are so new that evidence which might yield definite conclusions is only just being amassed, and we explain why privatization has advanced in recent years. Third, we address the controversies surrounding privatization and its underlying ideologies, indicating why privatization provokes such strong opposition or support, and what controversial issues are emerging and likely to emerge. In particular, we look at the No Child Left Behind (NCLB) Act, and how it undermines public education; we consider who benefits and who loses in the privatization of education. Finally, we look to the future and ask, "Which privatization reforms will keep growing?" "Which offer the highest probability of improving the nation's schools?" and "Is there a future for public education?"

THE ATTACK ON PUBLIC EDUCATION

The provision of public education is a complex matter. Until recently, "access to public education has been achieved with minimal intervention by the federal government" (Noguera, 2003). However, throughout the last decade, "education has been widely regarded as the most important domestic policy issue facing the nation. Even after the terrorist attacks of September 11, 2001, it continues to rank high as a concern among policy makers and the general public" (Noguera, 2003). It is also a source of great controversy.

Present-day society, demographics, student diversity, cultural and language barriers, funding, and fiscal restraint contribute to that complexity. Advocates of privatization are seeking to change the public's perception of education. "In rhetoric and reality," Robertson points out, "education is recast as a private good, not a public service. Those who have children in school are urged to judge the curriculum, teachers, and even other students on their contribution to personal advantage" (Robertson, 1999, p. 3). Globalization is used as "the all-purpose excuse to absolve decision-makers of responsibility" and "has replaced debt and deficit as the justification for dismantling the public sphere, for cutting welfare, for rolling back human rights legislation, and for ignoring environmental regulations. And of course, for reforming schools" (Robertson, 1999, p. 5).

When the public becomes convinced that the roles of consumer and citizen are synonymous, when privatized products, including education, become indistinguishable from public service (Robertson, 1999, p. 6), and when education and training become synonymous, not only is public education threatened, but so is our concept of democracy.

As Berkowitz (2003) reminds us, "America's public schools represent a multibillion dollar industry and the privateers desperately want their share." This is unsettling, particularly in a period where the most common word used to describe American corporations is "amoral" (Bracey, 2003a, p. 19).

On the surface, this controversy or "war" (Bracey, 2003a) on public education centers around accountability and the perception of the failure of public education to achieve the academic success that government deems basic to America's ability to compete in the global market. However, a closer look reveals that the underlying intent of replacing public education with private education may not be wholly related to raising students' achievement. It may be that government wants to divest itself of responsibility for education as it downsizes, based on the belief that less government is better government, and that education is an untapped source of profit for the private sector. There is also the suggestion that part of the motivation to privatize public education "is directed toward right-wing social engineering … to control the curriculum that future generations of American students must absorb" (Freeman, 2005a, p. 2). The ever-widening gap between the rich and the poor in America suggests the downsizing and possible elimination of the middle class even though it was "our commitment to education that helped to forge the broad middle class that is the pride of America's democracy and the foundation of its prosperity" (Borosage, 2004, p. 1).

Once the public is convinced that the public school system is "in crisis," privatization advocates are emboldened to introduce reforms to promote private sector provision. According to Dobbin (1996), "the charter school is one of the weapons that opponents of public education use to both undermine confidence in the public education system and to begin the actual erosion of that system" (p. 1). He sees the charter school "as the Trojan horse of those of who would transform public education into a commercialized, or even privatized system" (p. 1). Bracey (2003b) referred to the NCLB legislation, which advocates charter schools, as "a weapon of mass destruction used to launch a campaign of shock and awe against the schools and against the children" (p. 163). Dunbar (2004), referring to the cuts in funding to public universities, writes that "the search for weapons of mass destruction has yielded at least one: the increasing privatization of public education." In chapter 1 Spring describes the NCLB legislation as a "political fraud," for although it emphasizes accountability and standards, "the overall legislation was justified by the unproven claim that high-stakes testing and standards will improve schools or make American workers more competitive in the global market" (p. 15).

To get a sense of the tactics of those advocating privatization, note that Meese, Butler, and Holmes (2005) recommend, among other things, that in the provision of educational services in the rebuilding of New Orleans after the devastation of hurricane Katrina

> [T]he federal government should resist pouring resources into one-time school construction projects. Any new funding associated with rebuilding educational facilities should encourage state and local authorities to implement creative public-private partnerships through leasing arrangements. For example, education providers such as public schools (as well as charter and private schools and after-school tutoring companies) should be given opportunities to lease schools from private contractors through leasing arrangements.

Since that recommendation, Congress passed a "voucher program of nearly $500 million for the victims of Hurricane Katrina … [and] pays for 385,000 students to attend private schools" (Schemo in Kirkpatrick, 2006).

EDUCATION PRIVATIZATION

Technically, education privatization is the transfer of activities, assets, and responsibilities from government or public institutions and organizations to private individuals and agencies (Levin, 2001a). So, educational matters such as choosing a school previously decided by the government are now to be shifted to individual families, and school operations such as teacher recruitment and training are to be provided by private companies. This shift has substantial consequences: In the United States, there are over 55 million schoolchildren, and an amount of over $500 billion (Freeman, 2005a, p. 2) is spent annually on K-12 public education. Bracey's estimate (2003a, p. x) is $800 billion.

Chris Whittle is a leading advocate of privatization and founder and CEO of Edison Schools. In his latest book (Whittle, 2005), argues that

> The United States must embark on a concerted new investment strategy in education research and development. Only through enhanced and sustained R&D will the U.S. develop the breakthrough school designs that will be necessary to make leaps in student achievement (PR Newswire, 2005).

He then notes that "the federal government spends about 100 times more on healthcare research and development than it does on education." The same news release tells us that Edison Schools' president, Terry Stecz, "predicted that Whittle's book would create a new excitement about the future of public education and help us to move education back to its rightful place at the forefront of the U.S. agenda."

THE MANY TYPES OF EDUCATION PRIVATIZATION

It is important to recognize that the process of privatization is multifaceted; there is no single form of education privatization, although there is a set of reforms that can be classified as privatization.

Educational Vouchers

Historically, schools have been funded through taxes paid by local communities, by districts and states, or by the federal government; the total funds are then distributed to schools that provide an education to the children living in each community. A system of educational vouchers would be very different (Moe, 2001). Vouchers are educational coupons that entitle each student to a prescribed amount of schooling. With a voucher system each student is allocated an annual amount of funding that can be used to enroll at any eligible school. Purchasing power would be given to families, who could top up the voucher for extra educational services, such as after-school programs, tutoring, or summer school. Families could choose whichever school they preferred: the neighborhood public school, a private religious school, or a for-profit school. These schools would obtain revenues based on the numbers of students enrolling; they would be forced to compete for students. Thus, parents would be given more power, and schools would become more responsive to parents' wishes.

During most of the 1900s the only voucherlike system was in the smaller school districts of Maine and Vermont, where geographic isolation encouraged public school districts to cooperate with private schools to ensure all children would attend school (Hammons, 2001). (The system of special education funding also has some voucherlike components.) However, during the 1990s the momentum for vouchers grew. The first program was the Milwaukee Parental Choice Program in 1990. The program is limited to low-income families, and it began with a cap on enrollment; also, religious schools were not eligible. Both these conditions were removed during the 1990s, and, as the value of the voucher rose to $5,882 in the 2003–2004 school year, the number of participants rose to 12,778. Two thirds of these students were enrolled in religious schools.

Since 1990, new, smaller voucher programs have been established. In 1995, the Cleveland Scholarship and Tutoring Program was introduced. Again, low-income families were given preference, although the value of the voucher was set at only $2,250. Almost all the 4,000 participating students attend private religious schools. In 1999, the Florida Opportunity Scholarship Program was introduced. This program gave vouchers to children who attend low-performing schools, allowing them to switch out of those schools with a voucher worth $4,500. Take-up of the voucher has been relatively small, with less than 550 students using the voucher in 2002–2003. In January 2006, the Florida Supreme Court ruled this program unconstitutional. In 2003, the state of Colorado passed a voucher plan, to begin in Autumn 2004, to offer vouchers to students from low-income families with low academic performance located in poor-performing districts (see Lenti, 2003). However, the program has also been challenged in the courts on the grounds that it violates the state constitution. Finally, in 2004, a voucher program for Washington, DC, was introduced to provide at least 1,700 low-income students a chance to attend private and religious schools with taxpayer money (Kahlenberg, 2004). In the meantime, Section 8 housing vouchers, which help low-income and working-class families move to neighborhoods with good public schools, "is under attack by the administration" (Kahlenberg, 2004, p. 2).

Thus far, the total number of participants is a very small proportion of public school enrollments. (There is also a network of privately funded voucher programs, providing scholarship grants to over 100,000 students; see Howell and Peterson, 2002; Table 2.1.) Nevertheless, there is a consistent pressure both for more programs and the expansion of the programs currently operating.

Charter Schools and Public School Choice

Charter schools are schools funded through the public system but that are exempt from some state and local regulations in exchange for following a "charter" or contract. Each school draws up its own charter, which may reflect a particular pedagogy or educational philosophy. Charter schools may be exempt from regulations about hiring unionized teachers and have greater autonomy over school facilities (including virtual learning modules). However, because charter school legislation is intended to promote new schools that are responsive to local needs and the variations in family preferences, charter schools themselves are varied.

Not all states allow charter schools to operate (Miron and Nelson, 2002), but by 2002–2003, there were 2,556 such schools serving 685,000 students (www. edreform.org). Charter schooling is therefore a stepping-stone to vouchers: These schools can respond in some ways to parental expectations, and they can compete with public schools. However, because they are regulated and financed through the tax system, purchasing power is not transferred to families (Sugarman, 2002).

A related reform is the expansion of public school choice. This allows families to choose between public schools that have the same mission and are operating under the same set of regulations, but may differ for idiosyncratic reasons (e.g., their location). Public school choice gives families more options, but only on a few dimensions.

Private Contracting

Schools must provide many services that are not strictly instructional or educational but which support classroom programs. In theory, there is no reason why a school would provide these services itself if a private company can provide them at lower cost. Almost all schools contract with private firms for some of their day-to-day operations. Based on survey evidence, schools commonly hire outside contractors for catering, construction projects, refuse or waste management, and architectural or engineering services. Less frequently, schools may contract with private companies that provide retail and shopping services, auditing and accounting, printing and publications, teacher-training programs, and payroll and benefits services.

In many instances, this form of privatization is accepted: Students and their parents do not care whether the school cafeteria is run by a private company or by the school itself, assuming the food quality is adequate. However, in some cases the use of private companies is controversial, for example, when for-profit private businesses take over and manage schools. These educational management organizations (EMOs) manage entire schools under contract to school districts or to charter school boards. The EMOs have direct control over the instruction that the students receive. The highest-profile EMO is Edison Schools, which operates over 80 schools across the United States. However, the ostensible differences between Edison Schools and nearby public schools are not dramatic: Edison

Schools tends to hire relatively young, inexperienced teachers and offer more in-house training; they use a more scripted curriculum, but encourage greater use of computers; and they invest more in physical facilities and maintenance (Levin, 2001b). Each of these practices can be found in some public schools.

Tuition Tax Credits and Deductions for Parents

One way to advance privatization is to make parents pay (privately) for their children's school, bypassing the public financing of education altogether. This can be done either through tax credits or tax deductions on any educational expenditure (Belfield and Levin, 2003). A tax credit allows the total amount or some portion of the permissible expenditure to be subtracted from the amount of tax owed by the individual. A tax deduction allows the permissible amount to be deducted from the gross taxable assets of the individual. Over the last decade, 6 states have introduced tax credits (typically worth about $500), and 13 states have introduced tax deductions (of similar value). Clearly, if families get a tax break for sending their children to private school, they are more likely to do so. Hence, private funding leads to private schooling. Significantly, these tax changes only apply to families that pay tax; they do not apply to families whose income is so low that they do not pay income tax.

Homeschooling

The final form of education privatization is also the most fundamental: home-schooling. Here, families opt out of the (public or private) education system entirely. Privatization can mean education that is privately funded, privately regulated, and privately provided. Although the examples in the preceding text reflect some of these attributes, they all retain some element of government control and influence. In sharp contrast, homeschooling does not: It is funded, regulated, and (by definition) provided by individual families according to their own preferences.

Over the last two decades, every state has relaxed its laws on homeschooling (the last state to legalize homeschooling did so in 1993; see Stevens, 2001). Over this period, the numbers of homeschoolers have grown to approximately 1 million (NCES, 2004). The motivations for homeschooling are various: Some are motivated by religious belief, others by the costs of private schooling, others by the quality of public schools, and yet others according to a pedagogical preference (Lines, 2000). The homeschooling movement is now influential and actively promotes the practice across the country. Public support for homeschooling has also grown: Whereas in 1985, only 16% of families thought homeschooling a good thing, by 2001 this figure had risen to 41% (Rose and Gallup, 2001, p. 46).

WHAT DOES THE EVIDENCE SHOW?

Here, we review the evidence on the effectiveness of the privatization reforms outlined in the preceding text. Unfortunately, this evidence is mixed and does not lend itself either to a clear affirmation or rejection of these reforms. (However, opponents and advocates may selectively interpret the evidence to justify their preconceptions.)

On vouchers, the evidence is consistent: Voucher programs do not adversely impact student achievement, but they also appear to do little to enhance it. For the Milwaukee Parental Choice Program, there are only data available for the period 1990 to 1995: Of the three separate evaluations of the program during that period, one is very favorable, another shows no effect, and the third shows no gains in reading and a slight advantage for the voucher students in mathematics (Greene et al., 1998; Witte, 1999; Rouse, 1998). For the Cleveland Scholarship and Tutoring Program, a 5-year evaluation shows no achievement gain for the participants in the years from kindergarten to fourth grade (Metcalf et al., 2003). Because of small sample sizes, no evaluation of individual achievement in the Florida program has been carried out. Finally, in a randomized field trial of vouchers for families in three cities (New York, Washington, DC, and Dayton, Ohio), very small test score gains were found after 3 years (Howell and Peterson, 2002; Krueger and Zhu, 2004).

The evidence is also inconclusive on charter schooling, though given the heterogeneity of these schools, this is less surprising. Some studies identify excellent charter schools; other studies find that charter schools—particularly cyber- and non-classroom-based charter schools—report very poor achievement (Bifulco and Ladd, 2003; Buddin and Zimmer, 2003; Miron and Nelson, 2002).

Little academic attention has been paid to the other reforms. No direct research has been produced on the efficacy of private contracting, though the performance of the for-profit schools has been the subject of considerable attention. Mainly because of data restrictions, it has not been possible to perform a rigorous evaluation of the for-profit sector. Research simply describes the behaviors of the for-profit schools (Levin, 2001b). This research has raised many questions about the ability of the for-profit schools to outperform public schools that serve comparable students (Levin and Belfield, 2004). On tax credits, little is known because almost no evaluative research has been conducted. Finally, although there has been research on what motivates families to choose to homeschool (Houston and Toma, 2003), there are significant challenges in evaluating whether homeschooling is good for the children involved. (Data on test score differences between homeschoolers and public school students must be regarded with considerable caution; the samples of respondents are unlikely to be representative of all homeschoolers.)

More general evidence has been collated to frame the debate on privatization (Teske and Schneider, 2001). Over 40 studies have been carried out to assess whether competition between schools forces them to improve the quality of education offered. In reviewing these studies, Belfield and Levin (2002) found only modest effects of competition on student test scores. Competition does force schools to raise their standards, but it is not a panacea by any means. Finally, a number of studies have been undertaken to ascertain whether families appreciate the extra choices that privatization brings. Unsurprisingly, those families that do exercise choice—either through a voucher or attendance at a charter school—report favorably on privatization (Teske and Schneider, 2001).

WHY HAS EDUCATION PRIVATIZATION GROWN SO RAPIDLY?

Clearly, there are many reforms that could be part of an agenda for privatization. Some are complementary (e.g., vouchers for homeschooling families), but others can be undertaken independently (e.g., charter schools and tax breaks). This duality gives policymakers and planners who favor privatization a considerable advantage. First, there is flexibility in achieving the goal of privatization as a number of reforms can be introduced and implemented. Second, advocates can jump from reforms that are politically unappealing toward reforms that have political traction. Third, advocates can generate momentum as reforms are built up cumulatively (e.g., the legalization of homeschooling means that more families will favor tax credits on educational expenditures such as books and computers).

Families have also played a role in promoting privatization. Increasingly, education is viewed as an important way to gain social and economic advancement, particularly in the United States, where the labor market is flexible (Carneiro and Heckman, 2003). This raises the demand for education and the pressure for schooling that produces skills valued in the labor market. When public schools teach seemingly arcane topics or offer low-grade provision, families will switch to the private sector. Another set of parents may reject the public system because it does not foster the values that they wish their children to have. In growing numbers, parents are expressing preferences for differentiated choices.

Many families see the public school system as failing to offer a reasonable quality of education. Many urban schools have low graduation rates and may fail to provide a safe environment for students (Gootman, 2006). In spite of this, "last year's SAT scores were the highest in 30 years .... while the test-taking pool has gotten both larger and more diverse" (Freeman, 2005a, pp. 2,3). This is not to deny that there are problems, including low achievement. In part, this low achievement may reflect the economic circumstances of the families at the school (Hochschild and Scovronick, 2003), but other studies have been scathing about the waste of resources and inefficiency of the public school system (Segal, 2003).

Perhaps reflecting this view, support among the general public for further investments in education has been weak.

There are also more general reasons why privatization has grown in recent decades. Some advocates for privatization are motivated by an ideological commitment to individual rights over government intervention (Friedman, 1962). These advocates believe that a family's right to choose its own form of education is paramount and that the burden of proof should be on governments to explain why they would deprive parents of this right. Other advocates may stress efficiency (Hoxby, 2003); this has become an increasingly important consideration as per-student expenditures continue to rise faster than the rate of inflation and faster than wages (Hanushek, 1998). A third, relatively recent group of advocates regard the current public education system as unfair. The U.S. education system at present allows wealthy families to exercise school choice through their residential decisions (buying a house near a good school) or through opting out of the public school system entirely. They can also mobilize political support to avoid low-quality public schools (and to avoid integrating schools across racial or income lines). In contrast, low-income families are allocated places in low-quality urban schools. If privatization allows these families to attend any school with a publicly funded voucher, then they will be able to obtain the level of schooling previously available only to those in the wealthier suburbs. This view is typified by the statement of U.S. Supreme Court Justice Clarence Thomas in writing that "failing urban schools disproportionately affect minority children" and "many blacks now support school choice programs because they provide the greatest educational opportunities for their children in struggling communities" (Zelman v. Simmons-Harris, 2002). It is a view that is gaining support from others who see the public system as unfixable (see Sugarman and Kemerer, 1999; Vitteriti, 1999).

Overall, these factors driving privatization have been strong, largely unchecked by any countervailing forces leading to more state involvement (such as a belief that "common schooling" is important or that government schools best represent society's preferences; but see Wolfe, 2003). This explains the proliferation of policies and reforms. However, the privatization of education is not simply a technocratic problem to be easily solved by a more efficient school system.

IDEOLOGY

Education is not a neutral enterprise, but a political act (Apple, 1990). Nevertheless

> [c]urrent discussions over privatization and school reform are too often treated as technical matters, focused on questions of efficiency, standards and delivery of services. Such a focus leads to the neglect of the political and philosophical issues

that must be considered … . This neglect may prove costly for if the ideological assumptions associated with privatization are ignored, the long-term implications to the character of the state and the social democratic institutions of this nation— beginning with the provision of public education—may not be recognized until we have lost or severely undermined an important national resource (Noguera, 1993, Part 1, pp. 3,4).

There are many concerns related to the growing threat of privatization of our public schools and its impact on our citizenry and democracy. Noguera notes that so-called reformers "are unified by a common belief in the market as the pre-eminent regulator and guarantor of education quality" (Noguera, 1993, Part 1, p. 2). The NCLB Act is their prescription for reform. The original bill, which was introduced by the Bush administration in 2001, contained a voucher program that would have allowed children to attend private school at taxpayers' expense. Congress, in its wisdom, had this section deleted. However, the current administration has not given up on this prime educational goal and, as noted in the preceding text, cities and several states have introduced vouchers.

Nobel-prize-winning economist Milton Friedman (1995), the father of the privatization movement, has stated it as baldly as anyone. In his argument, Friedman indicates:

> I believe that the only way to make a major improvement in our educational system is through privatization to the point at which a substantial fraction of all educational services is rendered to individuals by private enterprise. Nothing will destroy or even greatly weaken the power of the current educational establishment—a necessary pre-condition for radical improvement in our educational system. (p. 5)

In his rationale for replacing public education with private, Friedman indicates that vouchers are not an end in themselves but a way to make the transition from a government to a market system in which families will pay for their children's education.

According to Moe (in Miner, 2002a, p. 2) of the Hoover Institution, "School choice allows children and money to leave the system, and that means there will be fewer public teacher jobs, lower union membership, and lower dues." The goal here is clearly the erosion of public education.

NCLB AND ITS TACTICS TO UNDERMINE PUBLIC EDUCATION

The NCLB Act is the current federal administration's response to the problems that have plagued the public school system for decades. Rather than reform, it is clear that NCLB is "part of a calculated political campaign to use achievement gaps to label schools as failures, without providing the resources and strategies needed to overcome them" (Karp, 2004, p. 54). The act, which comes up for review in 2007, is based on "two faulty assumptions. First, that standardized tests are the best way to measure academic success. Second, that schools are failing because they aren't trying hard enough and that the threat of sanctions will magically transform these troubled schools" (Miner, 2001, pp. 1, 2).

According to Darling-Hammond, "The biggest problem with the NCLB Act is that it mistakes measuring schools for fixing them" (Darling-Hammond, 2004, p. 9). Because NCLB is unconcerned with improving educational practice, some are convinced that it is a step toward the dismantling of the "problem-plagued" public education system. They view NCLB and its rhetoric as the Republican Party's endeavor to not only cater to the private sector, but also to drastically reduce the public sector, undermine teacher unions (a key base of support for the Democratic Party), and to win the support of African American and Latino voters to the Republican Party (Miner, 2002a; see also Nieto & Johnson, chapter 2 of this volume).

Senator Jim Jeffords, chair (1997–2001) of the Senate committee that oversees education, described the law as a backdoor maneuver "that will let the private sector take over public education, something the Republicans have wanted for years" (Kohn, 2004, p. 84). Bracey describes NCLB as "a trap. It is the grand scheme of the school privatizers; NCLB sets up the public schools for the final knock down" (Bracey, 2003c, p. 1). In an article titled "The NCLB wrecking ball," James McKenzie, a former school superintendent, says, "Misrepresented as a reform effort, NCLB is actually a cynical effort to shift public school funding to a host of private schools" (McKenzie, 2003).

Whatever the government's intent in legislating NCLB, the manner in which the law is being implemented could contribute to the undermining of public education, leading to the subsequent privatization of public schools. The following conditions are significant.

Underfunding of NCLB

Compliance with NCLB is voluntary; however, if states opt out, they forfeit federal money for educating disadvantaged students. Ironically, NCLB is underfunded by the federal government; the authorized funds have never been provided (Bracey, 2005, p. 151). There is disagreement as to the actual amount of the underfunding: Wood (2004) estimates it as $12 billion; the Democratic Staff Committee on Education and the Work Force, U.S. House of Representatives (2004), places the figure at $27 billion.

Member of Congress David Obey (2005) says that, "Unfortunately, the history of NCLB is one of broken promises to America's schoolchildren and their parents."

He anticipates that the NCLB shortfall will grow even larger under the Bush financial year 2006 budget with an additional projected shortfall of $12 billion.

The consequence of this serious underfunding, according to Darling-Hammond, is that the goal of having a qualified teacher in every classroom in the nation will not be reached. It has also prevented the recruiting of new teachers, the strengthening of teacher preparation, and the improving of teacher retention through mentoring programs.

> This underfunding of NCLB clearly impedes the accomplishment of the educational targets by schools as defined in the Adequate Yearly Progress (AYP). Undermining public education in this manner increases the possibility of its demise (Darling-Hammond, 2004, pp. 30,31).

Unequally Funded Schools

In some games, players may be given a "handicap" to level the playing field. However, the NCLB Act mandates that every school reach and maintain the AYP standards and ignores the uneven playing field of poverty and deprivation. There are students, teachers, and schools who, through no fault of their own, are doomed to failure with or without NCLB and AYP—students who are so disadvantaged that they have little possibility of achieving high school graduation. This inequality of educational opportunity in the public education system is often due to the unequal funding of public schools (see Kirch and Hunter, chapter 9 of this volume).

Broadcast journalist Bill Moyers (1996), in his documentary video, *Children in America's Schools: Flowers Growing in a Garbage Can* (based on Jonathon Kozol's *Savage Inequalities*, 1991), highlights the disparity in public educational opportunity that existed at that time between the affluent and the poverty-stricken people of this country, and which "ha[s] not lessened in recent years" (Darling-Hammond, 2004). Students in some of the poorest areas go to school in buildings that lack bathroom facilities, windows, and lunchrooms; students in affluent areas enjoy state-of-the-art facilities and an abundance of financial and human resources to support them in their pursuit of education. The existence of such extremes within a democratic society is not only difficult to understand but unpalatable.

Kozol, a longtime critic of inequality in educational opportunity, has written that not only do such schools represent a flagrant and ironical betrayal of the 1954 Supreme Court ruling in *Brown v. Board of Education* but, in some cases, have "not even lived up to the promise of the 1896 decision known as *Plessy v. Ferguson*, which sanctioned the principle of 'separate but equal'" (2000, p. 1).

In 1995, the General Accounting Office (GAO) estimated that it would require $112 billion simply to bring the schools up to safe standards (Borosage, 2004, p. 3). The NCLB Act does not address this critical issue of the underfunding of the public schools. If the funding allocated for NCLB had been utilized to upgrade those public schools that were destitute, might not the result have been increased educational opportunity for more of America's children?

Standardized Tests and the AYP: Being Set Up for Failure

At the core of NCLB is accountability through a system of standardized tests that serve as the basis for the AYP or individual school report cards. NCLB mandates the testing of children in grades three through eight in reading, mathematics, and, beginning in school year 2007–2008, science, and once during grades 10 and 12 (U. S. Department of Education, 2003). Based on these test results, schools are labeled as having made or having failed to make AYP. By 2014, all schools in the country will have to reach 100% proficiency in mathematics and reading. These tests present an almost insurmountable challenge to most public schools.

The American Federation of Teachers (AFT) describes the AYP targets as "not merely challenging, they are unrealistic" (2005a, p. 1). The "AYP does not measure the yearly progress of the same students over time" and "the evidence shows that whether or not a school makes the AYP does not necessarily depend on its effectiveness or the presence or absence or size of the achievement gap" (2005a, p. 1). In an earlier release the AFT says that AYP sets "predetermined benchmarks for students' proficiency without taking into account schools' starting points. Furthermore, its testing of students with disabilities and English language learners is neither valid nor reliable" (June 9, 2005, p. 1). In addition, AFT notes that "the narrow set of school improvement interventions are not research based and may be punitive rather than helpful to the school and the children they serve."

In the July 2003 QuEST keynote address, the late Sandra Feldman, former president of the American Federation of Teachers, stated that, "The [NCLB] law calls for 100 percent of students in general and in each of a number of subgroups—low income, racial and ethnic minorities, special education, and English language learners—to reach a 'proficient' level on tests of reading and math in grades 3–8 and at least one grade in high school. Science will soon be added" (p. 6). It is, therefore, not surprising that in 2004, 26,000 of the nation's 93,000 schools "failed to make adequate yearly progress" (Darling-Hammond in Meier & Wood, p. 5).

Robert Linn, in his AERA 2003 presidential address, showed with hard numbers how long it will take the country to attain 100% proficiency on AYP targets mandated by the NCLB Act:

> If the nation makes the same gains in proficiency on tests that it has made in the last decade, it will attain the required level of proficiency in fourth grade math in 2056, in the eighth grade math in 2060, and twelfth grade math in 2166. Conversely, if

the nation is to reach the NCLB targets by the required date of 2014, it must ratchet up improvement at grades 4 and 8 by a factor of 4. At grade 12, we must increase our rate of improvement by a factor of 12 (in Bracey, 2003b, p. 150).

Because standards vary from state to state regarding the type of tests administered and the cut-off grade used to determine adequate performance, studies have shown that students with exactly the same knowledge and skills would miss the proficiency targets in some states and easily surpass them in others (Helderman and Mui, 2003). Compounding the problem is the movement of students in and out of a given school or district. The criteria for making AYP are so stacked that "virtually no schools serving large numbers of low-income children will clear these arbitrary hurdles" (Neill, 2004, p. 85).

Kohn, described by *Time* magazine as the most outspoken critic of education's fixation on grades and test scores, says that NCLB

[u]surps the power of the local communities to choose their own policies and programs .... compromises the quality of teaching and learning by forcing teachers to worry more about raising test scores than about promoting meaningful learning ... punishes those who most need help, and sets back efforts to close the gap between rich and poor and between black and white (Kohn, 2004, pp. 79, 80).

In imagining how he might proceed in today's context if he wanted to become a privatizer of education, Kohn wrote:

If my objective were to dismantle the public schools, I would begin by discrediting them. I would probably refer to them as "government" schools, hoping to tap into a vein of libertarian resentment. I would never miss an opportunity to sneer at researchers and teacher educators as out-of-touch "educationists." Recognizing that it's politically unwise to attack teachers, I would do so obliquely, bashing the unions to which most of them belong. Most important, if I had the power, I would ratchet up the number and difficulty of standardized tests that students had to take, in order that I could point to the predictably pitiful results. I would then defy my opponents to defend the schools that had produced students who had done so badly. (Kohn, 2004, p. 81)

Many believe that Kohn's musings are actually a summary of what is happening today.

Feldman has described the AYP formula as "one which staggers the imagination and even human capacity." She believes that it "could put a large number of good schools on the "failing" list—which since states are then required to help them, could result in even less money to help schools which are really in trouble" (2003, p. 7). Feldman says that, consequently, the AYP would actually be working against the promised goals of NCLB. She considers that " ... accountability for that which is attainable is legitimate. But accountability for that which is humanly impossible, laudable as it may sound, is unacceptable" and calls for "world-class" rather than "the outer-space standards of AYP" (p. 7). In achieving the principles of NCLB, teachers " … need help. We need shared responsibility. We need politicians and administrators to be held accountable until they provide us with the tools and resources we have asked for repeatedly" (p. 9).

So Much Success and yet a Failure?

Huge numbers of schools have been labeled as *failing*, despite their continuing success in certain areas. An example of one of these, the Audubon public school in Cleveland, Ohio, "closed out the 2003–2004 school year on a strong note" (AFT, 2005a). All members of the school community had worked hard "to make a successful conversion from a traditional middle school to a K-8 building." There had been a significant improvement in discipline; many of the older students were meeting the challenge of being strong role models for students in the earlier grades; students appeared to be benefiting from the block scheduling and tutoring programs; and at both the fourth- and sixth-grade levels "the school posted across-the-board student achievement gains in mathematics, reading, writing, science, and citizenship from the prior years." The teachers believed that there was nothing they could not accomplish "no matter what came from downtown." The staff was more than a little frustrated when, despite these successes they "landed on the 'failed to meet AYP' list."

If Audubon continues as a School in Need of Improvement (SINI), it could find itself subjected to additional "reforms … . These include for-profit management, conversion to charter schools, wholesale reconstitution of the school, instructional staff and other steps driven more by ideology and political interest than by an evidence of proven effectiveness in the classroom" (AFT, 2005a, p. 2).

One of the weaknesses of the AYP is that it does not recognize that some students started far behind others and consequently did not reach NCLB's arbitrary benchmarks. Its implementation does not allow for "valid and reliable evidence of student progress" (AFT, 2005a, p. 2). Although "the AFT strongly supports the "disaggregation" of data as a necessary step to protect vulnerable student populations from being neglected in school improvement efforts," it recognizes that the "mechanisms for achieving this are still wanting" (AFT, 2005a, p. 2).

When schools such as Audubon, which are experiencing success by many other standards, fail to make the AYP target, it leaves little hope for other schools that are severely challenged. It is unfortunate, also, that in low-income urban communities, which have the greatest need for experienced, skilled, and committed instructors, for example, New York City, teacher pay is significantly lower than in the more affluent areas. The unbelievable conditions for education in many of these communities' schools include, but are not limited to, doubling of classes, half-day shifts, and the conversion of trailers, closets, libraries, and gyms into classrooms (Borosage, 2004). Such conditions do little to attract and retain teachers or to promote optimum learning.

Lobbying for NCLB

In the face of such reasonable opposition, the Bush administration has ratcheted up its efforts at lobbying in support of NCLB. Some of this lobbying has been of questionable legality. Lobbying is an accepted and regulated practice used by individuals, businesses, organizations, and governments to gain support when trying to change people's beliefs and attitudes toward proposed change. However, on January 6, 2005, *USA Today* reported that

> [s]eeking to build support among black families for its education reform law the Bush administration paid a prominent black pundit [and former aide to Supreme Court Judge Clarence Thomas, Armstrong Williams], $240,000 to promote the [NCLB] law on his nationally syndicated show and to urge other journalists to do the same (Toppa, 2005).

It was determined through a Freedom of Information Act that the Williams contract was "part of a $1 million deal with Ketchum that produced "video news releases" designed to look like news reports." Similar releases were used to promote the government's Medicare prescription drug program the year before. The Government Accountability Office called this "an illegal use of taxpayers' dollars" (Toppa, 2005).

In a front-page article in *The New York Times*, "Buying of News by Bush's Aides is Ruled Illegal," Robert Pear reported:

> The Bush Administration violated the law by buying favorable news coverage of its education policies by making payments to the conservative commentator Armstrong Williams and by hiring a public relations company to analyze media perceptions of the Republican Party … . The Government Accountability Office, an independent nonpartisan arm of Congress, said the administration had disseminated "covert propaganda" in the United States, in violation of a statutory ban (Pear, 2005, p. 1).

Pear noted that the Department of Education in March 2003 had directed Ketchum to use Mr. Williams as a regular commentator on Mr. Bush's education policies. "Ketchum had a federal contract to help publicize those policies, signed by Mr. Bush in 2002" (p. 3). According to the Government Accountability Office, such

[p]repackaged news stories are purposefully designed to be indistinguishable from news segments broadcast to the public. When the television viewing public does not know that the stories they watched on television news programs about the government were in fact prepared by the government, the stories are, in this sense, no longer factual. The essential fact of attribution is missing (Pear, 2005, p. 3).

THE PRIVATIZATION OF EDUCATION: WHO BENEFITS? WHO IS DISADVANTAGED?

In the privatization of education, there are some who benefit financially or in other ways; then there are those who will be disadvantaged. Bracey considers that two of the most powerful weapons in the battle against public education are private schools and the numerous private companies that manage "private" schools for profit (interview with Redovich, 2002). When education is conducted as a business venture, profit becomes the bottom line; in such a context, it is doubtful that there will be genuine concern for children and education within a democracy.

Public schools and schools run by EMOs are driven by very different ideologies and principles; they serve different purposes. Public entities exist for the common good, whereas profit-making entities exist for the increased wealth of their shareholders.

Testing Companies' Profit from Accountability through Standardized Testing

Profit increases for test-makers are ensured by accountability through standardized testing. It is estimated that the states are likely to spend $1.9 to $5.3 billion between 2002 and 2008 to implement NCLB-mandated tests, according to the nonpartisan general accounting office (GAO) (Miner, 2004/2005). Harcourt Educational Measurement, CTB McGraw, and Riverside Publishing have traditionally dominated the market for developing tests. However, new companies are appearing, the foremost being Pearson Educational Measurement. It is almost impossible to uncover the finances of these private companies (Miner, 2004/2005).

Profit-making opportunities for test-making companies continue to increase, as they are now producing software to help teachers prepare students for the testing. Further complicating matters, the major test publishers are said to have connections with current government administration. "Following [President] Bush's first election and his unveiling of the NCLB, testing companies' representatives descended on Congress to push for the type of standardized testing that Bush had made so popular in Texas" (Miner, 2004/2005).

Providers of Supplemental Educational Services (SES) Profit

SES provides $2 billion a year (Bracey, 2005) for the private sector. NCLB requires districts to make SES available to students from low-income families and who attend schools that, according to the AYP reports, have not made sufficient academic progress. To be eligible for SES, students must attend schools that have not made AYP for 3 consecutive years. The lowest-achieving students will receive these services, which are provided outside the regular school day and which may include tutoring, remediation, or other education interventions (AFT, 2005c, pp. 1,2). Individual states are required to select special services providers (SSPs) based on selected criteria. However, SSP staff members do not have to meet the definition of "highly qualified teacher."

Ironically, the regulations do not require the SSP to serve students with disabilities or limited English skills. The AFT therefore is concerned that providers will choose to serve the "easiest to educate" children, whereas those with the greatest needs will be left behind" (AFT, 2005c, p. 2). Another concern of the AFT is the protection of civil rights: SSPs are not required to adhere to federal nondiscrimination laws (AFT, 2005c, p. 2). Gootman, in the *New York Times* (March 8, 2006), reported serious problems with the tutoring program, including disclosure by school officials of confidential information such as children's telephone numbers and addresses, bribery of principals with projects for their schools, and the hiring of workers with criminal records. There is much to be lost if the implementation of the NCLB Act goes unchallenged by teachers and parents.

Through NCLB's SES, individual tutors and tutoring companies such as Sylvan and Kaplan stand to benefit excessively from the huge amounts of money promised by the federal government for the tutoring of some children. "Kaplan says revenue for its elementary and secondary school division has doubled since No Child Left Behind" (Kronholz, 2003). Assessment fees average $175 and hourly rates average $40 to $48 for K-12 tutoring in one of the two top tutoring services in North America. Washington lobbyists for test-making conglomerates and the owners of the private schools that replace public schools, as a result of AYP policy, will continue to draw lucrative salaries.

Moving from Being a Traditional Public School to an EMO School

When a school has been on the SINI list for 2 consecutive years, parents are given the choice of leaving their children there or sending them to another school. Meanwhile the district will develop a 2-year plan to turn the school around. If the school does not make adequate progress for 3 consecutive years, the board will continue to offer choices to the parents and the children from low-income families such as tutoring or remedial classes offered by private providers. After 4 years on the SINI list, the district must implement certain corrective actions to improve the schools. These actions may include replacing certain staff or fully implementing a new curriculum, while continuing to offer public school choice and supplemental educational services for low-income students. If a school fails to make adequate yearly progress during the 5th year, the school district must initiate plans for restructuring the school. This may include reopening the school as a charter school, replacing all or most of the staff, or turning the operation of the school over to either a state or private company with a record of effectiveness (U.S. Department of Education, 2003).

This is where for-profit companies such as Edison, the largest EMO in the United States, become players in the NCLB scenario. Edison's Web site contains the following information:

> Founded in 1992, Edison Schools is the nation's leading partner with public schools and school districts, focused on raising student achievement through its research-based school design, uniquely aligned assessment systems, interactive professional development, integrated use of technology and other proven program features. (Edison Web site, 2005) For the 2004–2005 academic year, Edison Schools Inc. served more than 250,000 public school students in over 20 states across the country and in the U.K. through its whole-school management partnerships with districts and charter schools; summer, after-school, and SES programs; and achievement management solutions for school systems. (Edison Schools, 2005)

The financial saga of Edison has been up and down. Over the years, it has received large amounts of government and private funding. On July 15, 2003, Henriques, of the *New York Times*, reported that

> After four roller-coaster years as a publicly traded company, Edison Schools, the nation's largest for-profit manager of public schools, announced yesterday that its board had accepted a bid of about $174 million by its founder and chief executive, H. Christopher Whittle, to take the company private. She noted that Edison's stock made its debut on Wall Street at $18 a share in 1999, closed as high as $36.75 a share in February 2001, and fell to 14 cents a share October 2002. Mr. Whittle remained the main shareholder.

Bracey (2003a, p. ix) reminds us that "as a publicly traded company, Edison's obligations are to its stockholders." It is "not to the parents of the children who attend their schools" (p. 19). "[Edison] is about the care and feeding of markets, not the education of children" (Bracey, 2005, p. 147). Also, Edison has been a failure; it has neither rewarded its investors nor increased educational achievement.

Freeman (2005b), formerly vice president of international marketing at Sybase and now a teacher of economics and history at Los Altos High School, reminds us that "[c]orporations are wonderful things, but they only work for a profit. To make a profit from our schools you need to do two things: increase efficiency and reduce costs" (p. 2). He says that "[i]ncreasing efficiency means removing variability while boosting output. This is a great formula for mass-producing hamburgers or semi-conductors. It is a disaster for producing intelligence and character in children" (p. 2). He believes that "if it is to make a profit, the only plausible vision that mass privatized education has to offer us [is] McStudents" (p. 2).

Despite these educational and fiscal failures, Steven Wilson, a senior fellow at the Kennedy School of Government at Harvard and a former school management entrepreneur, states, Edison's history notwithstanding, "Wall Street is extraordinarily close-minded about education as a business opportunity. There clearly is renewed private-equity interest that wasn't there a year ago." The backers of the educational management organizations industry "are fond of comparing it to the healthcare industry of 25 years ago, before the ascendancy of the health maintenance organizations (HMOs)" (Miner, 2002b, p. 2). Sandler, Chairman of Eduventures, an education industry research firm in Boston, believes that, "For the industry, having Edison out of the public limelight is an opportunity for the market to better digest the enormous opportunities that the different sectors of this industry offer" (Henriques, 2003). The appetite for privatization of the schools has not been diminished; on the contrary, it remains strong.

IS THERE A FUTURE FOR PUBLIC EDUCATION?

There is a future for public education, but only if educators and parents join in their efforts to protect it from those who wish to dismantle the system. The underlying ideology of public education continues to offer the possibility of moving toward Horace Mann's vision of public education as the "great equalizer of opportunity." As Ayers (chapter 12 of this volume) reminds us, authentic educational reform is concerned with the human and relational nature of teaching. Privatization, standardized testing, and the AYP of the NCLB Act ignore such considerations. The answer to Ayers' question "What and who do we see as we look out at our students?" determines the type of education that we strive to provide for them. Whereas privatizers may tend to see students as a source of profit, educators see students as human works-in-progress who along with their teachers can develop their potential within a democracy.

Ohanian notes (chapter 13 of this volume) that "this whole corporate-politico operation isn't about caring for children but about molding a workforce to be scared and compliant." She details how NCLB undermines the professionalism of teachers and the teaching profession and suggests that "one way for teachers to break out of their isolation is to understand the meaning of the assault on public education and to become active in a struggle against corporate power." But this effort to bring about authentic educational reform must be done with an awareness of the complexity of the task involved.

WHAT WE FAIL TO RECOGNIZE ABOUT THE ACHIEVEMENT GAP: SOCIAL CONDITIONS

Rothstein (2004), of the Economic Policy Institute, says that "the fact that children's skills can so clearly be predicted by their race and family income status is a direct challenge to our democratic ideals" (p. 6). He believes that the

> [c]ommonsense perspective—that the achievement gap is the fault of "failing schools"—is misleading and dangerous for it ignores how social class characteristics in a stratified society like ours may actually influence learning in school. It confuses social class, a concept that Americans have been loath to consider, with two of its characteristics, income and, in the United States, race. For it is true that low income and skin color themselves don't influence academic achievement, but the collection of characteristics that define social class differences inevitably influences that achievement (Rothstein, 2004, p. 6)[1].

Rothstein contends that "one of the bars to our understanding of the achievement gap is that most Americans, even well-educated ones, are inexpert in discussion of statistical distributions" (p. 8). He argues that

> The influence of social class characteristics is probably so powerful that schools cannot overcome it, no matter how well trained are their teachers and no matter how well designed are their instructional programs and climates. But saying that a social class achievement gap should be accepted is not to make a logical statement (Rothstein, 2004, p. 8).

Rothstein suggests three tracks that "should be pursued "vigorously and simultaneously if we are to make significant progress in narrowing the achievement gap. The first is "school improvement efforts that raise the quality of instruction in elementary schools"; second, "expanding the definition of schooling to include crucial out-of-school hours in which families and communities now are the sole influences … . Implementing comprehensive early childhood, after school, and summer programs;"[2] and third, "social and economic policies that enable children to attend school equally ready to learn … health services for lower-class children and their families, stable housing for working families with children, and the narrowing of growing income inequalities for American society" (Rothstein, 2004, pp. 11,12).

LOOKING TO THE FUTURE: TEACHERS, PARENTS, AND CITIZENS SPEAK OUT

With the continuing ascendancy of conservative thought, the threat to public education is likely to increase. At issue, here, is how best to respond to this pressure and, at the same time, move education forward.

Monty Neill, executive director of the National Center for Fair Open Testing (Fair Test) in Cambridge, Massachusetts, argues that

> NCLB is a fundamentally punitive law …. It must be transformed into a supportive law that really promotes school improvement and makes good on the promise to leave no child behind. The legislation must be reconsidered and rewritten, particularly in the areas of assessment and accountability. But given the current climate, this won't be an easy task (Neill, 2003, p. 1).

Neill believes that to change this law, if indeed we can, "we will have to build a powerful national alliance among education and civil rights organizations and strengthen our public engagement. Advocates can start by recognizing there is wide public concern around some key components of NCLB" (2003, p. 4). According to Neil, these components include the one-size-fits-all nature of testing; the unfairness of making decisions about students, teachers, and schools based only on test scores; and the danger of teaching to the test. Neill recognizes that "education organizations alone cannot do it alone. Individual teachers must take an active and prominent role in educating the public about the law and its negative impact. They can reach out to the public and parents."

Kohn contends that

> NCLB [rechristened by some as No Child Left Untested] usurps the power of local communities to choose their own policies and programs. It represents a power grab on the part of the federal government that is unprecedented in the history of U.S. education … compromises the quality of teaching … [and] … punishes those who most need help (Meier & Wood, 2004, p. 79).

A rallying cry might focus on the meddling of the federal government in the affairs of the local schools and the negative consequences of this usurping of traditional prerogatives. To ensure that NCLB as it now exists is altered to adhere to principles that are educationally sound and democratic, teachers, parents, and concerned citizens must speak out: Our voices must be heard as advocates for America's children. We need to remind the government and the privatizers, referred to by Berkowitz (2003) as "privateers" and by Freeman (2005a, p. 2) as "prophets of profit," that "public education is not only the most important democratizing institution in America today. It is the foundation of our economic future as well" (Freeman, 2005a, p. 5).

The improvement of public education is indeed a "task for the nation" (Borosage, 2004). Recognizing this and regardless of the ideology that is driving the NCLB legislation, we, as educators, parents, and citizens, must challenge the government on the fundamental flaws inherent in NCLB. It is our responsibility to become the counterforce to privatization and demand that government critically reexamine the basic assumptions underlying NCLB, and create legislation that will truly improve the education of all children. This includes not only looking at the school- and classroom-related issues but looking for solutions to the serious problems that are considered by government to be external to the school: poverty, health, housing, and other issues that impact education and the well-being of our children. In shirking this responsibility, we become complicit in the dismantling of public education; we become accessories to the crime.

REFERENCES

American Federation of Teachers (AFT). (2005a). *Adequate Yearly Progress (AYP)*. http://www.aft.org/topics/nclb/ayp.htm.

AFT (2005b). *Public school choice & supplemental education services*. http://www.aft.org/topics/nclb/ses.htm.

AFT. (2005c). *Public school choice & supplemental education services*. http://www.aft.org/topics/nclb/ses.htm.

Apple, M. (1990). *Ideology and curriculum*. New York: Routledge, Chapman & Hall.

Belfield, C.R., & Levin, H.M. (2002). The effects of competition on educational outcomes: A review of the U.S. evidence. *Review of Educational Research, 27*, 279–341.

Belfield, C.R., & Levin, H.M. (2003). The economics of tuition tax credits for US schools. *NTA Proceedings*, 95th Annual Conference on Taxation, 1–15.

Berkowitz, B. (2003, January). Edison Schools going under? *Z Magazine Online, 16*(1). http://zmagsite.org/Jan2003/berkowitzprint0103.shtml.

Bifulco, R., & Ladd, H. (2003, November). *Charter school impacts on student performance: Evidence from North Carolina*. APPAM Paper.

Borosage, R. (2004). Why high quality-education is the democratic challenge of our time. http://www.prospect.org/web/page.ww? section=root&name=ViewPrint&articleId=6997.

Bracey, G. (2003a). *What you should know about the war against America's public schools*. Boston: Allyn and Bacon.

Bracey, G. (2003b, October). The 13th Bracey Report on the condition of public education. *Phi Delta Kappa.*

Bracey, G. (2003c). *The No Child Left Behind Act, a plan for the destruction of public education: Just say no.* A Gerald Bracey report on the condition of education. Education Disinformation Detection and Reporting Agency. http://www.america-tomorrow.com/bracey.

Bracey, G. (2005, October). The 15th Bracey Report on the condition of public education. *Phi Delta Kappa.*

Buddin, R., & Zimmer, R. (2003, November). *Student achievement in charter schools: New evidence from California*. APPAM Paper.

Carneiro, P., & Heckman, J.J. (2003). Human capital policy. In J.J. Heckman & A.B. Krueger (Eds.). *Inequality in America: What role for human capital policies?* Cambridge, MA: MIT Press.

Chin, T., & Philips, M. (2004). *Season of inequality: Exploring the summer activity gap*. http://www.aft.org/pubsreports/american_educator/issues/summer2005/chin.htm.

Committee on Education and the Workforce (2004). Democratic Staff. U.S. House of Representatives. September 24. http://edworkforce.house.gov/democrats/brokenpromisesreport.html.

Darling-Hammond, L. (2004). From "separate but equal" to "No Child Left Behind": The collision of new standards and old inequalities. In D. Meier & G. Wood (Eds.). *Many children left behind: How the No Child Left Behind Act is damaging our children and our schools.* Boston: Beacon Press.

Dobbin, M. (1996). The charter school threat to public education in Canada, in *Issues In Ontario education.* http://www.osst6f.on.ca/www/issues/charter/charter.html

Dunbar, G.L. (2004, June). Privatization of public education: The real weapons of mass destruction. *The Journal of Undergraduate Neuroscience Education, 2*(2), E2.www.funjournal.org.

http://www.ed.gov/print/about/overview/budget/budget06/nclb/index.html.

Edison Schools. (2005). http://www.edisonschools.com

Feldman, S. (2003). QuEST Keynote address. http://www.aft.org/presscenter/speeches-columns/speeches/feldman071003.htm.

Freeman, R. (2005a). Is public education working? How would we know? *Common Dreams News Center.* http://www.commondreams.org/cgi-bin/print.cgi?file=/views05/01103-22. htm.

Freeman, R. (2005b). *Getting our money's worth in public education: Are we buying our "McStudent" lie?* http://www.commondreams.org/cgi-bin/print.cgi?file=/view05/0118-28htm.htm.

Friedman, M. (1962). The role of government in education. In *Capitalism and freedom.* Chicago: Chicago University Press.

Friedman, M. (1995). *Public schools: Make them private.* CATO Briefing Papers. Downloaded from http://www.cato.org/cgi-/bin/scripts/ printtech. cgi/pubs/briefs/bp-023.html.

Gootman, E. (2006). Report assails tutoring firms in city schools. New York Times, Metro Section, B1 & B6. March 8.

Greene, J.P., Peterson, P.E., & Du, J. (1998). School choice in Milwaukee: A randomized experiment. In P.E. Peterson & B.C. Hassel (Eds.). *Learning from school choice.* Brookings Institution, Washington, DC.

Hammons, C.W. (2001). *The effects of town tuitioning in Vermont and Maine.* Mimeo, Milton & Rose D. Friedman Foundation. http://www.friedmanfoundation.org.

Hanushek, E.A. (1998). Conclusions and controversies about the effectiveness of schools. *Federal Reserve Bank of New York Economic Policy Review, 4,* 1–22.

Helderman, R.S. and Mui, Y.Q. (2003). View on school's progress unclear. Washington Post (September 25).

Henig, J.R. (1994). *Rethinking school choice: Limits of the market metaphor.* Princeton, NJ: Princeton University Press

Henriques, D.B. (2003, July 15). Edison Schools' founder to take it private. *The New York Times.* http://www,nytimes.com/2003/07/15/business/15EDIS.html?ei=5007&en=538146c2b3303963&e.

Hochschild, R., & Scovronick, N. (2003). *The American dream and the public schools.* New York: Oxford University Press.

Houston, R.G., & Toma, E.F. (2003). Home-schooling: An alternative school choice. *Southern Economic Journal, 69,* 920–935.

Howell, W.G., & Peterson, P.E. (2002). *The education gap. Vouchers and urban public schools.* Washington: Brookings.

Hoxby, C.M. (Ed.). (2003). *The economics of school choice.* Chicago: University of Chicago and NBER Press.

Kahlenberg, R. (2004). *Schools of hard knocks.* http://www.prospect.org.org/web/printfriendly-view.ww?id=7637.

Karp, S. (2001). Bush plan fails schools: Wrapped in compassionate rhetoric, the President's proposals center on mandatory testing vouchers programs that would leave millions of children behind. *Rethinking Schools* Online. http://www.rethinkngschools.org/special_reports/bushplan/Bush153.shtml.

Karp, S. (2004a). NCLB's selective vision of equality: Some gaps count more than others. In D. Meier & G. Wood (Eds.). (2004). *Many children left behind: How the No Child Left Behind Act is damaging our children and our schools.* Boston: Beacon Press.

Karp, S. (2004b). Taming the beast. *Rethinking Schools.* Summer 2004. http://www.rethimkingschools.org/archive/18_04/tami184.shtml.

Kirkpatrick, D.D. (2006). Hanging in: he's battered but his agenda isn't beaten. New York Times (Mar. 5). Week in Review (Section 4, pp. 1, 3).

Kohn, A. (2004). NCLB and the effort to privatize public education. In D. Meier & G. Wood (Eds.). (2004). *Many children left behind: How the No Child Left Behind Act is damaging our children and our schools.* Boston: Beacon Press.

Kozol, J. (1991). *Savage inequalities: Children in America.* New York: Crown Publishers.

Kozol, J. (2000). *The shame of the nation: A savagely unequal school system betrays New York's ideals.* http://www.refuseandresist.org/resist_this/060500kozol.html.

Kronholz, J. (2003). Education firms see money in Bush's school-boostlaw. Wall Street Journal (December 24). http://pipeline.com/~rgibson/educationfirms.html.

Krueger, A.B., & Zhu, P. (2004). Another look at the New York City school voucher experiment. *American Behavioral Scientist, 47,* 658–698.

Lenti, L. (2003). *New wave of voucher programs? The Colorado Opportunity Contract Pilot Program.* Occasional Paper, National Center for the Study of Privatization in Education.

Levin, H.M. (2001a). *Privatizing education: Can the market deliver freedom of choice, productive efficiency, equity and social cohesion?* Boulder, CO: Westview Press.

Levin, H.M. (2001b). Thoughts on for-profit schools. Occasional paper, National Center for the Study of Privatization in Education, http://www.ncspe.org.

Levin, H.M., & Belfield, C.R. (2004). The marketplace in education. *Review of Research in Education,* forthcoming.

Lines, P. (2000). Home-schooling comes of age. *The Public Interest,* 140, 74–85.

Linn, R. (2003). Accountability: Responsibility and Reasonable Expectations. AERA 2003 Presidential Address. Educational Researcher, Vol. No. 7, pp. 3–13.

McKenzie, J. (2003). *The NCLB wrecking ball.* http://www.nochildleft.com/2003/nov02wrecking.html.

Meese, E. III, Butler, S.M., & Holmes, K.R. (2005). *From tragedy to triumph: Principled solutions for rebuilding lives and communities.* RESEARCH: Government Reform. Special Report No. 05. September 12, 2005. http://www.heritage.org/Research/GovernmentReform/sr05.cfm.

Meier, D., & Wood, G. (Eds.). (2004). *Many children left behind: How the No Child Left Behind Act is damaging our children and our schools.* Boston: Beacon Press.

Metcalf, K.K., West, S.D., Legan, N.A., Paul, K.M., & Boone, W.J. (2003). *Evaluation of the Cleveland scholarship and tutoring program,* Summary Report 1998-2002. Bloomington: Indiana University School of Education.

Miner, B. (2001). Bush's plan is shallow and ignores critical details. In *Rethinking Schools Online.* http://www.rethinkngschools.org/special_reports/bushplan/bush.shtml.

Miner, B. (2002a). Why the right hates public education. *Rethinking Schools Online*. http://www.rethinkngschools.org/special_reports/bushplan/rightPRO.shtml.

Miner, B. (2002b, January/February). Privatization: Rip-offs and resistance. Business goes to school: The for-profit corporate drive to run public schools. *Multinational Monitor, 23*(1&2). http://multinationalmnitor.org/mm2002/02jan-feb/jan-feb02corp2.html.

Miner, B. (2004/2005). Keeping public schools public: Testing companies mine for gold. *Rethinking Schools Online*. http://www.rethinkngschools.org/special_reports/bushplan/test192.shtml.

Miron, G., & Nelson, C. (2002). *What's public about charter schools?* Thousand Oaks, California: Corwin Press.

Moe, T.M. (2001). *Schools, vouchers and the American public*. Washington, DC: Brookings Press.

Moyers, B. (1996). *Children in America's schools with Bill Moyers*. Film based on J. Kozol's *Savage inequalities*, J. Hayden & K. Cauthen (Producers) & J. Hayden (Director). South Carolina: ETV.

NCES. (2004, July). *Home-schooling in the US*. Issue Brief. http://www.nces.ed.gov.

Neill, M. (Fall 2003). Don't mourn, organize! Making lemonade from NCLB lemons. *Rethinking Schools*. http://www.rethinkingschools.org/special_reports/bushplan/nclb181.html.

New York Times (2006, March 5), Week in review, p. 3.

New York Times (2006, April 6), p. 1.

Noguera, P. (1993). Confirming the challenge of privatization in public education. *In Motion Magazine*. http:/www./inmotionmagazine.com/pnpriv1.html.

Noguera, P. (2003, August 13). Taking on the tough issues: The role of educational leaders in restoring public faith in educational issues. *In Motion Magazine*. http://www.inmotionmagazine.com/er/pn_leaders.html.

Obey, D. (2005, April 15). House Appropriations Committee. Letter to colleagues and attachments. http://www.house.gov/appropriations_democrats/press/pr_050421.htm.

Ohanian, S. (2004). *NCLB in your face: Ten changes needed to improve NCLB*. http://www.susanohanian.org/show_nclb_stories.html?id=140.

Pear, R. (2005, October 1). Buying of news by Bush's aides is ruled illegal. *New York Times*. http://www.nytimes.com/2005/10/01/politics/01educ.html.

PRNewswire. (2005). Penguin Group publishes new book by CEO Chris Whittle. August 23. New York: Riverhead Books, Penguin Group (USA).

Redovich, D. (2002, April). *Commercializing education*: Interview with Gerald Bracey, author of *The war against America's public schools*. Center for the Study of Jobs & Education in Wisconsin and the United States.

Robertson, H. (1999). Shall we dance? (The privatization of education). www.creativeresistance.ca/awareness/1999-aug-13-privatization-of-education.

Rose, L.C., & Gallup, A.M. (2001). *33rd poll of the public's attitudes toward the public schools*. http://www.pdkintl.org/kappan/kimages/kpoll83.pdf.

Rothstein, R. (2004). *Class and schools: Using social, economic, and educational reform to close the black-white achievement gap*. New York: Teachers College Press.

Rouse, C.E. (1998). Private school vouchers and student achievement: An evaluation of the Milwaukee Parental Choice Program. *Quarterly Journal of Economics, 113*, 553–602.

Segal, L.G. (2003). *Battling corruption in America's public schools*. Boston: Northeastern University Press.

Stevens, M.L. (2001). *Kingdom of children: Culture and controversy in the home-schooling movement*. Princeton, NJ: Princeton University Press.

Sugarman, S.D., & Kemerer, F.R. (Eds.). (1999). *School choice and social controversy: Politics, policy and law*. Washington, DC: Brookings Institute.

Sugarman, S.D. (2002). Charter school funding issues. *Education Policy Analysis Archives, 10*(34). http://www.epaa.asu.edu/epaa/v10n34.

Teske, P., & Schneider, M. (2001). What research can tell policymakers about school choice. *Journal of Policy Analysis and Management, 20*, 609–632.

Toppa, G. (2005, January 6). Education Department paid commentator to promote law. *USA Today*. www.SATODAY.com—Education Dept. paid commentator to promote law.

U.S. Department of Education. (2003). *NCLB. A Parents Guide*. Washington, DC.: ED Pubs, Education Publications Center.

U.S. House of Representatives. Democratic Staff, Committee on Education and Workforce. Sept. 24, 2004. http://edworkforce.house.gov/democrats/brokenpromisesreport.html.

Vitteriti, J.P. (1999). *Choosing equality*. Washington, DC: Brookings Institution.

Whittle, C. (2005). Crash course: Imagining a better future for public education. New York: Riverhead Books, Penguin Group (USA).

Witte, J.F. (1999). *The market approach to education*. Princeton, NJ: Princeton University Press.

Wolfe, A. (Ed.). (2003). *School choice: The moral debate*. Princeton, NJ: Princeton University Press.

Wood, G. (2004). A view from the field: NCLB's effects on classrooms and schools. In D. Meier & G. Wood (Eds.), *Many children left behind: How the No Child Left Behind Act is damaging our children and our schools*. Boston: Beacon Press.

Zelman vs. Simmons-Harris. (2002). U.S. Supreme Court, 00751.

NOTES

1. For a detailed discussion of Rothstein's analysis, please see Rothstein (2004) or go to http: www.epinet.org.

2. To learn more about the potential of quality summer programs to "bring greater equity to the summer season," please see Chin and Philips (2004) or go to http://www.aft.org/pubsreports/american_educator/issues/summer2005/chin.htm.

4

High-Stakes Testing and No Child Left Behind (NCLB): Conceptual and Empirical Considerations

PATRICK B. JOHNSON

With the passage of NCLB and its emphasis on accountability to ensure students' academic achievement, student assessment has taken on far greater significance and urgency. In addition to providing a measure of whether a student has success-fully reached some arbitrary standard or benchmark, assessment also provides a measure of whether a teacher's class as a group has reached a similarly arbitrary standard. With the passage of NCLB, failure to achieve the standard carries seri-ous negative consequences both for students and teachers. For the student, it may result in mandated summer school, tutoring, or grade retention. For the teacher, it may result in special mentoring, after-school workshops, and increasing job insecurity. These consequences are all triggered by students' scores obtained on single tests given at one point during the school year. According to Spring (2004), a high-stakes test "refers to an examination that determines a person's future academic career and job opportunities" (p. 36).

HIGH-STAKES TESTING: HISTORICAL, CONCEPTUAL, AND EMPIRICAL ANALYSES

High-Stakes Testing: Recent Background

Much of the current concern about American academic performance and its ulti-mate impact on national competitiveness in the global economy can be traced to the publication of *A Nation at Risk: The Imperative for Educational Reform* (National Council on Excellence in Education, 1983). This report decried the mediocrity of American education and contrasted it with Japanese schools. Although the political motives behind this report have been widely circulated (Bell, 1988; Berliner & Biddle, 1995), for unknown reasons, most educators accepted the validity of the report and its indictment of American schools. Cremin (1989), an exception, suggested that the report "is at best a foolish and at worst a crass effort to direct attention away from those truly responsible for doing something about competitiveness and to lay the burden instead on the schools. It is a device that has been used repeatedly in the history of American education" (pp. 102, 103).

To provide additional historical perspective, Bracey (2003) suggested that any thoughtful analysis of subsequent economic history would have strikingly demonstrated the fallaciousness of the report's assumptions, findings, and conclusions. Shortly after the publication of *A Nation at Risk*, Japan's economy fell into a long period of decline at precisely the same time that the American economy surged to become the standard to which other nations aspired. Interestingly, during this time or subsequently, little was said about the role American schools played in this unanticipated economic reversal (Bracey, 2003).

It is in this context that one should seriously question the current despair and hand-wringing regarding the poor quality of American education and the poor comparative performance of American students in international studies. According to Berliner and Biddle (1995), the poor performance of American students in such studies can be explained, at least partially, by the fact that in the United States all public school students participate in these tests; whereas in other countries, only those students attending academically rigorous schools are included. Clearly, such an apples-to-oranges comparison places American students at considerable academic disadvantage compared to students from other countries.

It is also in this context that one needs to understand the emergence of NCLB in 2001 and the central emphasis it places on testing our way to successful academic achievement. Although there appears to be little, if any, relationship between academic competitiveness and a nation's economic competitiveness (Bracey, 2003; Spring, chapter 1 of this volume), today the American public is once again being inundated with propaganda to the contrary, as special interest groups including the testing industry and tutoring companies line up to make a killing at the expense of generally dedicated teachers and hard-working and overstressed children.

It should also be added, however, that an additional rationale for NCLB can be found in the long-standing racial disparities observed in American education (NCLB, 2001, Sec. 101) and an apparent desire by policymakers to enhance the academic performance of all groups (Kim & Sunderman, 2005). Accordingly, school districts must now disaggregate performance scores separately for different racial, ethnic, and socioeconomic groups to ensure that all groups are making adequate yearly progress (AYP). Unfortunately, because the law also requires that academic progress be determined by mean group proficiency scores, schools with large populations of economically disadvantaged students and racially diverse student populations are more likely to fall short of their AYP requirements, as recently demonstrated in the analyses of Kim and Sunderman (2005). This is because the mean accords greater weight to extreme scores than would the median score.

High-Stakes Testing: A Conceptual Analysis

The term *high-stakes testing* does not appear in the hundreds of pages of the NCLB law. A central focus rests instead on accountability and holding key constituents responsible for educational outcomes. The general idea is that unless students and their teachers are held accountable for poor academic performance, performance will continue to suffer or further deteriorate. From this perspective, it is the specter of these negative consequences or stakes that are supposed to motivate students to learn more and teachers to transmit information more effectively. It is the fear engendered by these consequences that will ensure that "no child is left behind." Now, of course, should a child fail to perform to standard, he or she, in reality, can be summarily left behind their current peer group.

B.F. Skinner, the most influential learning theorist of the 20th century, conducted countless studies on the differential impacts of carrots (reinforcements) and sticks (punishments) on learning. And, let us not kid ourselves about the true meaning of the current high-stakes-testing environment, in which children are being threatened with the ultimate academic punishment—grade retention. According to Skinner (1951), punishment is a wholly ineffective technique because its most immediate effect is to suppress rather than eliminate unwanted behavior. How suppression could move a child from ineffective to effective learning strategies is not readily apparent. Nor has anyone identified specific studies that demonstrate fear and punishment produce more effective learning or a desire for lifelong learning.

Now, Skinner did identify "extraordinary" circumstances in which punishment was effective at eliminating unwanted behavior, such as when severe punishment was applied. However, he warned that the side effects of severe punishment were so unpredictable that it should never be used to facilitate learning (see examples under "The Impact of High-Stakes Testing on Students" below).

Not surprisingly, short-sighted policymakers, looking for a quick fix to solve the "problems" of American education, have ignored this warning and plunged ahead without considering the likely consequences of severely punishing large numbers of children. Although it can certainly be argued that high-stakes testing ultimately will hold teachers and administrators, or even parents, responsible for the poor education of American children, the harsh reality is that in its most immediate impact, it is the children, especially those from disadvantaged socio-economic circumstances, who are being held responsible and being severely punished when they fail to perform well on these tests.

According to Spring (2004), using high-stakes tests to motivate schoolchildren is an attempt to motivate them by fear of failure. Unfortunately, a central problem with fear-of-failure motivation is that the best way to avoid failure is simply to avoid putting yourself in an achievement situation (Weiner, 1992). Following from this, one obvious way to avoid academic failure would be to drop out of school, a solution increasingly resorted to by students following the introduction of high-stakes testing in Chicago (Roderick, Nagaoka, & Allensworth, 2005) when social promotion was eliminated, and in Louisiana, the first state to mandate such tests statewide, a state in which approximately 1 in 3 students drop out before completing high school (Harvard University, 2005).

High-Stakes Testing: An Empirical Analysis

In the current educational environment with its emphasis on evidence-based practice and data-driven decision for teachers, it seems only reasonable that a momentous policy decision such as mandating high-stakes testing for all public school children would be based not just on the results of a few studies, but rather on an avalanche of supportive findings. This is especially true given Skinner's findings on the dangers associated with using punishment to modify learning. However, as Joel Spring points out (chapter 1 of this volume), actually there is no data to support the contention that the use of such testing will enhance student learning or improve teachers' teaching.

Unfortunately, our political leaders are not being held to the same evidentiary standards as the teachers they so often and easily criticize. Nor are these leaders required to be responsive to evidence that runs counter to their beliefs about the need to subject children to high-stakes testing. A particularly egregious example of this know-nothing, antiempirical approach can be found in the recently enacted New York City public school policy to end social promotion. Despite considerable evidence suggesting that such a policy was doomed to failure based on countless studies, including a recent 9-year study of the detrimental effects of a similar policy change in Chicago (Roderick et al., 2005), the mayor of New York and his hand-picked school chancellor, neither of whom had any background in education, imposed this policy on the largest school district in the country. Both dismissed the Chicago findings by emphasizing that New York City was not Chicago—a true but irrelevant point, given that both are large, urban school districts with large numbers of poor, minority students. They contended instead, possibly based upon some intuitive "knowledge," that the policy of ending social promotion and imposing high-stakes testing for third-graders would be successful in New York.

Although there is no evidence indicating that high-stakes testing will improve learning and teaching, there is a great deal of empirical evidence on the negative correlated consequences of such testing both on students and their teachers.

THE IMPACT OF HIGH-STAKES TESTING ON STUDENTS

High-stakes testing impacts students in terms of their educational choices and options, their academic performance and intellectual development, and their psychological health. With regard to educational choices, empirical studies have repeatedly demonstrated positive associations between the introduction of high-stakes testing and increased student dropout rates (Darling-Hammond, 2000; Haney, 2000; Madaus & Clarke, 2001). The associations have been especially strong among poor and minority students, according to Madaus and Clarke (2001). They pointed out that the most negative academic effects of high-stakes testing, including grade retention and school dropout, are not experienced equally by all children but fall disproportionately on the small shoulders of those who possess special needs or who are most economically disadvantaged.

It is important to acknowledge, as Nieto and Johnson suggest (chapter 2 of this volume), that many poor parents are strong supporters of NCLB. They support it because they correctly perceive that they and their children have been seriously disadvantaged by an educational system seriously biased against them in terms of the inadequate resources and supports provided. Many of the parents believe, or at least hope, that NCLB will correct these inequities. Unfortunately, what we know about the impact of high-stakes tests is that their negative educational consequences—retention and dropout—will be disproportionately borne by their children under the current NCLB legislation. This was dramatically demonstrated in Haney's (2000) reanalysis of the "Texas educational miracle" data, which demonstrated the disproportionate numbers of Hispanic and African American students among those who dropped out following the advent of high-stakes testing in Texas in the 1990s.

A great deal of attention has also focused on the psychological impact of high-stakes testing on American children and adolescents. Much of this attention has revolved around the stress engendered by such tests, including general psychological distress and the test anxiety first identified by Mandler and Sarason (1952). Many students are intimately acquainted with the sympathetic nervous system signs of test anxiety, including sweating palms, nausea, and inhibited concentration and recall (Gregor, 2005; McCarthy & Goffin, 2005). For the many afflicted with this test-taking malady, high-stakes testing is not a recipe for academic success but rather a recipe for physical discomfort and poor test performance.

General psychological distress is another common concomitant of high-stakes tests. According to Abrams, Pedulla, and Madaus (2003), "increased levels of anxiety, stress, and fatigue are often seen among students participating in high stakes testing … " (p. 20). Other examples of the psychological consequences for children can be found throughout B. Johnson and D. Johnson's (2002) compelling book on high-stakes testing. For example, "As the children begin the first timed test, Kevin vomits in his hands and runs to the bathroom." "Gerard takes one look at the first section and begins to cry" (p. 141). Learning that they have failed the tests, "most of the children are crying." "One little girl in the room next door tells her friend, 'I'm going to kill myself'" (p. 177). They also cite a headline in a local paper that read, "Failure of LEAP Test Prompts Suicide Attempt by Fifteen Year Old Student" (p. 42).

There is also evidence that suggests some children may turn to alcohol and drugs to self-medicate the emotional distress produced by these tests (Morehouse, 2004). Then, too, some have suggested that rather than providing the necessary assistance that "at-risk" students certainly deserve, teachers particularly resent such students because of the threat they pose to the class's test average and the teacher's job security or salary advancement (Johnson & Johnson, 2002).

Some might argue that high-stakes tests and the negative consequences associated with failure will teach children that school is serious business to which they need apply themselves. The recently released summary of findings on Chicago's 9-year experiment to eliminate social promotion suggests otherwise (Roderick et al., 2005). Results revealed increased dropout rates among those children retained in the third grade. This is the same pattern observed by Haney (2000) in Texas following the advent of high-stakes testing in that state.

For all of these reasons, our current system of high-stakes testing must be seriously questioned. But those who have imposed and expanded this system are either ignoring this information or simply ignorant of it. As Kohn (2000) has passionately argued, it is our responsibility to educate them through whatever means will most expeditiously and effectively gain their attention.

An educational practice that increases the likelihood of school dropout rather than enhancing student's academic performance surely must be questioned. To label such a program No Child Left Behind is nothing less than cynical political propaganda. But there may be other serious, unintended consequences associated with use of such testing procedures.

The introduction of high-stakes tests produces a narrowing of the school curriculum (Horn, 2003; Madaus & Clarke, 2001). In a high-stakes testing environment, rather than offering students a full range of courses, what becomes emphasized is a narrow range of material focused on the material and subject matter to be tested.

Kohn (2000) has suggested that such narrowing has led to shallowness or superficiality in student thinking that inhibits their ability to think deeply about complex content material (Anderman, 1992). If true, this is certainly not helpful to our students as they prepare to compete against their counterparts from other technologically advanced societies. As Klein, McNeil, and Stout (2005) recently pointed out, "This emphasis on mastering a standardized, uncontroversial curriculum ... is killing off exactly the qualities our children need most to appeal to future employers, who want not just 'reading,' 'riting, and 'rithmetic,' but innovation, initiative, and flexibility" (p. 32).

THE IMPACT OF HIGH-STAKES TESTING ON TEACHERS

Teachers are the other group of educational stakeholders most immediately impacted by the tidal wave of high-stakes tests. The effects of such testing on teachers have been widely reported and here will only be briefly summarized.

A frequent and commonly reported complaint is that high-stakes tests force teachers to "teach to the test" or to focus their classroom instruction on the material likely to be covered on the test (Popham, 2001). This position was often voiced by teachers at the 2004 "Authentic Educational Reform" conference, as evidenced by Baghban and Li and by Zarnowski, Backner, and Engel (chapters 7 and 8 of this volume). For example, Baghban and Li emphasize that the "increasing, unceasing emphasis on testing and assessment" (p.) leads to the "imposition of highly scripted programs that tell them exactly what to do and what to say ... " (p. 105). Or, quoting a teacher from Zarnowski et al., "I have a lot of pressure from my administration to focus on test prep all day long" (p. 121).

Recently, an eighth-grade science teacher described the pressure she was feeling to produce lessons that emphasized the material to be tested either on the math or English Language Arts portions of New York's high-stakes tests. She had been asked repeatedly by her principal to focus on these materials, especially when the English teacher was absent. As Zarnowski and her colleagues have pointed out, increasingly, content areas such as science and social studies are being ignored, only focused upon when they are included on the tests.

Not surprisingly, a recent article in the *New York Times* (Saulny, 2005) revealed that middle-class parents are becoming restive about the restrictive educational practices currently in wide use in New York City. They "have complained of an increasing focus on test prep and remedial work, of a decreasing focus on science education ...." (Saulny, 2005, p. A1).

The emphasis on test-score-driven instruction forces teachers to ignore important academic areas and focus exclusively on those that will be tested. B. Johnson and D. Johnson (2002) highlight this tendency, as teachers are explicitly told to ignore science and social studies because they will not be on the tests.

High-stakes testing impacts teachers and teaching in other less direct ways. For example, the increased pressure on first-year teachers to produce positive test results heightens the stress in an already stress-filled first year. Terzian (2002) quotes a new teacher: "The pressures a first-year teacher faces are stressful enough; suddenly, I had to worry about keeping my job even before I had begun to teach." Such effects may be even more acute in teachers working in schools located in poor areas. Reporting on the reactions of these teachers, Wright (2002) concludes:

> The teachers are stressed and overwhelmed by all the curricular changes and pressure to teach to the test and raise scores. ... . They experience additional stress when helping students in poverty deal with problems within their families and neighborhoods. They are insulted when monetary awards are disbursed to schools and teachers of more privileged students. They are frustrated when they watch good teachers leave the school, and sometimes teaching in general (p. 12).

In addition, this pressure may negatively impact the relationships between teachers, both new and old, and their low-performing students, who may be subjected to additional strain in a high-stakes environment. Although teachers normally might focus additional attention and provide more academic support for low-performing students, in the high-stakes testing classroom such attention takes valuable time away from teaching those students likely to bring up the class average. In line with this, on more than one occasion I have heard school administrators recommend that teachers focus their attention on students most likely to show the most improvement in their scores or to move from one performance category to another even if they do not show a great deal of improvement. The implication here is clearly that it is not efficient to spend too much time with the lowest-performing students.

This also appears to be the position taken by states generally; many exclude large proportions of special-needs and second-language learners from their state-testing requirements. A recent U.S. Government Accountability Office report (2005) estimated that the average proportion of special-needs students excluded by states was close to 40%. The effect of such exclusionary policies is, of course, to artificially enhance state-test scores (Herman, 2000). At the same time, many states have requested variances to allow similar exclusions for NCLB-mandated tests, and in many instances these requests have been granted (Olson, 2005). In so doing, the Department of Education is clearly violating both the letter and spirit of NCLB. One unintended benefit of granting these exclusions has been that at least the children in these groups are spared the stress and travails associated with high-stakes testing. However, in requesting and in granting these exclusionary requests, federal and state educational leaders and administrators are once again marginalizing special-needs and second-language students.

In light of these and other practices, it is hardly surprising that many of the best teachers decide to leave the profession. Many became teachers because they wanted to educate children and teach them the skills necessary to be successful in life. They are now being asked to be complicit in a process that is antithetical to these goals and so choose to leave rather than participate (Spring, 2004; Wright, 2002).

In such an educational environment, it is likely that it will become increasingly difficult for schools to attract those who previously wanted to become "teachers" but now realize that "teaching" is not possible in the current climate. If this occurs, our educational system will have further reduced the availability of its most important resource: competent, effective teachers.

ALTERNATIVE ASSESSMENT METHODS

In the controversy surrounding high-stakes testing, the distinction between testing and assessment is often blurred or ignored altogether. In contrast to the considerable controversy surrounding the academic value of high-stakes testing, most educators involved in this debate recognize the value of educational assessment. Without accurate assessment, it is impossible to know if children are learning or to determine how best to help them to learn more or to do more efficiently. To assess something means to measure or quantify it, and there is little argument regarding the necessity of measuring student learning in some fashion. The real debates revolve around whether assessments should be summative and only provide information about what or how much a child has learned, or formative and provide information about how to enhance teaching and learning (Roddy, 2005). Then, too, debates continue regarding the most accurate, fair, and educationally sound method of conducting such assessments, and the determination of what precisely should be taught, and what assessed.

It is important to understand, therefore, that those educators, parents, policymakers, and students who are opposed to high-stakes testing are generally not opposed to assessment. They are simply convinced that reliance on single-moment assessments that mostly measure specific disconnected pieces of information or dead knowledge is not the best way to assess our children and to enhance their educational progress. Moreover, many are convinced that this approach may in fact be counterproductive when it comes to enhancing our children's knowledge base and their higher order cognitive skills (Popham, 2001).

For example, the National Research Council's committee on appropriate test use has stated: "An educational decision that will have a major impact on a test taker should not be made solely or automatically on the basis of a single test score" (Heubert & Hauser, 1999, p. 15).

Moreover, the International Reading Association (2006) and the National Council of Teachers of Mathematics (2006), organizations that represent reading teachers and mathematics teachers in this country, are both on record opposing high-stakes testing; each also recognizes the intrinsic value of assessment. The Reading Association's position is that "assessment should be used to improve education and benefit students rather than compare and pigeonhole them." According to the National Council of Mathematics Teacher' statement on high-stakes testing, "When assessments are used in thoughtful and meaningful ways, students' scores provide important information … . The misuse of tests for high-stakes purposes has subverted the benefits these tests can bring if they are used appropriately" (p. 1). It is worth noting that these two organizations represent the disciplines initially impacted by the high-stakes testing associated with NCLB.

At the same time, opposition to high-stakes testing in no way indicates opposition to standards-based instruction, but rather to the current preoccupation with mindless test prep and administration with serious consequences for students and teachers that have little to do with classroom instruction or learning. In emphasizing the distinction between standards and high-stakes testing, Horn (2003) described high-stakes testing as the "evil twin" of the current-standards movement.

From this perspective, there is little disagreement regarding the importance of identifying appropriate educational standards to be achieved. Serious and deep divisions arise, however, regarding whether high-stakes testing enhances or actually impedes the likelihood that children will achieve the standards.

High-stakes testing has been mandated throughout American primary and secondary schools to ensure the accountability of students and teachers. The underlying assumption of this educational model is that by holding these groups accountable, the apparent problems with student achievement will be overcome. One obvious difficulty with such thinking is that because it focuses exclusively on the end point of the educational process or achievement scores, it ignores the processes involved in student achievement and the teaching required to support it. Figure 1 provides a simple schematic of this mindset.

This says nothing about the process of learning and the impact of teaching on this process. Nor does it provide any information about how to improve scores other than to repeat the mantras, "more testing" or "higher stakes." This is an example of a summative approach to assessment or evaluation (Roddy, 2005). Summative assessments seek to measure the end point or culmination of the learning process.

High-stakes testing>>>>accountability>>>>enhanced student achievement

Figure 1   A summative model of achievement.

Effective teaching and classroom supports>>>>enhanced student learning>>>>
assessment>>>>improved teaching>>>>more enhanced learning and so on

Figure 2   A formative model of achievement.

However, because learning is a process in which teaching is intimately involved (Vygotsky, 1978), a more accurate model might utilize a more formative approach to assessment. In formative assessment, the primary purpose is to modify and improve the process of teaching and learning (Roddy, 2005). Assessments are used to modify teaching and improve learning. This formative approach might look something like Figure 2.

Such a model acknowledges the essential importance of teachers to learning and of feedback to the improvement of the teaching process and to the improvement of student learning and achievement (Morrison, 2006). It also acknowledges the ongoing, iterative nature of teaching and learning. Teachers are certainly accountable, to a considerable degree, for student learning. But to focus our attention on test scores as the primary method for gauging a teacher's effectiveness is to diminish the importance of teaching and, in so doing, to distort the educational process. To do so in poor school districts with unprepared students, little academic support, and overwhelmed teachers represents educational malpractice at its worst and a cynical ploy to make it appear that tests with consequences will somehow miraculously improve student achievement in the absence of resources and effective teaching. Darling-Hammond (2000) persuasively makes the same point.

In contrast to the high-stakes-testing approach with its emphasis on summative assessment, there are examples of state programs that have clearly recognized the appropriateness of formative assessments and highlighted the importance of teaching and support to student learning and the local nature of this process. Rhode Island (Thompson, 2001) and Connecticut (Darling-Hammond, 2000) are two that have worked to improve their educational practices and whose students' learning has been enhanced as a result. Interestingly, both have been successful although emphasizing low-stakes rather than high-stakes testing, in which assessment is used primarily to provide feedback to enhance teaching and thereby enhance student learning.

Many educators agree that there are problems in the American educational system today. But as Madaus and Clarke (2001) have suggested it, is simplistic to assume that we will be able to test our way out of these problems, especially if we rely on summative rather than formative assessments. Instead, a careful and systematic approach needs to be developed, one that provides teachers with the information they require to better educate children and with the economic and material supports only the most affluent school districts possess today.

CONCLUSION

Accountability and the high-stakes tests that are supposed to provide it are not new (Callahan, 1962; Darling-Hammond, 2000). What has changed recently is the age of the children being required to take these tests, the universality of their administration, and the belief that summative tests will somehow magically enhance student learning. Although tests are mandated, there is little consideration given to explaining how more and more testing will improve student understanding of key content areas including math and science. It is easy to demand more testing and student and teacher accountability and to exact stiff penalties for failure to "perform." But it is difficult to see how simply giving more consequential tests is going to help students to learn more or teachers to teach more effectively. The absurdity of the current situation has been amplified by reports highlighting widespread scoring errors that "raised fresh questions about the reliability of the kinds of high-stakes tests that increasingly dominate education at all levels" (Arenson & Henriques, 2006).

An oft-stated rationale for the move to high-stakes testing is the concern of policymakers regarding the much-discussed poor relative performance of American students on international math and science comparisons. Although serious questions have been raised about the validity of this concern (Berliner & Biddle, 1995), there can be little doubt that it has played a critical role in creating an unprecedented and deeply unsettling era of high-stakes testing.

This concern with comparative test scores is most certainly linked to the belief among business leaders and policymakers that if our students cannot compete academically against those from other countries, this will ultimately have serious negative consequences for the nation's economic competitiveness. This is, of course, the same concern raised in *A Nation at Risk* over two decades ago about how American schoolchildren and their academic failures would ultimately destroy our economic superiority if we did not change the educational system. As previously discussed, this position was wrong then, and it is wrong now.

As Cremin (1989) emphasized then, the nation's economic competitiveness is far more "a function of monetary, trade, and industrial policy, and of decisions by the President and Congress … ." Today, the economic future of the country is imperiled not by our schoolchildren's scores on international comparisons, but by the nation's astronomical trade imbalance, tax policies, and profligate personal spending, and meager personal savings (Krugman, 2006; Phillips, 2006). By redirecting the focus to schools, students, and teachers, the business and political leaders are attempting to abnegate their responsibility for the nation's current economic crisis.

The American public and all involved in the American educational process must now demand more thoughtful educational policies from their national and local policy leaders. These "leaders" need to be held accountable for the serious damage caused by high-stakes testing, especially in the lives of the nation's poor and most vulnerable children.

At a 2001 press conference, President Bush stated, "Too much precious time has lapsed in this for us to achieve what we want: every child being able to learn. Testing every child every year is the way to stop the cycle. We must care enough to ask how our children are doing" (G.W. Bush, press conference, January 2001).

Incessant testing with serious consequences is not the way to guarantee that children will learn what they need for success in the 21st century. In fact, for many the lesson learned will be extremely negative and counterproductive to their prospects for lifelong learning. Although it is certainly important to ask how our children are doing, it is far more important to provide them with the resources necessary to improve their educational experiences and to enhance their current learning while motivating them to continue learning in the future. High-stakes testing is not a solution to our current problems, but rather a symptom of what is wrong with current educational policy. Rather than focusing so much time, energy, and scarce school dollars on test prep and testing, all involved in schools should work together to focus more directly and systematically on teaching and learning and on ways to make the American educational process more fair and equitable for all students.

Unfortunately, the sad irony is that the real legacy of NCLB legislation is likely to be that those economically disadvantaged groups that most support it will be more disadvantaged because of it. Given the current realities of the American social structure, although this is sad, it is hardly surprising.

REFERENCES

Abrams, L.M., Pedulla, J.J., & Madaus, G.F. (2003). Views form the classroom: Teachers' opinions of statewide testing programs. *Theory into Practice, 42*, 18–29.

Anderman, E.M. (1992, December). *Motivation and cognitive strategies uses in reading and writing.* Paper presented at the National Reading Association Conference, San Antonio, TX.

Arenson, K.W., & Henriques, D.B. (2006, March 10). Company's errors on SAT scores raise new qualms about testing. *New York Times.*

Bandura, A. (1995). *Self-efficacy in changing societies.* New York: Cambridge University Press.

Bell, T.H. (1988). *The thirteenth man: A Reagan cabinet memoir.* New York: Free Press.

Berliner, D.C., & Biddle, B.J. (1995). *The manufactured crisis: Myths, fraud, and the attack on America's public schools.* Reading, MA: Addison-Wesley.

Bracey, G. (2003). April foolishness: The 20th anniversary of *a nation at risk. Phi Delta Kappan, 84*, 616–621.

Bush, G.W. (2001). Press conference, January.

Callahan, R.E. (1962). *Education and the cult of efficiency.* Chicago: University of Chicago Press.

Cremin, L.J. (1989). *Popular education and its discontent.* New York: Harper & Row.

Darling-Hammond, L. (2000). Transforming urban public schools: The role of standards and accountability. ERIC Document Reproduction Service No. Ed-459290.

Gregor, A. (2005). Examination anxiety: Live with it, control it, or make it work for you? *School Psychology International, 26,* 617–635.

Haney, W. (2000). The myth of the Texas miracle in education. *Education Policy Analysis Archives, 41.* Retrieved February 14, 2006, from http://epaa.asu.edu/volume3/.

Harvard University. (2005). *The Civil Rights Project.* Retrieved at http://www.civilrightsproject.harvard.edu/research/dropouts/dropouts_south05.pdf.

Herman, J.L. (2000, July). Making high-stakes testing systems work for kids and you. Presentation to the AASA Suburban School Superintendents Conference.

Heubert, J.P., & Hauser, R.M. (Eds.) (1999). *High stakes: Testing for tracking, promotion, and graduation.* Washington, DC: National Academy Press.

Horn, C. (2003). High-stakes testing and students: Stopping or perpetuating a cycle of failure? *Theory into Practice, 42,* 30–41.

International Reading Association. (2006). *High-stakes assessments in reading.* Retrieved from http://www.reading.org/resources/issues/positions_high_stakes.html.

Johnson, D.D., & Johnson, B. (2002). *High stakes: Children, testing, and failure in American schools.* New York: Rowman & Littlefield Publishers.

Kim, J.S., & Sunderman, G.L. (2005). Measuring academic proficiency under the No Child Left Behind Act: Implications for educational equity. *Educational Researcher, 34,* 3–13.

Klein, B., McNeil, J.D., & Stout, L.A. (2005). The achievement trap. *Education Week, 25,* 32.

Kohn, A. (2000). Standardized testing and its victims. *Education Week,* September 27, 47.

Krugman, P. (2006, February 13). Debt and denial. *New York Times,* p. A23.

Madaus, G., & Clarke, M. (2001). The adverse impact of high stakes testing on minority students: Evidence from 100 years of test data. In G. Orfield & M. Kornhaber (Eds.), *Raising standards or raising barriers? Inequality and high stakes testing in public education.* New York: The Century Foundation.

Mandler, G., & Sarason, S.B. (1952). Some correlates of test anxiety. *Journal of Abnormal Psychology, 47,* 810–817.

McCarthy, J.M., & Goffin, R.D. (2005). Selection test anxiety: Exploring tension and fear of failure across the sexes in simulated selection scenarios. *International Journal of Selection and Assessment, 13,* 282–295.

Morehouse, E. (2004). Personal communication.

Morrison, G.S. (2006). *Teaching in America.* New York: Pearson.

National Council of Teachers of Mathematics (2006). *High-stakes tests.* Retrieved from http://www.nctm.org/about/position_statements/highstakes.htm.

National Council on Excellence in Education. (1983). *A nation at risk: The imperative for educational reform.* Washington, DC: U.S. Department of Education.

NCLB. (2001), Pub. I. No. 107–110.

Olson, L. (2005) States revive efforts to coax NCLB changes. *Education Week, 24,* 29.

Phillips, K. (2006). *American theocracy: The peril and politics of radical religion, oil, and borrowed money.* New York: Viking.

Popham, W.J. (2001). Teaching to the test? *Educational Leadership, 58,* 16–20.

Roddy, M. (2005). Assessment in high school at the start of the twenty-first century. In S.J. Farenga & D. Ness (Eds.). *Encyclopedia of education and human development* (Vol. 2, pp. 558–560). Armonk, New York: M.E. Sharpe.

Roderick, M., Nagaoka, J., & Allensworth, E. (2005). Is the glass half full or half empty: Ending social promotion in Chicago. *Yearbook of the National Society for the Study of Education, 104,* 223–259.

Saulny, S. (2005, December 27). In middle class, signs of anxiety on school efforts. *New York Times.*

Skinner, B.F. (1951). How to teach animals. *Scientific American, 185,* 26–29.

Spring, J. (2004). *American Education.* New York: McGraw-Hill.

Terzian, S. (2002). On probation and under pressure: How one 4th-grade class managed high-stakes testing. *Childhood Education, 78,* 282–284.

Thompson, S. (2001). The authentic standards movements and its evil twin. *Phi Delta Kappan, 82,* 358–362.

United States Government Accountability Office. (2005). *No Child Left Behind Act: Most students with disabilities participated in statewide assessments, but inclusion options could be improved.* Retrieved online at http://www.edweek.org/links.

Vygotsky, L. (1978). *Mind in society.* Cambridge, MA: Harvard University Press.

Weiner, B. (1992). *Human motivation.* Newbury Park, CA: Sage Publications.

Wright, W.E. (2002). The effects of high stakes testing in an inner-city elementary school: The curriculum, the teachers, and the English language learners. *Current Issues in Education.* http://cie.ed.asu.edu/volume5/number5/.

5

Educational Reform and the Child With Disabilities

Mikki Malow-Iroff, Michael Benhar, and Sonya Martin

Educational reform is an issue that is of concern to many people owing to discontent over the state of the country's educational system. Reform is not a new concept to teachers; it is a natural extension of the reflective practice that has been part of the professional teacher-training curricula throughout the country. As teachers, we are taught to think about our classroom practices, evaluate what is working and what is not, and to make adjustments accordingly in our work with students. However, educational reform at the federal level seeks to impose changes not based on best practices in individual classrooms, but on greater accountability of all classrooms to the federal government. Thus, the reforms proposed and implemented by well-intentioned policymakers have implications for all students and their parents, including those students with special needs.

Students with special needs have often been the neglected part of the school population. However, special education teachers know that what works best for this group of students is to focus on each individual student's needs in the classroom. William Ayers (chapter 12 of this volume) has said that "it is essential to begin with a particularly precious ideal—the belief that education at its best is an enterprise geared to helping every human being reach the full measure of his or her humanity, inviting people on a journey to become more thoughtful and more capable, more powerful and courageous, more exquisitely human in their projects and pursuits." Teachers who work with students with special needs have known this all along; they labor to meet their students' needs at their present skill level and engage these students to take the next step in the learning process. Current educational reforms, such as the No Child Left Behind (NCLB) Act, are implementing changes in teaching practice that will impact how these students are taught, who teaches them, where they will do their learning, and how they will be assessed. With these changes comes the growing realization among general educators that special education is no longer the sole domain of the special education teacher. Practices of including students with special needs in general education classrooms have become the norm. As such, the practice of inclusion, as mandated by federal legislation and reforms such as NCLB, requires all teachers to have a working knowledge of special education—past, present, and future. Thus, this chapter will briefly outline the history of special education, discuss the two major pieces of legislation that govern the administering of services to students with special needs (the Individuals with Disabilities Education Act [IDEA] and the NCLB Act), present some of the central controversies in special education and the opinions of teachers and leading authorities in the field and, lastly, take a look at future trends and policies.

A BRIEF OVERVIEW OF THE HISTORY OF SPECIAL EDUCATION

One of the first instances of a government attempting to distinguish among the ability levels of students came from the French ministry at the turn of the last century. In 1905, the French government recognized a need to distinguish slow learners from the general student population and employed Alfred Binet and Theodore Simon to do so. As a result, Binet and Simon created one of the first measures of intelligence to predict academic performance in school. Subsequently, the Binet–Simon Scales were revised and standardized at Stanford University by Lewis Terman and published in 1916 as the Stanford–Binet Intelligence Scale.

It was partly due to the use of the Stanford–Binet Intelligence Scale that awareness of individual differences progressed throughout the early 1900s. Programs were established to address the requirements of students with special needs, specifically those with a loss of hearing or sight and slow learners. Typically, students with special needs were placed either in a separate classroom within a school that served the general population, or they were placed in a separate school. Those children who were perceived as being unable to benefit from these segregated placements were simply excluded from the educational system. During the 1930s, special classes emerged for children with physical disabilities; and by the 1950s, separate schools that provided facilities for this population such as ramps, elevators, and desks emerged. Throughout the early 20th century, although the educational system began to service children with some physical disabilities and those thought of as slow learners, mental hospitals remained the only viable alternative for children with severe emotional problems.

In the 1950s, a change began to emerge in the United States, largely through the efforts of parents who had children with special needs. The goal was to implement more effective practices in order to improve the services to this population. In support of this expansion in services, research emerged that addressed the validity and benefit of having separate classrooms for students with special needs. Research conducted by Johnson (1962) contended that there was no difference in academic achievement or social adjustment for children with mental retardation if placed in a general or special education classroom. In fact, the separate special education classroom was perceived as possessing several distinct advantages, which are still perceived today: (a) low teacher–pupil ratios, (b) a specially trained teacher, (c) a homogeneous classroom that contained greater individualization of instruction to meet the specific needs of the child, (d) an increased emphasis on social and vocational goals within the curriculum, and (e) greater expenditure and allocation of funds for each student (Johnson, 1962).

The validity of the separate special education classroom was not questioned until Dunn (1968), a special education professor at Peabody College (now Vanderbilt University), wrote an article that questioned the validity and efficacy of separate classrooms for children with mild disabilities. Although the scholarly aspect of the work in this article was called into question by MacMillan (1971), Dunn's contention caused many other researchers to join in and advocate the abandonment of the separate special education classroom (Christopolos & Renz, 1969; Lilly, 1970; Deno, 1970). Despite the increasing research on the inclusion of students with special needs in general education classrooms, empirical evidence advocating for a placement that was less restrictive than the separate special education classroom was anything but conclusive (Guskin & Spicker, 1968). Today, the debate continues as to what is the best placement of a child with special needs, the general education setting or a special education setting. Best practices in education suggest that this is a decision based on an individual child's needs and circumstances.

SPECIAL EDUCATION LEGISLATION

Historically, children with special needs have been discriminated against in two ways (Turnbull & Turnbull, 2000). First, schools either did not admit this population of students or, if they were admitted, they were not always provided with what experts would call an appropriate education (Yell, Rogers, & Rogers, 1998). Second, students who belonged to culturally and linguistically diverse groups were frequently misclassified as possessing a disability that they did not have or were given the wrong classification, a type of mislabeling (Sarason & Doris, 1979).

As a result of this blatant discrimination, families of children with disabilities, civil rights lawyers, and parent advocacy organizations sued state and local school officials in the 1970s for misclassifying and excluding students, a violation of their rights to receive equal educational opportunities as guaranteed by the U.S. Constitution (Turnbull & Turnbull, 2000). One early piece of legislation that came about as a direct result of public advocacy was the Education of All Handicapped Children Act of 1975, also known as Pub. L. No. 94-142. This law advocated for the rights of children with special needs and provided for a free and appropriate public education (FAPE) for all children aged 5 through 21. In addition, the law required a comprehensive, nondiscriminatory evaluation to identify the specific needs of the child, a written individualized education plan (IEP), and placement in a classroom representing the least restrictive environment (LRE) for that child.

In 1990, the IDEA, also known as Pub. L. No. 101-476, was passed in Congress. This law updated the terminology of the Education for All Handicapped Children Act to reflect the ideology that the disability does not define the person, but that students with special needs are individuals with disabilities, who need to be served. IDEA was amended in 1997, providing an expanded role for parents in the decision-making process, including parents on the team that makes educational placement decisions. Additionally, schools were required to create and bear the cost of a system of mediation to resolve conflicts between schools and families. The most recent reauthorization of IDEA occurred in December 2004 with President Bush signing into effect the Individuals with Disabilities Education Improvement Act of 2004. In this reauthorization, some of the changes include the definition of a highly qualified teacher for both general and special educators, a plan to reduce the amount of paperwork that now exists in special education programs, the inclusion of special education students in the testing system that establishes accountability and a recommitment to the funding of special education as outlined by these laws.

The reauthorization of IDEA in 2004 refines many of the constructs of the earlier legislation; however, the basic premise of Pub. L. No. 94-142 and the IDEA legislations consists of six main principles that are designed to identify students in need of services. The passage of each new law has reauthorized and extended these basic rights. The six main principles of IDEA are the following:

1. Zero-exclusion principle: The zero-exclusion principle prohibits schools from excluding children from the age of 3 to 21 with disabilities from receiving a free and appropriate public education, no matter how severe their disabilities.
2. Nondiscriminatory evaluation: A nondiscriminatory evaluation of each student is required to provide a multifaceted and comprehensive assessment in order to determine if the child has a disability. Historically, children from culturally and linguistically diverse backgrounds have experienced discrimination in the assessment process (Dunn, 1968). As part of nondiscriminatory evaluations, evaluations must be conducted in the student's primary language.
3. Free and appropriate public education (FAPE): FAPE must be provided to each student. To accomplish this end, an individualized education program is designed that is tailored to the specific requirements of the student with special needs. For babies and toddlers from the ages of 0

to 3, this plan is called an individualized family service plan (IFSP). For students from the ages of 3 through 21, the plan is called an IEP. There has been much debate about the meaning of an appropriate education (Yell & Drasgow, 2000). The basic premise of FAPE is that a student should be making substantial progress that produces a beneficial educational experience (Turnbull & Turnbull, 2000).

4. Least restrictive environment (LRE): LRE contends that a student with a disability will be educated to the greatest extent possible with peers without disabilities. The LRE is often interpreted as the general education classroom, but historically, this interpretation was not clearly defined as the only accepted one. The most prevalent notion is that the school may not remove a student from the general education classroom unless school officials can prove that even with the provision of supplementary aids and support services, the student is not benefiting to the maximum extent and warrants a more restrictive placement (Bateman & Chard, 1995). Therefore, schools must offer a continuum of placement options that range from less to more restrictive. This continuum is generally understood as (from least restrictive to most restrictive): the general education classroom, general education classroom with resource room or other related services, separate special education classroom, separate special education school, homebound instruction by a special education itinerant teacher, and hospital or institutional placement.

5. Procedural due process: Procedural due process seeks to make the parents and school partners in their responsibility to each other for ensuring that the rights of both the student and parents are protected as guaranteed by the IDEA legislation. If a parent or the school does not agree with the placement decision and services that are to be provided, a hearing is organized and is conducted before an impartial arbitrator. The loser of the due process hearing maintains the right to appeal the ruling to a higher court.

6. Parental and student participation: Finally, parental and student participation is required in the special education process in order to facilitate shared decision making. Written informed consent is required to be given by the parent to the school in order to conduct an evaluation and to implement an IEP, as well as the verbal assent of the student during the process of an IEP evaluation. These steps are taken to ensure parents and students are participants in the development of the educational plan and are not simply informed of school-based decisions.

In addition to the six main principles of IDEA, this federal law requires that a student with special needs be classified into 1 of 13 classifications of disability.

High Incidence Disabilities
Specific Learning Disabilities   50%
Speech or Language Impairment   18.9%
Mental Retardation   10.6%
Emotional Disturbance   8.2%

Low Incidence Disabilities
Other Health Impairments   5.1%
Multiple Disabilities   2.1%
Autism   1.4%
Orthopedic Impairments   1.3%
Hearing Impairments   1.2%
Visual Impairments   .4%
Developmental Delay   .5%
Traumatic Brain Injury   .3%
Deaf Blindness   .0%

Figure 1   Federal classifications of special education and the percentage of students served.

These classifications can be thought of as existing in two groups: high-incidence disabilities and low-incidence disabilities. High-incidence disabilities are those classifications that represent the highest percentage of students receiving special education services, and low-incidence disabilities represent students in classifications that are not seen as frequently. The federal classifications and the percentage of special education students that were served by them in the 2000–2001 school year are detailed in Figure 1.

The implementation of federal laws involves agencies at the federal, state, and local levels. Each state presents a plan to the U.S. Office of Special Education Programs to ensure compliance with federal regulations in order to receive federal funding. Although the state laws must comply with the federal laws, the implementation, description, and criteria for classifying children with special needs is slightly different from state to state. At the local level, departments of education and early intervention agencies are responsible for the delivery of special education services. As a result of the many layers of governmental involvement for the implementation of special education services, the laws related to special education are complex.

NCLB LEGISLATION

In addition to the federal laws that specifically pertain to special education, governing agencies are continually reauthorizing and refining education legislation that pertains to all students. One example of this, the latest version of the Elementary and Secondary Education Act of 1965 known as the NCLB Act of 2001, redefined the federal role in education from kindergarten through grade 12. The NCLB Act of 2001 was specifically intended to support schools in four distinct ways: (a) provide stronger accountability of academic results, (b) implement scientifically based curriculum and practices, (c) give more options to parents on how and where their children will be educated, and (d) expand flexibility on how school districts can allocate their federal funding. The goal of NCLB is to make schools accountable for the federal dollars spent on education. The four major provisions of the NCLB legislation are detailed in Figure 2.

1. **Accountability.**
   Each state has developed standards that must be met for every child. In order to establish that each child is learning, test data is collected on all groups of students and schools are evaluated for adequate yearly progress (AYP). In 2006–2007, every student will be tested in math and reading every year, starting in 3rd grade. In 2007–2008 science will be tested once in elementary, middle and high school. Additionally, this provision stipulates that teachers must be highly qualified, which includes a bachelor's degree, state certification, and demonstration of subject matter competency.

2. **Scientifically Proven Practice.**
   NCLB emphasizes the implementation of teaching methods. Federal funding is provided to purchase scripted lessons and standardized school curriculums. Established the *Reading First* program, a federally funded research based reading program for children in kindergarten through grade three and the *Early Reading First* program, which targets early childhood education.

3. **Options for Parents.**
   Published detailed school report cards will provide parents with information on each school's AYP. If a local school fails to meet state standards of AYP it becomes identified as "in need of improvement." Parents are then given the option to place their children in better performing schools outside of their zoned school.

4. **Flexibility.**
   There is flexibility in how the state and local districts can allocate up to 50% of the federal formula grant funds that come from this act. This flexibility is designed to allow the school to use the money as they determine in order to serve the community better.

Figure 2   Major Provisions of *No Child Left Behind* Act of 2001

REFORM CONTROVERSIES WITHIN SPECIAL EDUCATION

Although the goal of educational reform is to effect change in school policy and practice, the NCLB reform poses difficulties for special education practice, students, and teachers. Many special educators wonder if it is wise to require students with special needs to meet the same standards as their general education peers. Most people agree that setting high standards for students is a good thing; however, it needs to be recognized that not everyone will meet those standards. These difficulties have stirred a controversy within the special education community, as professionals find ways to work within the constrictions of NCLB. Some of the specific areas of controversy include issues surrounding curriculum, assessment practices, and teacher certification.

Curriculum

The NCLB reform requires students with disabilities to have access to and participate in the same standardized curriculum as regular education students. For example, the general education curriculum requires students to read by the third grade. A difficulty with this requirement is that some students with special needs will not read by the third grade. This practice promotes tracking of students and is based on ease of instruction and testing, rather than the benefit to the child. The issue of individualization of instruction has always been built into special education practices because of the need to develop an IEP for each child. With an emphasis on the inclusion of students with special needs into the general education classroom and with classroom teachers required to use standardized curriculum, one concern is the loss of the individualization of the learning process. Most teachers now spend instructional time teaching to the mandated tests that students take. As the number of tests increases, the amount of instructional time teaching to these tests increases, and there is less time remaining for the individualized instruction so necessary for students with special needs. Joel Spring (chapter 1 of this volume) highlights that we as a nation are unaware of the long-term effects of an educational system that is driven by a reliance on testing. He questions whether the effect will be a reduction in " … students' creativity and willingness to take risks." This could prove to be a devastating blow to many students with special needs, who are already unwilling to take risks academically due to chronic failure in the classroom.

Another worry that special educators have voiced is in regard to the concept of adequate yearly progress (AYP) that is built into NCLB. The structure of the standardized curriculum and the NCLB legislation require students to make a year's worth of progress in a year's time. For many children with special needs, this may be an unrealistic standard, as they are working on an individualized set of annual goals as defined in their IEP. In addition, the IEP annual goals are frequently not synchronized with the structure of the standardized curriculum. IEP goals are usually constructed by employing general statements about the academic and behavioral attainments desired, but lack any significant specific steps on how to achieve them. For example, an IEP goal may consist of increasing the attention span of a child in a classroom setting with only vague specifications of how this is to be done, such as having the child work on a specific assignment for 10 min, and then ultimately increasing the time at work to a 30-min period. The goal and subgoals are clearly identified (i.e., increasing attention span for longer increments of time), but how the gap is supposed to be diminished is left in vague terminology, such as employing behavioral methodologies to keep the child on task. Additionally, as this example illustrates, the IEP goal has nothing to do with standardized curriculum content. Thus, measuring the AYP of many IEP goals would not be beneficial, as they have nothing in common with standardized curriculum.

One important characteristic of students with special needs that is easily lost in the NCLB legislation is that many children within this population learn differently. As such, a current debate among special educators is whether or not these trained professionals should function as instructional strategists or as content specialists. However, if it is determined by NCLB that they serve best as content specialists, then this undermines the profession's role in establishing teacher qualification standards.

Assessment

The policy of including special education students in city and state assessments as mandated by NCLB has received support from some special education professionals. However, the one-size-fits-all assessment policy that is currently in place may not allow students with special needs to demonstrate what they know. For assessment to be successful, it must be matched to the individual student's skill set. Although the NCLB reform mandates that students with special needs must be tested and evaluated just as regular education students are, there are several testing options available to individual students, as shown in Figure 3.

Although alternative assessments are an option, 95% of the school's population, including the subgroup students with a disability, must be assessed using the same general education guidelines in order to show AYP as determined by NCLB. The difficulty with these assessments is that these test results determine a child's promotion and graduation. In addition, some children do not do well on the tests, and often a school's funding and incentive structure is tied to the children's performance. One major concern about the use of standardized assessments is whether test results are pushing struggling kids out of school, forcing them to choose to drop out of school early.

Testing options

1. Receive exactly the same assessment in the same way.
2. Receive the same assessments, but with modifications. These modifications must be specified on the IEP. Examples include extended time, computerized testing, and oral exams.
3. Take an alternative assessment that relates to the same curriculum specifications as the grade the student is in currently. Examples include a portfolio, a paper, or some sort of authentic assessment.
4. Use an alternative assessment method that can either be on grade level or on a level that is specified by the IEP. Again, the alternative assessment could be a portfolio, a paper, or an authentic assessment devised for this purpose.

Figure 3   Standardized testing options for students with special needs.

The idea that struggling students are forced out of school due to accountability for school test scores is highlighted by Susan Ohanian (chapter 13 of this volume). She recounts an event that occurred in Birmingham, Alabama, in early 2000 in which 522 low-performing high school students were dropped from the school enrollment records. This event coincided with the threat by the state of Alabama to take over the Birmingham high schools if test scores did not improve. This example is but one illustration of the idea that poor performance on mandatory standardized tests may cause struggling students to drop out of school early.

Other educational scholars have joined with Susan Ohanian to question the validity of linking standardized school testing to the preparation of the future American workforce. Joel Spring (chapter 1 of this volume) calls into question whether the linking of the American economy to national academic standards "… will improve the ability of American workers to compete in a global workforce." William Ayers (chapter 12 of this volume) argues that testing functions make students invisible and voiceless when they really should be asking themselves, "Who in the world am I? What place is this? What will become of me here? What larger universe awaits me? What shall I make of what I've been made? What are my choices?"

Teacher Qualifications

The federal reforms of IDEA 2004 and NCLB have called for all teachers to be highly qualified. Although, in principle, everyone would agree that it is important to have highly qualified teachers in the classroom, the difficulty lies in the uncertainty over what *highly qualified* means for special education teachers and the short time frame within which they are required to meet that goal. By the

2005–2006 school year, all special education teachers must meet this requirement. To be highly qualified according to the NCLB reform, special educators must possess at least a bachelor's degree and be certified to teach in their state. Although these two requirements are standard and all states required special educators to meet these guidelines in the 2002–2003 school year, the problem for most special educators and the schools who employ them is that the NCLB legislation also requires special education teachers to demonstrate competency in each core academic subject they teach. Special educators are exempt from this regulation only if they do not directly instruct students in core academic subjects. The difficulty with meeting this requirement is that most special educators teach not only multiple subjects but also multiple grade levels. Some states have started to take steps to help their special education teachers comply with these standards by establishing alternative evaluation methods. The concern is whether they will be able to meet the requirements in a timely fashion.

Looking to the Future

The community of professionals involved in teacher education has long advocated a standard of practice known as *reflective teaching*. Teacher trainers require their student teachers to think about what they are doing in the classroom setting and make decisions about whether their practices are working or not. If the conclusion that the student teachers arrive at is that the current practice is not working, then they are advised by their teacher trainers to abandon it and try something else. Even though this process often can seem like a process of trial and error, it should be repeated until the student teacher finds what is most effective in any given situation. Although educational reform can often seem like a series of haphazard trial-and-error mandates, what needs to be remembered is that it is in response to current practices that do not appear to be working. In addition, the overarching goal of educational reform is to improve the state of the educational system for the majority of students. What needs to be remembered in this process is that students with special needs are not the majority. They do not learn in the same way as general education students and so cannot be assumed to be able to master the same curriculum in the same way. Thus, assessment results of special education students' knowledge and skills will necessarily be different than those of the general education population. What must be maintained and fostered throughout all educational reforms is the idea of individualization.

Individualized instruction has been a hallmark of special education since the Education of All Handicapped Children Act of 1975 first mandated an individualized education plan. Even in the inclusive setting of a general education classroom, an IEP's content goals must be honored by teaching professionals. Some professionals, including the authors of this chapter, hold out the hope that the concept of individualization will spread to general education and that the principles of individualization will be applied in dealing with all students. An example of this is currently taking place in Miami Dade County public schools in Florida. In this school district, those students who are not performing up to grade-level standards and are not being serviced with an IEP receive extra services with individually tailored academic intervention plans. In this way, the teaching professionals serve the individual needs of an at-risk population. This innovative project should be commended and used as a model program for inserting a level of individualization that students need.

Additionally, with the reauthorization of IDEA in 2004, special education professionals can look forward to less paperwork relating to special education needs and more time to spend on instruction with students. IDEA 2004 has established a 15-state demonstration program in which state departments of education can put together proposals for pilot programs aiming to reduce the time-consuming tasks of completing special education paperwork and noninstructional time burdens. The efficacy of these pilot programs will be determined, and final regulations will be instituted at the end of the 4-year trial program. At that time, training and information about effective ways to reduce time burdens and increase instructional time will be made available to all states. Until this initiative is in place, special education teachers will benefit from a small reduction in their paperwork requirements. Another component of IDEA 2004 calls for the removal of short-term objectives from IEPs of students who will not take alternative assessments tied to alternative achievement standards. Instead, teachers will be able to report only on how progress on meeting annual goals will be measured. In these ways, special education professionals can focus more time and energy where it should be placed—on serving the educational needs of students.

The information in regard to background, legislation, and controversies of special education practice under NCLB was presented to current and aspiring teachers at a workshop for a conference examining issues of educational reform. In concluding the workshop, the general educators and special educators in attendance discussed what was needed in looking to the future for special education under NCLB. Five areas were identified in which these teaching professionals felt that they needed more knowledge and support from their school administration, support staff, and the department of education. These areas included how to incorporate the mandates of NCLB such as standardized testing for students with special needs, classroom management, staff development, home–school collaboration, and technology. The teaching professionals suggested topics under the five areas discussed that they would like to see addressed in professional development workshops. The suggestions are detailed in Figure 4.

In conclusion, in the wake of NCLB, students with special needs can no longer be an invisible part of the school community, and this is an important benefit.

Standardized testing concerns

1. Information on individualized accommodations such as how to obtain them and how to administer them.
2. Information on promotion policies on standardized tests for students with special needs.
3. Strategies to implement mandated instructional practices based on results of standardized tests for students with special needs.

Classroom management

1. Where to go for help with classroom control and discipline issues.
2. How to enlist administrative support on discipline issues.
3. How to manage classroom time for students having academic difficulties with the standardized curriculum.
4. How to deal with issues related to problems with transitioning.

Staff development seminars relevant to students with special needs

Seminars that address
   a. concerns about classroom management issues.
   b. concerns about academic issues and curriculum.
   c. techniques to individualize learning needs.
   d. legal issues and policy.
   e. how to read an IEP and teach utilizing a child's IEP.
   f. the various related service personnel in the school available to consult with you about the students with special needs in your classroom.
   g. technology available for the special needs students in your classroom.
   h. how to refer a child for evaluation for special education services.

Ideas for the inclusion of parents of children with special needs

1. Conduct a variety of workshops in the school.
2. Invite parents to participate in class.
3. Send letters home to keep parents informed.
4. Hold regular meetings either in person or by telephone.

Use of technology in the classroom for this population

1. How to gain access and use of
   a. computers.
   b. specific computer software.
   c. laptop computers for class and home use.
   d. communication boards.
   e. assistive listening devices.
   f. personal digital assistants or other organizational devices.

Figure 4   Teacher needs for effective practice.

However, the strictures of the legislation, the narrow approach toward assessment, and the punitive aspects of the law work directly against the well-being of children with disabilities. Administrators, teachers, parents, and students need to work together in order to facilitate the most effective learning environment for each individual. William Ayers (chapter 12 of this volume) stated that teachers need to endeavor to accomplish two things with their students: "One is to convince students, often against a background of having attended what we might call 'obedience training school,' that there is no such thing as receiving an education as a passive receptor or an inert vessel—in that direction lies nothing but subservience, indoctrination, and worse. All real education is and must always be self-education. The second task is to demonstrate to the students and to yourself, through daily effort and interaction, that they are valued, that their humanity is honored, and that their growth, enlightenment, and liberation are the paramount concern." In light of educational reform that seeks to impose higher standards, frequent assessments, and standardized criteria for all students, educational professionals must keep this tenet of education in sight. The best way to do this is to see all students as individuals who come to school with their own level of knowledge and skills. Then, we as educational professionals schooled in reflective practices can build our instructional relationships with that as our starting point.

REFERENCES

Bateman, B., & Chard, D.J. (1995). Legal demands and constraints on placement decisions. In J.M. Kauffman, J.W. Lloyd, P. Hallahan, & T.A. Astuto (Eds.), *Issues in educational placement: Students with emotional and behavioral disorders* (pp. 285–316). NJ: Erlbaum.

Christoplos, F., & Renz, P. (1969). A critical examination of special education programs. *Journal of Special Education, 3*, 371–379.

Council for Exceptional Children. (2004, November). *The new IDEA. CEC's summary of significant issues.* Retrieved January 10, 2005, from http://www.cec.sped.org.

Council for Exceptional Children (2004). Special education at a crossroads. *Today, 11.* Retrieved January 10, 2005, from http://www.cec.sped.org.

Council for Exceptional Children (2004). Special education teachers struggling to meet NCLB. *Today, 11.* Retrieved January 10, 2005, from http://www.cec.sped.org.

Deno, E. (1970). Special education as developmental capital. *Exceptional Children, 37,* 229–237.

Dunn, L.M. (1968). Special education for the mildly retarded: Is much of it justifiable? *Exceptional Children, 35,* 5–22.

Guskin, S.L., & Spicker, H.H. (1968). Educational research in mental retardation. In N.R. Ellis (Ed.). *International review of research in mental retardation* (Vol. 3, pp. 217–278). New York: Academic Press.

Herszenhorn, D. (2004, September 13). Bloomberg faces payoff year on school plans. *New York Times.* Retrieved October 8, 2004, from http://www.nytimes.com.

Johnson, G.O. (1962). Special education for the mentally handicapped: A paradox. *Exceptional Children, 19,* 62–69.

Krashen, S. (2001). Bush's bad idea for bilingual ed. *Rethinking Schools Online.* Retrieved October 8, 2004, from http://www.rethinkingschools.org.

Lilly, M.S. (1970). Special education: A teapot in a tempest. *Exceptional Children, 37,* 43–49.

MacMillan, D.L. (1971). Special education for the mildly retarded: Servant or savant? *Focus on Exceptional Children, 2,* 1–11.

New York City Department of Education. *Children first.* Retrieved October 8, 2004, from http://www.nycenet.edu/Administration/Childrenfirst/default.htm.

New York State Education Department. Just the facts for NY parents. *The No Child Left Behind Act—An overview.* Retrieved October 8, 2004, from http://www.emsc.nysed. gov/deputy/nclb/parents/parents.htm.

New York State United Teachers Division of Research and Educational Services (2002). *No Child Left Behind Act of 2001: Reauthorization of Elementary and Secondary Education Act, Fact Sheet 1-7.* Retrieved October 8, 2004, from http://www.nysut.org.

Sarason, S.B., & Doris, J. (1979). *Educational handicap, public policy, and social history.* New York: Free Press.

Turnbull, H.R., & Turnbull, A.P. (2000). *Free appropriate public education: The law and children with disabilities.* Denver: Love Publishing.

U.S. Department of Education (2002). *24th Annual report to congress on the implementation of the individuals with Disabilities Education Act. Students ages 6 through 21 served under IDEA.* Retrieved October 15, 2004, from http://www.ed.gov/print/ about/reports/annual/osep/2002/index.html.

U.S. Department of Education (2004). *No Child Left Behind: A toolkit for teachers.* Retrieved September 29, 2004, from http://www.ed.gov/print/teachers/nclbguide/toolkit.html.

Yell, M.L., & Drasgow, E. (2000). Litigating a free appropriate public education: The Lovaas hearings and cases. *The Journal of Special Education, 33*(4), 204–214.

Yell, M.L., Rogers, D., & Rogers, E.L. (1988). The legal history of special education: What a long, strange trip it's been! *Remedial and Special Education, 19*(4), 219–228.

III

REPORTS FROM THE FIELD: THE IMPACT OF COMPASSIONATE CONSERVATISM ON TEACHING AND LEARNING

The push for accountability, implemented through high-stakes testing, has profoundly altered the educational landscape in American public schools. For teachers, the imposition of scripted curricula has undermined their ability to respond to their students' needs. With this has come a diminished sense of professionalism and decreased collegiality. For children and their families, the threat of negative consequences for poor test performance has changed the view of school from safe and supportive to demanding and punitive. With this has come increased suspicion and uncertainty about the goals and intentions of educational institutions. The first three chapters in this section draw upon evidence from field settings to explore concretely the impact of compassionate conservatism on the experiences of teachers, children, and families in American public schools today. The last three chapters in this section offer some illustrations of efforts in the field to improve educational experience for the children ostensibly targeted by NCLB.

In chapter 6, Richard Meyer gives us the story of Kesha, whose teacher provided a learning environment in which Kesha was able to participate actively while addressing a very urgent personal concern. Meyer examines the difference between classrooms in which teachers can openly design a learning environment that accommodates the needs of individual students and those in which teachers must find ways to "fit in" what they believe is important around what they are required to do.

The reactions of teachers and parents in New York City to current educational "reforms" are reported by Marcia Baghban and Harriet Li in chapter 7. Once again, the frustration of teachers who are no longer treated as professionals is apparent. Also apparent is the concern of parents about whether a one-size-fits-all approach to education will really benefit their children.

The pernicious effect of current educational policies, especially high-stakes testing, on curricular issues is detailed in chapter 8 by Myra Zarnowski, Amie Backner, and Liba Engel. Detailing the breakdown of time in a typical New York City classroom, they highlight how testing dictates what subjects are covered regularly, and what subjects are no longer included in the regular school day.

One of the problems confronting school systems such as New York City's is the cost of providing adequate facilities and instruction for a burgeoning and disproportionately high-needs population. The Campaign for Fiscal Equity (CFE) has sought, for over 10 years, to obtain an equitable allocation of state education funding for New York City. In chapter 9, Susan Kirch and Molly Hunter discuss some of the steps that the Campaign for Fiscal Equity (CFE) has taken since 1993 to ensure that every child in New York State has the opportunity for a "sound basic education" through significant school funding reform.

Critical to the maintenance and healthy sustainability of community and school–community partnerships is community voice. However, education policy initiatives, curriculum, and education organizational structures are too often formulated without input from the community. In chapter 10, Lisa Scott and Angela Love discuss how community development impacts the academic success and socioemotional well-being of all students through the mobilization of human and material resources, the building of relationships between school personnel and community members, and community development. In chapter 11, Penny Hammrich and Michelle Myers report on innovative programs that seek to increase the participation of girls and underrepresented populations in science.

6

Leaving Sanity Behind: How Scientific Are the Scientific Phonics Programs?

Richard Meyer

This chapter presents two different views of how children come to be readers and writers in first grade. The first view is through the lived experiences of one child, as she exerts agency and becomes instrumental in learning to write and writing to learn prior to the influences of the No Child Left Behind (NCLB) Act. The second view is from the perspective of a group of children whose literacy learning is strictly controlled by a district mandate following the thrust of NCLB. The two views are juxtaposed in an effort to demonstrate that the teaching and learning of reading involve much more than what is suggested by the recent push toward intensive, systematic direct instruction in phonics as prescribed by the Reading First section of NCLB. The Reading First section demands that reading programs be scientifically based on research that is reliable and replicable. The narrow definition of science is devastating thoughtful teachers, reflective children, and sound reading programs such as the one in which Kesha flourished.

KESHA'S LITERACY LEARNING ENVIRONMENT

Kesha arrived in the first grade quite shy, both orally and in reading and writing, prior to the impositions on reading instruction that are rooted in NCLB. She rarely volunteered when her teacher, Kim, asked questions of the class. Kesha rarely took risks as a reader or writer, preferring to read and reread familiar texts and not venturing into new ones until the teacher or a first-grade colleague reviewed the new text quite a bit. Kim was not overly concerned about Kesha's hesitancy to read. "She'll find herself in a while," Kim said, relying on her 10 years of teaching experience and ever-increasing familiarity with first graders.

Ridgeway Elementary School, where Kim teaches and Kesha attends first grade, is a diverse school in a small city in the Midwest United States. Over 15 languages are spoken in the homes of the children attending the school, and over 75% receive free or reduced lunch (a figure included to represent the level of poverty in the neighborhood). Most of the children walk to the school. The principal of the school explains the linguistic diversity at Ridgeway: "Any place there's been a war, we have children from that country." There are church groups in the neighborhood and surrounding area that work to save families in war-torn countries. As a result, there are children from the former Soviet Union, the former Yugoslavia, Arab-speaking countries, and others. With such a broad range of language groups, bilingual education is not feasible. There are English as a Second Language-(ESL) certified teachers who address the needs of the English language learners at Ridgeway. Kesha's first language is English, and she lives with her mother and younger sister.

Kim's approach to literacy teaching and learning is holistic (Meyer, Brown, DeNino, Larson, McKenzie, Ridder, & Zetterman, 1998). She earned a master's degree in reading, and I was one of her professors in that program. Working with colleagues at her school, Kim and I were part of a study group that investigated ways in which children might develop literacy, using their interests and passions as a point of origin for literacy instruction (Short & Harste, with Burke, 1996). Kim uses miscue analysis (Goodman, Watson, & Burke, 2005) to assess her students' reading and to make decisions about what to teach. During the year that Kesha is in her classroom, Kim's principal is very supportive of her professional decision making.

Kim structures her day to support her students' literacy learning. The children arrive and engage in interest centers for 30 min. During this time, they learn math, science, reading, writing, and more as they engage in areas Kim has constructed that are reflective of their interests. They write about what they are learning as part of their activity at those centers. The children then move to a whole-group activity that includes songs on charts or in teacher-made songbooks, sharing of activities from the centers, and sharing about things that happened at home. Following whole-group activity, they move to individual reading, which is something they also keep track of. After recess, they work at literacy centers that involve books they are mastering; these are texts that are challenging or "intensive" (Peterson & Eeds, 1990). They spend a week learning the book, receiving instruction from Kim, and developing a project around the book. The children work at writers' workshop for 30 min each day. They spend a half hour prior to lunch discussing texts that the teacher reads to them, including fiction and nonfiction books, poems, newspaper articles, and others. After lunch, they work in math groups, have special classes (art, physical education, etc.), hear a chapter book, and work in inquiry groups.

Inquiry groups were not always a part of the children's day. These groups emerged as children's interests increasingly dominated conversations prior to writers' workshop (Meyer, 1999/2002). Kim suggested the children write about their interests, but their passions demanded more exploration and inquiry prior to writing. Kim invented inquiry groups as a place in which the children could pursue their interests and passions—their "great virtues" (Ayers, chapter 12 of this volume). Through inquiry, her students would respond to the questions that Ayers suggests all teachers support their students in addressing: "Who am I in this world?" and "Where in the world am I?" Kim required that they read, write, and interview people inside and beyond the school, and search extensively for ways to follow their interests and present their learning. For example, one group worried about spiders in the basement of the school. One member of this group suggested that if the spiders in the basement "pee on you, you can't move." He explained this to the group and froze in place to demonstrate what would happen. This small group of concerned first graders worked with the principal to make a videotape of the basement to demonstrate to their friends in the classroom that there were no dangerous spiders in the basement. They also wrote a book for the school library, in case others were worried about spiders that were, indeed, not a threat to the safety of those in the school.

KESHA IN THE CAT GROUP

Kesha quietly agreed to be in the cat group as the class was organizing for a new round of inquiry studies. They recently had project presentations where they presented inquiry activities in which they had been engaged for almost 6 weeks. Children presented their learning about rats, sharks, dinosaurs, spiders, and more. The success of their learning, as evidenced by the reading and writing they accomplished, led the class and Kim to decide that they would engage in more inquiry. The children sat and brainstormed areas they wanted to study.

"Fish," called out one child. "I want to learn more about fish. And I want to make centers for the other kids in the class to learn about fish, too."

Other children agree to study fish and that inquiry group is formed. Children call out other areas of interest. Some want to study cats, others the human body, and yet others want to learn about mermaids because of the popularity of a new movie. Kim makes lists on chart paper to show which children agreed to be in which groups. Kesha agrees to be in the cat group because one of her friends tells her it will be fun. "Okay," she assents quietly. Her friend tells Kim that Kesha wants to be in the cat group. Kim asks Kesha if this is true, and Kesha shakes her head, indicating yes.

A few weeks into the study of cats, the group has made many literate decisions. They will use books that have good pictures of cats and will make pictures of cats.

They will also make clay models of cats and have labels for these. One member of the group suggests that they bring in a real cat, "in a cage, so we can look at it and stuff." Kim explains that bringing a cat to school is a good idea if no one is allergic, and if they can arrange it so that the cat is only present during their study time and not in school all day. They discuss how to arrange the cat's visit to meet their teacher's criteria. After the discussion, they turn to some books and begin to decide which child will make a model of which cat. There is much to be figured out, because they have learned that lions, tigers, and other big animals are in the cat family. After their decisions seem firm, the children in the group sit with books and clay and begin to produce models of their cats. Kesha seems only tangentially interested, perfunctorily looking at the book in front of her, and squeezing the clay in her hands to soften it.

Kim tells the class that their inquiry time is over for the day, an announcement followed by moans of surprise as the children (and I) wonder how the time has passed so quickly. The clock confirms that it is almost time for dismissal. They have a few minutes to write in their inquiry daily logs. The children in the group each have their own log, and some write quite a bit; Kesha typically writes things like, "I'm making a cat from clay" [spelling conventionalized].

KESHA WRITES

The next day during inquiry time, the cat group eagerly begins kneading their clay to ensure that it is soft enough to work into cat shapes. They open their various reference books, and each refers to the cat he or she selected. Kesha begins to work alongside her friends. One of the first graders in the group looks around to assess her colleague's progress.

> "Hey," she says to Kesha, "that's not a cat. It only has two legs. All cats have four legs."

> "I don't care," Kesha replies. "I'm not making a cat. I'm making my grandmother."

> "You can't make your grandmother," another member of the group insists. "She isn't a cat. You have to make a cat."

> "Well, I'm not making a cat. I'm making my grandmother and I quit this group."

> Immediately, calls go out for Kim to address this radical departure from the group's goal of studying cats. Kim arrives at the scene and asks what is going on.

> "She's making her grandmother!" one member of the group points at Kesha. Kesha is shyly looking at her in-progress model, not looking at her teacher. This is the first time that a group member has ever—in the history of this first-grade class—so radically departed from the goals of an inquiry group.

Kim turns to Kesha. "Your friends are pretty upset. What do you want to do?"

Kesha is, much to Kim's delight, tenacious in her desire to make her grandmother. "I want to study my grandmother," she tells her teacher.

"Well," Kim begins, "you can. You'll have to be in a group of your own, but if you're much more interested in your grandmother, you certainly may study her. You just have to explain that to your group so they're not hurt or angry."

Kesha is quiet. This is the type of moment that she dreads, because she feels that she is in the spotlight and must assert herself in front of other children. She looks up at their solemn faces and says, "I really need to study my grandma now." The group's silence seems to weigh down on Kesha as her colleagues consider what she has said. Kim offers to help: "Inquiry is about studying what you really want to learn about," she reminds the group. "Okay," one of the members of the group says. Kesha looks up and smiles, seeing the other members of the group shaking their heads in agreement.

"You'll have to write about your grandmother," Kim reminds Kesha.

"I know," she smiles.

Kesha turns her body a bit, and that movement seems to be sufficient withdrawal from the group to follow her interests in her grandmother. She completes the model of her grandmother as Kim requests that the children write about their inquiry work on this day. Throughout what follows, Kesha's writing is transcribed as it was written, following the places she changed lines, using upper- and lowercase letters as she did, adhering to spelling as she presented it, and using punctuation and spacing (Hall, 1996) as she did. Each piece is followed by a conventional presentation of her work. On this first day of studying her grandmother, Kesha writes:

GranDmA WiLLA
GrAnDMA
She OWAiS Boey seDHd
Me Four A Laecg TAM
I MeA going To MiSS
MY GranDmA FourA Laecg
TAM I LOVe MY GranDmA
From Kesha [illustration of Kesha, smiling]

(She always babysitted me for a long time. I am going to miss my grandma for a long time. I love my grandma.)

This first piece is rich in data, which Kim will use in planning lessons for Kesha. The lessons will include a celebration of Kesha's voice as Kim says, "This sounds like you. It sounds so happy that you love your grandmother." It will lead to lessons about words, because Kesha seems to have thought that *am* should be spelled *M*, but then realized there were not sufficient letters to make a word. She added other letters to fill out the word, indicating her growing sense of what words should look like. She used her mouth to sound out *always* and wound up using letters that fit the position of her mouth as she wrote (Read, 1971). Within this one piece rests a wealth of information about Kesha's use of phonics, grammar, lexicon, and semantics to build a cohesive and coherent text (Martens, 1996).

An important piece of this story arose after school, when Kim and I spoke and realized that Kesha's grandmother died a few weeks ago. Kesha was writing to grieve over, remember, and deal with her grandmother's death. Over the course of the next few weeks, Kesha wrote about her grandmother in ever-deepening ways. One example:

> my grandma was very very
> very sitck sitck and very
> because she was sitck I
> miss she was very very
> very sitck sitck sitck [up to here done on word processor]
> sHe HAD A stroke
> She DieD in FeB.
> WillmAm DieD 3 [the '3' reversed]
> YeArS A go
> He WAS my
> GrandqA
> He Saied someTHing
> To my mommy
> I wiLL aLWAYS Be
> WiTH you
> She sAid thAnk
> You GranDqA
> Said thank you
> Mommy sAid
> I Love you

(My grandma was very very very sick sick and very because she was sick. She had a stroke. She died in Feb. William died 3 years ago. He was my grandpa. He said something to mommy. "I will always be with you." She said, "Thank you." Grandpa said, "Thank you." Mommy said, "I love you.")

Kesha's grandfather died 3 years before her grandmother, yet she knew about a conversation between her grandfather and his daughter (Kesha's mother). Kesha knew this, because she was asking questions at home. She wanted to know more about her grandparents, and her mom was telling Kesha family stories that made Kesha feel connected to loved ones who had died.

Kesha's sense of story is developing, as evidenced by the differences between the pieces immediately above and the first one presented. She includes dialogue and dialogue carriers in the second piece. She tells the story from her mother's perspective. She spells many words conventionally and indicates, again, her growing knowledge of the relationships between sounds and letters in the English language, and from this piece, Kim decides to teach Kesha words in the *ick* family so that she will know how to spell *sick* conventionally in the future.

One day during inquiry time, Kesha drew things that her grandmother loved. She drew a couch, a TV with a football game on it, a bathtub, a water bed, and continued on to a second page with more drawings. Each drawing was labeled, "She liked—" with "green" or "her house" written in the blank. There was an illustration of Kesha, next to which she wrote, "And she really loved me." On the second page of her illustrated and labeled work for the day were three long rectangles and one short one. Above the short rectangle was a word, *baby*, with an arrow pointing toward the rectangle. Next to one of the longer ones was an arrow pointing and labeling the rectangle *grandma*. We asked Kesha about these, and she explained that they were coffins.

Kesha had been excluded from the funeral of her grandmother, a decision that her mother made in Kesha's best interest. Her mother was concerned about Kesha being traumatized by the funeral. But Kesha had questions, so her mother took her to the funeral parlor to see a coffin like the one in which grandmother was buried. While there, Kesha also saw a coffin used for children. Kesha's mother was listening to Kesha's needs and interests, and at school we were seeing the documentation of Kesha's findings as she and her mother addressed those interests. The family stories and trip to the funeral parlor helped Kesha remember her grandmother and put her death into a context with which she could live.

FAMILY–SCHOOL RELATIONSHIPS

As the children completed almost 6 weeks of study in this round of inquiry, Kim called the class together to try to put closure on it. The children discussed ways which they could present their learning to others and decided on a fair. The sixth grade had recently completed a science fair, and many of the children in Kim's class had attended with their older siblings. The first graders wanted a fair similar to the one that the sixth graders presented. They wrote to the principal and got permission to hold a fair during the school day.

On the day of the fair, the children set up cafeteria tables along the first-grade hallway. Each child had much to show. Kesha had all the writing that she had completed about her grandmother and the clay model she had made. A few minutes before the start of the fair, Kesha's mother arrived at the school with a poster. Kesha waved from the table where her clay model and writing rested, and Kesha's mother walked over to her. She hugged her daughter and placed on the table an item that brought tears to her teacher's and my eyes. Kesha and her mom made a large poster of their family. In the middle are 12-in. photos of Willa and William. Surrounding them are photos of their children and grandchildren, cousins, and even some friends. Kesha and her mom explained the poster to visitors passing by during the first-grade fair.

After the fair, on an evaluation sheet that Kim constructed, Kesha's mom wrote:

> Kesha, what a wonderful job you did! If grandma could talk, she would say, "Oh, Kesha, you did that? What a big, growing, smart girl!" But in my heart I know a part of grandma was there every single day when you worked on a project about her and you can bet she's doing nothing but smiling. It is important for all who lose someone they love to keep some part of that memory alive. Thank you to all of her teachers and thank you Kesha for doing just that! This will remain in my heart forever. You did great Kesha!!!! I love you. Your Mom xoxoxo

A TEACHER'S WORK

Kim composed her classes with children in a way that addressed their literacy needs with depth, passion, and integrity. She kept careful track of each child's growth and crafted literacy lessons that addressed their needs. In terms of phonics, Kesha clearly understood most consonants and was working on how vowel and consonant blends work, phonic elements that Kim helps Kesha understand. Kim documents Kesha's growing understanding of letter–sound relationships, and Kesha's many pieces of writing serve as points of reference for that documentation. Consistent with what language is really for—to make meaning—Kim also addressed Kesha's understanding of words, sentences, vocabulary, and other elements. In other words, Kim understood language development, reading, and writing sufficiently to assess and make pedagogical decisions about her students. At times, Kesha was grouped for a writing lesson with other first graders. At times, Kim worked with her individually. Sometimes Kesha and her colleagues taught the entire class strategies that they were learning as emerging readers and writers.

The present fear about children's lack of use or understanding of phonics (National Reading Panel, 2002; executive summary) is a manufactured crisis (Berliner & Biddle, 1995). As a reader and writer, Kesha grew because of her intense need to use language to be heard and understood. She understands what language is for and is learning the conventions of written language under the guidance of an expert teacher and from other children in the class.

WINDS OF CHANGE

My interest in first graders engaging in inquiry was interrupted one year after Kesha moved to second grade. The district's reading scores appeared in the newspaper in April and, consistent with the federal pressure to adhere to the Reading First view of reading, an intense backlash against teachers (claiming they cannot or do not teach) and children (claiming they are not learning to read) surfaced (see Ohanian, chapter 13 of this volume). Salespeople from intensive phonics program publishers arrived in the district and began courting the curriculum decision makers at the district office. They claimed to have scientifically proven programs that would fix the students' scores and provide teachers with foolproof methods of teaching reading. By the end of the year, a new phonics program was adopted and mandated: All kindergarten through third-grade teachers would use the program. All children would participate, regardless of reading performance, second-language learning, special education needs, or any other reason. No child was to leave the room for services (reading, speech, etc.) during the phonics lesson.

Karen (pseudonym) invited me to visit her classroom, because she was exploring the use of inquiry with her children, until the mandate arrived at her school. At that point, she no longer had time for inquiry. The phonics lessons, which the publishers claimed would take 20 min each, often took more than an hour to complete. Karen and her first graders did not have time for inquiry. They often did not have time for writers' workshop. Karen and her colleagues attempted to challenge the soundness of the decision to have all children participate in the program. She explains what happened when she raised the issue at a district-wide in-service: "I was told by [a district reading administrator] that for too long teachers in this district have thought that their job was to create curriculum. I was told that is not our job. Our job is to deliver curriculum."

At the same meeting, teachers were told that they are "not self-employed." I asked Karen what that meant, and she explained that it was another way for the phonics company to demand that teachers follow the program and not think for themselves. Just as Galileo capitulated (see Ayers, chapter 12 of this volume), Karen bracketed her talent for "teaching toward freedom" in order to keep her job. The following section is a brief recounting of a typical phonics lesson. The analysis of this lesson is presented in greater depth in another publication (Meyer, 2001).

THE PHONICS LESSON

Karen moves swiftly through the many parts of the phonics lesson. The lessons are scripted, meaning that the exact words that she is to use are written in the guide that she holds on her lap. Even though she works to complete the lesson in

20 min, on the day that I observe, it takes just over an hour. She pauses midway in the lesson to have the children write in journals and read books that reflect their interests and reading abilities. She is not supposed to stop during a lesson, but she finds it impossible to let the lesson go uninterrupted.

The lesson starts with a blending story in which Karen says the phonemes of every fifth word of the text she reads from the publisher's guide. For example, she says, "Once there was a c-r-ow," making the sounds for *c*, *r*, and the long *o*. The children have to call out the word as soon as they recognize it. They do this for an entire story without stopping to discuss the content of the text. Then, they focus on the marker board on which Karen writes and changes words. For example, she writes *superman* and waits for a child to read it. Her precocious readers take on that task. Then, Karen erases the *n* and puts a *d*, making *supermad*. When a child asks what it means, Karen is about to say she does not know, but one of the children suggests that if you are very mad at someone, you "are supermad at them." Karen erases the *d* and puts the *n* back, but then adds an additional *d*, making *supermand*, a nonword. Using real words and erasing the final consonants, she asks the children to read: baboot from baboon, alphabed from alphabet, school bun from school bus, and so on. One of the children suggests that at school they serve hotdogs on school buns. The children are searching for meaning, because during the other parts of the school day, Karen demands that reading make sense.

Karen explains, "I won't call that reading. It's not reading." Karen believes that reading is about making sense, not simply reproducing the sounds that letters might make when they are next to each other. Still, the lesson goes on. The children are told to look at the puppet that comes with the program. The puppet says a sound after each word that Karen says. When she says, "maze," the puppet says, "zzzzzz." When she says, "place," the puppet says, "sssss." The children realize, with the help of a precocious reader, that they are to echo the last sound in the word that the teacher says, just like the puppet. They do that for a few more words. Then, they hear a very short story about the sound of the letter *d*, and how to pronounce the sound that the letter makes.

The lesson them moves to the children saying the sound of *d* when they hear it in a story Karen reads. Then, they shift to saying whether or not a word that is read has a *d* at the beginning (e.g., dance vs. treat). They make words with cards that have single letters on them and read a short story that is printed on a sheet of paper that can be folded to look like a little book; the lesson goes on and on and the behavior of different children becomes quite significant.

Some of the children are tuned into the lesson and do what Karen asks, providing words, sounds, and reading as asked. Others work to echo those children that are tuned in. If the lead children say "duh" for the sound of *d*, these children will echo that. If the lead children say a word, the followers quickly say that word. There is a small group of children that does not participate at all, sitting and not engaging with what is requested.

Some of the children begin to rock back and forth during the lesson. Others stroke their ears or pick their noses. One child raises his hand and lowers it while making the sound of bombs dropping. Others braid their friend's hair, poke their friends, suck on their clothing, and one child pulls strings of thread out of his socks. In analyzing these behavior, I wrote:

> The children's behaviors indicate their responses to the content of the lesson. Finding phonics cognitively and affectively barren, many initiate and communicate (by their actions) a search for stimulation, contact, and meaning (Snell & Brown, 2000). They find it in their noses, along their ears, and in their clothing. They find it as they suck a bracelet or touch a friend. Their behaviors communicate the mismatches between learners, curriculum, and the interactions children expect in a social learning setting (Durand, 1990). The phonics lesson forces kids to have "tunnel vision" (Smith, 1994) about reading as they focus on sounds rather than reading to construct meaning. In contrast, large group lessons (composed by Karen when she teaches literature from a big book) allow for all to participate, because children can learn a broad spectrum of reading strategies as they learn about the reading process (Meyer, 2002, p. 458).

UNDERSTANDING THE DIFFERENCES

Looking across the two first-grade classrooms provides much insight into the state of reading and, more specifically, the use and understanding of phonics instruction. In Kim's classroom, phonics is one cueing system that is taught specifically to the children's needs. In Karen's classroom, the students' needs are not considered because the program is a "one-size-fits-all" (Ohanian, 1999) view of teaching and learning. The specificity that Kim could provide Kesha, reflective of Kesha's needs, is not present in Karen's classroom. Previously, Karen's and Kim's classrooms were quite similar, as children engaged in inquiry and participated in lessons specific to their needs and interests. The mandate stripped Karen of her professional decision making, and she was forced to defer to the program or leave the school. Her principal and the district office administrators made that clear to her.

Teaching, within the context of the phonics program, involves the delivery of the packaged curriculum via the materials and script provided. Deviation from that program is grounds for dismissal due to insubordination. The teacher, Karen, serves as a conduit for the curriculum provided to her. She knows that her students have a variety of needs and seeks to address those during other times of the day if and when there is time. The children in Karen's classroom read books of their choice, and she develops strategy lessons for individuals and groups, but she does that work *around* the phonics program. There is no time for inquiry.

Curriculum, then, comes from a place (a publisher) far from the children in the local setting. This means that individual, linguistic, and cultural differences are bracketed, and that the company's program drives classroom activity. The motivation for this is clear: profit (Altwerger, 2005); publishers make a lot of money from districts that purchase their consumable and nonconsumable products. In this context, children like Kesha—children with interests, emerging voices, and tentative agency in their own literacy development—are forced into programs that make school boring, irrelevant, and divorced from preparing children to participate in a democracy.

Readers often are taken aback when I suggest that participation in a phonics program like the one that Karen is forced to use might actually influence a student's ultimate participation in a democracy. However, as Strauss (2005) points out, students are learning more than what appears to be the superficial lesson when they are involved in a learning experience. Some children may learn the sounds of letters in Karen's classroom during phonics lessons. But, they are also learning to be compliant; whether they understand the lesson or not, they are supposed to sit and act as though they understand. The echoing group of students is evidence of such a lack of understanding. Karen explains that during the rest of her day, the children are encouraged to question things they do not understand, but during phonics there is no place in the script that offers explanation of babbot, alphabed, school bun, and so forth. Her students' questioning of some of the nonwords suggests there is some overflow from other times of the day, but as the year progressed, children withdrew, echoed, or complied during phonics. The political fraud that Spring explains (chapter 1 of this volume) has transformed into curricular fraud that leaves Karen and her children cognitively lifeless. If we agree with Dewey (1938) that school should *be* life, not some readiness program for life, then the lives being lived in Karen's classroom do not suggest the cultivation of thoughtful, responsive citizens.

The children in Karen's classroom love her and she loves them. Karen cried when she recounted one facet of the phonics lesson in which she distributed cards to the children. The letters m, n, c, d, and a are written, one per card, with consonants in black and the vowel in red. The children are to make words with the cards. Some of her first graders do not know English well enough to understand what is occurring; others are very strong readers who enjoy playing with the cards. One of her stronger readers says, "I could make 'candy' if we had a y." Karen looks at me, retelling this story, saying, "This program is just not appropriate for all of my students." She resents giving important instructional time, the rare time when all of her students are present in the room (and not at various pull-out programs), to this program.

The home–school connections that Kim's inquiry-based classroom cultivated will not grow in Karen's classroom this year. Karen's students are not engaged in learning that raises questions and provokes curiosity in ways that follow children home. Karen feels isolated from her students' home lives, because the program simplifies teaching and learning to the point at which there is little to discuss with families. In previous years, Karen had much to discuss with her students' families, but now her professional soul aches (Popkewitz, 1998) as she lives out, with her students, a program that serves them superficially at best.

"BACKLASH PEDAGOGIES" AND HOPE

As I reflect upon teachers like Kim and Karen, smart teachers who are informed about the reading process, writing pedagogy, and the power of inquiry, it is hard to understand why anyone would get in the way of what they are doing. When I consider profit or the push toward compliance as motives, I become angry. The need for publishers to make money, as well as their complicity in the cultivation of compliant workers (Strauss, 2005), seems too pernicious to comprehend. Lakoff (2002) suggests that the agenda of compliance is rooted in one of the metaphors we have for our country, a metaphor based on the family. He suggests that the "strict father" metaphor demands that the children (or teachers or students) remain compliant. Such a metaphor, once it becomes part of the general public's way of thinking, virtually demands that those in power have ultimate power and that those under them comply. This force toward compliance helps perpetuate the distribution of power and wealth as they are defined now, barring access to these by others. Any type of progressive thinking results in a "backlash pedagogy" (Gutierrez, 2001, p. 568) that pushes to maintain the status quo.

Backlash pedagogies are strict and demanding. Sadly, once teachers and researchers comply with them, they become complicit in maintaining the unequal distribution of power and wealth that the backlash seeks to preserve. Yet, in the midst of all the tension and pain, of some of the greatest literacy researchers' ideas being dismissed, of the attacks on children and teachers that are being perpetuated daily, I have hope. The corner in which hope rests at present is a critical corner that needs to be saturated with the kind of hope that Paulo Freire (1970) and Max Van Manen (2003) talk about. This is a hope that is based in the fundamental decency and goodness, and sense of fairness and equity that thrive deep within the human heart; and here I do mean a figurative heart, one that is truly in our minds and connected to others. Hope grows from self-knowledge, knowledge of texts, knowledge of contexts, knowledge of relationships, and reflection on action and in action. Hope is about conscientization or consciousness-raising;

it is also about believing in the potential for things to change; it is about belief in one's agency, even entitlement during hard times; and hope is about a vision of and for change. All four facets of hope (consciousness, potential, agency, and vision) are here, today, in teachers' hearts and minds. We have all the conditions necessary to keep hope alive and to live out a vision for literacy teaching and learning that is rooted in the passions of children and the expertise of teachers.

WHAT DO WE DO?

We cannot be silenced. We must ask questions of imposed curriculum, talk to each other socially, form or continue study groups, and always pay attention to and talk about our students. The stories of our students, of children like Kesha, are what teaching is about. Meier (1997) calls teaching "a big ball of rolling stories" (p. 82). Our stories and the stories of our children's lives in and out of school are the stories that need to drive our schools. These are stories specific to individuals and settings and should not be homogenized into a generic curriculum provided to us by someone far from the sites at which we teach and learn from children. We need to attend conferences, put on conferences, engage in political action, make demands of our professional unions and organizations, and do whatever else we can to demand that teaching and schools remain one of the true cornerstones of a democratic nation.

We must understand that every act is a political one. Not talking is political. Not responding is political, and may easily be construed as complying or agreeing. A phonics program imposed upon us and our students by a district office that neither listens to nor honors what we know about our students is a political act. When mean-spirited and punitive laws like NCLB are passed—laws that employ flawed science to hold children and teachers hostage—we need to tell our legislators and anyone else who will listen that children are being hurt, and it must stop. We need to partner with other teachers and supporters of public education to demand that our professional thinking and reflective praxis be honored and supported in order to preserve our democratic tradition and cultivate the possibilities for a democratic future.

REFERENCES

Altwerger, B. (2005). *Reading for profit: How the bottom line leaves kids behind.* Portsmouth, NH: Heinemann.

Berliner, D.C., & Biddle, B.J. (1995). *The manufactured crisis: Myths, fraud, and the attack on America's public schools.* Reading, MA: Addison-Wesley.

Dewey, J. (1938). *Experience and education.* New York: Collier Books, Macmillan.

Durand, V.M. (1990). *Severe behavior problems: A functional communication training approach.* New York: Guilford.

Freire, P. (1970). *Cultural action for freedom*. Cambridge, MA: Harvard Educational Review and Center for the Study of Development and Social Change.

Goodman, Y., Watson, D., & Burke, C. (2005). *Reading miscue inventory: From evaluation to instruction* (2nd ed.). Katonah, New York: Richard C. Owen.

Hall, N. (Ed.) (1996). *Learning about punctuation*. Portsmouth, NH: Heinemann.

Lakoff, G. (2002). *Moral politics: How liberals and conservatives think*. Chicago: University of Chicago Press.

Martens, P. (1996). *I already know how to read: A child's view of literacy*. Portsmouth, NH: Heinemann.

Meier, D. (1997). *Learning in small moments: Life in an urban classroom*. New York: Teachers College Press.

Meyer, R. (1999/2002, October). Spiders, rats, and transformation. *Primary Voices K-6, 8*(2) [October 1999], pp. 3–9. Retrieved October 7, 2002, from http://www.ncte.org/pdfs/members-only/pv/0082-oct99/PV0082Spiders.

Meyer, R. (2001). *Phonics exposed: Understanding and resisting systematic direct intense phonics instruction*. Mahwah, NJ: Lawrence Erlbaum Associates.

Meyer, R. (2002). Captives of the script: Killing us softly with phonics. *Language Arts, 79*(6), 452–461.

Meyer, R., Brown, L., DeNino, E., Larson, K., McKenzie, M., Ridder, K., & Zetterman, K. (1998). *Composing a teacher study group: Learning about inquiry in primary classrooms*. Mahwah, NJ: Lawrence Erlbaum Associates.

National Reading Panel. (2002). *Report of the National Reading Panel: Teaching children to read*. Washington, DC: National Institute of Child Health and Human Development.

Ohanian, S. (1999). *One size fits few: The folly of education standards*. Portsmouth, NH: Heinemann.

Peterson, R., & Eeds, M. (1990). *Grand conversations: Literature groups in action*. Ontario, Canada: Scholastic.

Popkewitz, T. (1998). *Struggling for the soul: The politics of schooling and the construction of the teacher*. New York: Teachers College Press.

Read, C. (1971). Preschool children's knowledge of phonology. *Harvard Educational Review, 41*, 1–34.

Short, K., & Harste, J., with Burke, C. (1996). *Creating classrooms for authors and inquirers* (2nd ed.). Portsmouth: Heinemann.

Smith, F. (1994). *Understanding Reading*. Hillsdale, NJ: Lawrence Erlbaum Associates.

Snell, M.E., & Brown, F. (2000). *Instruction of students with severe disabilities*. Columbus, OH: Merrill.

Strauss, S. (2005). *The linguistics, neurology, and politics of phonics: Silent "E" speaks out*. Mahwah, NJ: Lawrence Erlbaum Associates.

Van Manen, M. (2003). *The tone of teaching*. London, Ontario, Canada: Althouse.

7

"I Thought I Was a Professional": Teachers' and Parents' Reactions to NCLB in New York City

Marcia Baghban and Harriet Li

INTRODUCTION

The federal and state governments have traditionally experienced an uneasy relationship in determining responsibilities for education in the United States.

The Tenth Amendment to the Constitution states that "the powers not delegated to the United States by the Constitution, nor prohibited by it to the states, are reserved to the states respectively, or to the people" (Legal Information Institute). Using this amendment as justification, states have assumed primary responsibility for education within their jurisdictions. However, the federal government has often used money to influence the underfunded and undersupported educational systems. Since 1965, the federal government has attempted to solidify a steady role in directing education (Lazerson, 1987).

The Republicans gained impetus for such a role with the publication of *A Nation at Risk*. Although Ronald Reagan was opposed to a federal role in education, he assembled the National Commission on Excellence in Education; its report, *A Nation at Risk,* noted that our educational system was producing mediocre results. In fact, as Spring states (chapter 1 of this volume), the report not only unjustifiably holds schools responsible for the U.S. failure to compete in international markets but also blames schools for a weakened U.S. future. One recommendation from the report is the establishment of a common curriculum. This task, of defining a basic set of knowledge that students were expected to achieve by certain grade levels, Reagan assigned to the states.

Prompted by Reagan's assignment of common curriculum to the states, in 1989 former President George Bush held the National Education Summit. The governors of the states attended and established six objectives to reach by the year 2000. In addition, the president created the National Education Goals Panel, whose purpose was to monitor and report on the progress made toward meeting the six objectives. One objective contributed to the formation of extensive assessments. By the year 2000, it declared that students would leave grades 4, 8, and 12 with demonstrated competency in challenging subject matter, including English, mathematics, science, history, and geography. It further stated that every school in America would ensure that all students learn to use their minds so that they might be prepared for responsible citizenship, further learning, and productive employment. This vision of students' learning would be accomplished by extensive standards and testing.

The emphasis on assessment and accountability led to the development of the No Child Left Behind (NCLB) Act. In 1994, President Clinton signed the Improving America's Schools Act. This act also made demands of the states. Among its requirements was the mandate for the development of challenging content standards for what students should know in mathematics and language arts and accompanying performance standards. President George W. Bush built upon the policies of this act to invest in standards and assessments as a means of holding schools more accountable for student performance. Both Republicans and Democrats supported the NCLB, and President George W. Bush signed it into law on January 8, 2002.

The bipartisan support for NCLB surprised legislators and educators alike. As Spring states (chapter 1 of this volume), some Republicans voted for the legislation merely to support President Bush, not to support the act itself. Both Democrats and Republicans claimed that curriculum standards coupled with high-stakes testing would provide American workers with the skills needed to compete in a global economy. Unfortunately, as Spring emphasizes, "we do not know the long-term effects of an educational system driven by standards tied to high-stakes testing." There is no evidence that "world-class standards" and "American achievement tests" would make America more competitive. To blame students and teachers for an economy of greed, Ohanian states (chapter 13 of this volume), is simply a business plan for the schools.

NCLB purports to improve public schools by enforcing a system of standards and accountability through high-stakes testing of students and sanctions for poor school performance and noncompliance. Far from improving public schools and increasing the ability of the system to serve poor areas and poor children, the law is doing exactly the opposite. In fact, many educators believe that the law is more about dismantling support for public education, increasing use of vouchers, and privatizing public schools, thereby reducing the size of the public sector and weakening the teachers' unions. Spring also argues that although NCLB has spawned new opportunities for a diverse testing industry, it more dangerously has protected prayer in public schools, the antigay agenda of the Boy Scouts of America, and abstinence-based sex education. To piggyback the Republican religious agenda on legislation that emphasized accountability and standards in education is, as Spring emphasizes, "political fraud."

NCLB IN NEW YORK CITY: THE PARENT–TEACHER PERSPECTIVE

In 2002, major management and political changes took place in New York City that mirrored many of the educational power struggles at the federal level. That August, Mayor Michael Bloomberg, in an attempt to wrest control of the New York City public schools from the 32 local school districts and central board of education, a system long considered to be a bloated, top-heavy bureaucracy, sought and received approval from the state to make the chancellor of education responsible directly to the mayor's office. Neither the mayor nor his newly named chancellor had much experience with educational research and philosophy, with educators, or with the realities of managing a public education system, and the newly renamed Department of Education saw a number of significant changes take place in a very short period of time.

By 2004, Leonie Haimson, parent activist and head of the public school advocacy organization Class Size Matters, felt strongly enough to publicly declare, "We all know that things have gotten substantially worse in the last couple of years." At a conference to discuss issues facing parents and professional educators, Ms. Haimson, joined by New York City educators Debbie Aizenstain and Ms. Angela Iannocone, veteran teachers of almost 20 years, cited policies and practices contributing to this deterioration, all of which are the same factors that have been blazoned widely in the national media and which eerily echo NCLB legislation: a top-down approach to management and instruction with mandated standards and curricula; increased, unceasing emphasis on testing and assessment; a punitive, aggressive, and expanding retention policy to combat social promotion; and a lack of funding to enact recommended reforms such as reductions in burgeoning class size.

MANDATED CURRICULA

The practice that rankles teachers the most is the administration's imposition of highly scripted programs that tell them exactly what to do and what to say; in short, not just *what*, but *how*, to teach. All teachers in New York State go through a rigorous certification process, which is one of the most demanding in the nation. All are holders of masters' degrees in their field of specialization and many continue on to postgraduate coursework. Yet, the rigid nature of New York City's mandated math and literacy programs does not allow teachers to draw on their knowledge of child development, theories of cognitive awareness and affective behavior, or learning styles and multiple intelligences. Nor are teachers able to respond to the needs, strengths, and weaknesses of the child as an individual. Rather, teachers are required to read verbatim from a scripted, prepared lesson and regurgitate it for the entire class. Feeling is widespread that there is no need to rely on the research and training that teachers went through for their master's degrees (Aizenstain, cited in Li, 2004). As Ohanian indicates (chapter 13 of this volume), this is not professionalism but powerlessness.

Perhaps most important and most frustrating for teachers is that this rigid, authoritarian approach to education does not see the student as an individual. Instead, it flies in the face of all that experience and research on child development have to say us about best practice in the classroom, by not allowing for individual students' strengths, weaknesses, experiences, or interests. As Professor Rafael Olivares noted:

> The prescriptive curriculum assumes equal students, equal situations, equal everything, and we know that the schools of New York are not equal. We know that every classroom in New York has a diversity of students with ethnic diversity, cultural diversity, and linguistic diversity … and *that* is a *real* problem because that has *not* been considered in the testing situation, that has *not* been considered in the prescriptive curriculum at all (quoted in Li, 2004, p. 16).

If the new programs ignore differences in learning style, they do the same for teaching style. Not only has the rigidity of the curriculum incurred teachers' wrath, but the senseless repetition of meaningless trivia, from the rote nature of the teacher's scripted "Hello" each day ("Good morning Readers and Writers!") to the students' movement to prescribed mandated spots in the classroom for each lesson, has become a joke to teachers and students alike. Veteran teacher Debbie Aizenstain noted:

> A lot of the time spent during the day is moving—from the rug … to the chairs … to the rug … to the chairs. For math we have to move, for the math message, to the rug, then we move back to the chairs to do partner work, then we move back to the rug to do sharing. Then we go into the reading workshop, then we move back to the rug for the mini-lesson, and then we go back to do individual work, then we come back to the rug to share again. I spend more time moving back and forth than I do teaching. The kids know this. They're not stupid. They're really very smart. They've got street savvy. They *know* that this is a time waster. They're falling right into it: "Well, if the teacher's going to waste time, I might as well waste time as well" (Li, 2004, pp. 10,11).

TESTING, TESTING, TESTING ...

To counteract what is seen as the ineffectiveness of the curriculum, teachers often teach using several programs at once so that the children learn the material and do not suffer at testing time because they are ill-prepared. Between this parallel curriculum and

> all the emphasis on assessment and testing, [teachers] spend much of their time on that, and they have little time left for instruction ... There is barely enough time to teach the math curriculum ... and do the reader's workshop and writer's workshop ... . I find it difficult to do social studies [and] science has been almost outlawed in my building except for the science cluster [teacher] who does science once a week. This is unbelievably poor education (Aizenstain, quoted in Li, 2004, p. 4).

Perhaps, but it *does* emphasize the subjects required by NCLB to be tested, math and literacy, although, as Zarnowski amply documents (chapter 8 of this volume), at the expense of educating our children in other subjects. In some schools, the emphasis on "Back to Basics" is so overwhelming that children are required to take their journals with them to lunch and write in them after they are finished eating (Iannacone, cited in Li, 2004). Gone are the days when children ran and played and got some exercise for their growing bodies each day after lunch. They write whether or not they have something to say, and the lesson on how to lead an active as opposed to a sedentary lifestyle is learned rather differently from what experts on child development and physical fitness might wish. Emphasis is focused almost exclusively on "teaching to the test."

TESTING AND RETENTION: CHILDREN "AT RISK"

This "increased, relentless pressure on testing," as parent advocate Haimson puts it, is felt by teachers, parents, and children alike, and nowhere do the feelings of frustration make themselves more evident than with respect to the third- and now the fifth-grade retention policy, New York City's answer to the end of social promotion. As Haimson notes,

> every single educational expert and researcher across the country has called and thinks [the policy] is "a terrible idea." Many of them called it "educational malpractice" because the research is so overwhelming that it leads to higher dropout rates and lower student achievement. But the mayor went ahead anyway. In terms of how that is affecting parents' lives – it used to be that 4th grade was the worst grade because of the 4th grade tests. Now it's 3rd grade, 4th grade, 5th grade. I can just tell you the pressures of retention and the possibility that their kids have been held back is *extremely* difficult for both parents and kids to deal with ... I can tell you when the policies were announced I had parents who were absolutely frantic.

In many cases ... kids who had gotten straight A's on their report card and because of one bad result on an interim assessment were considered now "at risk." There were thousands of parents out there who were absolutely *shocked* to get this letter, who didn't understand why the kid's results on one test should change their futures forever, and were not being offered *anything* by the school. So there were lots of parents out there who were absolutely distraught and horrified and scared to death (Haimson, quoted in Li, 2004, pp. 2–6).

Here, of course, is the real difficulty—certainly, not all children who are said to be "at risk" end up being held back; however, for those who are, there is no comprehensive plan for how to bring these children to the level of their peers. Haimson reports that at the Panel for Educational Policy meeting when they voted to impose the fifth-grade retention policy, a question was asked about what had happened to third graders who were held back and what they were getting that was different from or in addition to other students, a question that no one present could answer. "So," Haimson notes,

this was this great plan, that all these kids who were held back were going to get all these extra services and all this special treatment to make sure that they succeeded this time, and they have absolutely *no* plans for these kids and no idea about what special treatment they are being given (Haimson, quoted in Li, 2004, p. 7).

At times, even when there is an attempt to establish a program for helping these students, decisions are made in a top-down fashion with what appears to be a lack of substantiating research, of resources, and sometimes even of focus. Here again, Haimson provides the perfect example in the announcement of Saturday academies for fifth graders:

[When this was presented to the panel, it was said,] "These kids are going to be in there Saturdays. They're going to be in there holidays. We're hoping that we get some teachers to sign up for this .... One of the things we're going to do is bring middle school principals to the Saturday academies to tell these kids how great middle school is, so they really have to work hard if they don't want to miss out on the opportunity to go to middle school." As though [Haimson reports] it was just a matter of their *attitude*, like they didn't care about graduating. It was pretty outrageous and it just shows you how badly thought out the whole program was from beginning to end (Haimson, quoted in Li, 2004, p. 7).

In short, notwithstanding the horrible self-image of a child who is held back once, twice, and even three times, the point is that we are failing these children miserably because there is no effective plan to help them. When we implement programs without reference to the unique problems that caused the individual children not to test well initially, we position them for failure time and time again, no matter how much money we spend.

BUDGET BATTLES

Lack of funding and austerity budgets are political and economic realities that both parents and teachers acknowledge and with which they have largely come to terms. What they have not come to terms with is the way in which spending is allocated. This is not just an indictment of the choice of curriculum, but rather a frustration with scarce monies being spent on programs that could be cut back or painlessly eliminated and used on other programs that could reap demonstrated quantifiable results. For example, Haimson tells us,

> this administration has put *tremendous* emphasis and a *tremendous* amount of resources and dollars to professional development in terms of math and literacy coaches in every school, more time in the school day and the school year specifically devoted to professional development, and the response from teachers as a whole is overwhelmingly negative. Like 80 percent [of teachers surveyed by the union] said they think that professional development is much worse now than it was before (Haimson, quoted in Li, 2004, p. 9).

This reaction occurs because many of the coaches have no more experience in the classroom than the teachers they are coaching. They are learning the new programs just like the teachers and do not always understand what it is they are supposed to be modeling. Implementation and understanding of the programs' particulars are evolving, and what is learned one day often has to be discarded the next (Aizenstain, cited in Li, 2004). Teachers, as professionals, find it very demeaning being lectured to (Iannacone, cited in Li, 2004), and, as Aizenstain states, "resent having to waste [their] time."

A perfect example of contention over educational spending is the plan put forth by the mayor for spending the anticipated Campaign for Fiscal Equity (CFE) funds, funds that had been anticipated as being used to hire additional teachers, create additional classes and classroom space, and thereby reduce class size. These monies were due the city by the state as a result of a judicial decision that found that New York State had consistently underfunded urban schools in New York City for years. A detailed account of the CFE case is provided by Kirch and Hunter in chapter 9 of this volume. Haimson reports that the city is expected to receive between $4 and 5 billion extra per year from the state, but the mayor has already filed a compliance plan with the court that outlines a plan to buy "laptops for every student in the New York City public schools ... and also [to hire] thousands of additional specialists and administrators who will be housed outside of school buildings in leased office space" (Haimson, quoted in Li, 2004). Despite the fact that the city has "the largest class sizes by far in the state and the highest needs student population," despite the fact that the situation in high school is even worse than in elementary school, with "over 11,000 classes which violate the union contractual limit of 34 (which means kids who are in classes of up to 40 or more)," and despite the fact that we've known that "class size makes a tremendous difference, not just in terms of student achievement but to teachers being able to do their jobs effectively in the classroom"; despite all this, the proposed compliance plan includes lowering average class size in no grade higher than the third (Haimson, quoted in Li, 2004).

I THOUGHT I WAS A PROFESSIONAL

On a personal level, teachers have found that life in the New York City public school system is very different from what it was a few years ago. In imposing lockstep scripted programs, politicians and administrators with little experience or training in education have ignored teachers' scholarship and credentials and have treated them as assembly-line process workers rather than professionals. Teachers may never have had much control over the larger educational system, but, as documented in this volume by Meyer in chapter 6 and Ohanian in chapter 13, they now have little or no voice in their own schools, and virtually no autonomy even in their own classrooms.

Interestingly enough, many of these issues that are so irksome to teachers and parents are the outgrowth of programs and reforms that those same teachers and parents agree are conceptually well conceived. Rather, it is the actual implementation of these programs and reforms that has been significantly flawed. For example, Haimson, speaking of overcrowding and smaller class size, cites the recent trend:

> [I]n an ideal world, that would be a great initiative to have small high schools where kids get to know their whole administration better and generally they get smaller classes as well. It's a very good reform in an ideal world. But what we're seeing is small schools being put into already overcrowded large buildings. The kids in the small schools are getting small classes, more resources, laptops, Internet access, special programs, while kids in the large schools are getting squeezed into bigger and bigger classes, double and triple shifts, five classes being given *at once* in the library or the auditorium, and those kids are feeling justifiable resentment against the kids in the other small schools, leading to increased levels of school violence throughout the system. So really, a lot of these reforms in an ideal world, with more resources, with more room, with smaller classes, make sense, but in the general environment of New York City public schools, they're making things worse, not better (Haimson, quoted in Li, 2004, p. 5).

Additionally, it has been generally agreed that the emphasis and resources the City has placed on professional development, especially with new curriculum, make a great deal of sense. In reality, however, "the problem is that people who are in charge of doing the staff development don't quite know what they're doing either" (Iannacone, cited in Li, 2004). The curriculum itself, as the chancellor of education envisioned it 2 years ago, would provide teachers with much-needed direction, but also leeway for creativity. At the time, he rejected rigid, scripted teaching, saying the system needed teachers who were creative and empowered (Goodnough, 2003). Yet all schools were required to adopt the new curriculum except for the "top-performing" 200 schools, some of which adopted the program voluntarily. In a few cases, middle and high schools have been asked to use the same model, including such absurdities as "lessons on the rug," even though it was really developed for elementary schools. Compellingly, Haimson makes the point that it is in the implementation, not the conceptual framework, that New York City has fallen short:

> What's interesting to me as a parent is the model for professional development and the curriculum to some extent that the administration imposed citywide was based upon the model in District 2 which is where my kids go to school. My understanding and my experience is that it was never meant to be a lockstep approach. In fact, it was supposed to be something else altogether. I never experienced it the way these teachers are describing it. The balanced literacy was supposed to be *different* from the scripted programs ... that teachers really hated because it told them exactly what they had to say and measured out their lives in minutes and seconds and was a straitjacket for their ability to use their skills. So it sort of surprises me that this is how it's being imposed in the city as a whole because it was never *meant* to be that kind of a program ... So, what they did is they took a model that was semi-successful in District 2 among a very specific population of kids and was not enforced in a rigid way by any means in my experience, and they took that model and they imposed it in a very *stupid* and authoritarian way on the city as a whole and it obviously makes no sense (Haimson, quoted in Li, 2004, p. 11).

THE FUTURE OF DEMOCRACY

These, then, are some of the descriptors of public education and the public education system in New York City today: rigid, lockstep, scripted, and authoritarian. It is precisely this one-way communication, coupled with this almost total disregard of what experienced educators can contribute in the way of solutions, that has become pandemic throughout the educational system, a fact that teachers find not just frustrating, but frightening. Teachers and low-level, untenured administrators are often afraid of questioning or criticizing because of the fear of repercussions (Aizenstain, cited in Li, 2004). Parents, too, are often just as powerless to obtain answers or to evoke even the slightest bit of administration concern over issues that they themselves see as vital:

> We had parents talking about how when their child was in third grade in a class of over 30, the teacher instructed them that they weren't allowed to ask any questions of the teacher until they had asked two other students first. When the child protested and the parent protested that they weren't allowed to ask questions directed at the teacher anymore, the school principal said, "Maybe you should consider putting your son in private school" (Haimson, quoted in Li, 2004, p. 3).

Unfortunately, this cavalier attitude toward those who raise questions and issues is not just confined to Department of Education administration. During the afternoon session of the conference cited in this chapter, two elected officials, both members of the City Council Education Committee, sat with the rest of the panel on stage. One received and took numerous phone calls in full view of the audience. Both listened while the guest speakers addressed their remarks to the audience, and, following the lead of their fellow panel members, introduced themselves and their own personal views on education. Yet neither acknowledged nor in any way validated remarks made by the other speakers. Both left the proceedings early without making any attempt to enter into meaningful, informed dialogue with the members of the educational community who were there for that purpose.

The message sent here was a chilling reminder to all the educators present that the most frightening aspect of the current repressive educational environment is in the unspoken implications it holds for the future of our democracy. For, if educators who are themselves trained professionals have no freedom to question, how can we in good conscience believe we are preparing children for citizenship in a democratic society? How can we fool ourselves into thinking we are providing a strong democratic model when the ends justify the means, when questions are discouraged, and personal opinions are not valued? How can we say we have done justice to our students and valued their uniqueness and diversity, qualities that make this nation great, when our educational system is struggling so mightily to have them all fit into the same mold, to have them all march to the beat of the same drum? If the future of our nation is our children, then we must provide authentic models of democratic principles for them to learn from. As Ayers (chapter 12 of this volume) so eloquently states, "democracy, like education … must be achieved over and over again by every individual and each successive generation if it is to live at all."

FINAL THOUGHTS

With NCLB, Democrats and Republicans united to guarantee success in schools. However, the vision of school success offered by NCLB is a narrow one, defined in terms of performance on standardized tests. This view presupposes that there is a universally agreed upon list of skills and knowledge that each child must possess. Experts do not agree on the skills and knowledge that constitute such learning nor the timeline of such learning. Where then is the scientifically based practice that supports such a limited view of human learning (Murphy, 1998; Coles, 2000, 2003; Smith, 2003)? Moreover, as Spring (chapter 1 of this volume) explains, an emphasis on high-stakes testing only results in improving the ability of students to take standardized tests, not their skills and knowledge.

In fact, the federal Department of Education uses the term "research-based" to enforce directives and limit choices, as it did when it vetoed the reading program selected by New York City schools. It is quick to impose "research-based" curriculum on public schools, but it is even quicker to exempt its own pet projects from scientific thinking or judgment (No Child Left, 2004). In October 2004, more than 60 leading scientists, including Nobel laureates, leading medical experts, former federal agency directors, and university chairs and presidents, issued a statement calling for regulatory and legislative action to restore scientific integrity to federal policymaking. According to the scientists, the Bush administration has suppressed and distorted scientific analysis from federal agencies and taken actions that have undermined the quality of scientific advisory panels (No Child Left, October 2004).

In addition, NCLB's approach to success depends solely on punishment. No worthwhile psychologist or educator would establish such a system (Bracey, 2004). NCLB punishes the many for the few. If a school's special education students fail to make "Adequate Yearly Progress," the whole school fails. If a school's English language learners fail to make "Adequate Yearly Progress," the whole school fails. If 95% of any group fails to show up on the test day, the whole school fails (Bracey, 2004). What gets tested is then taught. Teachers teach to the tests and specifics get taught, not higher level thinking. Once again, how do students ever become independent decision makers?

Although NCLB claims to be enhancing the quality of education for low-income and minority group students by requiring highly qualified teachers, there is nothing in NCLB to attract teachers or administrators to poorly performing schools. Poor and minority children have families that cannot afford the private tutoring that is buffering the effects of NCLB in wealthier districts. The option of federally financed tutoring is offered at poor schools that have been deemed "failing" for 2 years in a row. Hundreds of new providers have been established to take advantage of the law. Experts say that these groups will earn as much as $200 million this school year. Because families choose from a list of state-approved providers, some tutoring groups have reacted with aggressive soliciting, promising computers and gift certificates to parents who often do not have the English facility to understand the agreements. In New York City, where more than 81,000 students are tutored, officials began an inquiry into all the providers to be completed by summer 2005 (Saulny, 2005, p. A1). In addition, there is a lower standard for tutors than for teachers, and documented cases of absent tutors, unqualified tutors, and tutors with no understanding of schools accumulate daily. Yvonne Jones, the mother of an eighth-grade student at an East Harlem middle school, describes her shock when after 1 month of tutoring, her daughter arrived home with a letter from the state-approved tutoring group that it was closing (Saulny, 2005, p. A18). Shirlene Little, the PTA president at Middle School 22 in the Bronx, lists the many observations of unqualified tutors and wonders if the tutors do any good. When she took her son for tutoring in math, she states, "the only thing he seemed to do was cut up and play" (Saulny, 2005, p. A18). The law's silence on such issues is not an oversight. "We want as little regulation as possible so the market can be as vibrant as possible," Michael Petrilli, an official with the federal education department told tutoring company officials at a recent meeting (Saulny, 2005, p. A1).

The focus on reading, writing, and math at the expense of social studies, the arts, and foreign languages makes for a narrowed curriculum. Reports from different parts of the country cited by Zarnowski, Backner, and Engel state (chapter 8 of this volume) echo the experiences of New York City. The elementary school curriculum is so off balance that it has even squeezed out the one subject, social studies, explicitly designed to teach the knowledge and skills students need to become effective citizens. Moreover, low-income minority students are excluded from the liberal arts curriculum that their more privileged counterparts receive. "In our effort to close achievement gaps in literacy and math, we have substituted one form of educational inequity for another, denying our most vulnerable students the kind of curriculum available routinely to the wealthy" (Bartlett & von Zastrow, 2004). When you tilt education in the direction of areas most easily measured, you impose a kind of starvation, which is difficult to notice at first, on the very children and families who can least afford the damage (No Child Left, 2004). By failing in school to provide minority children with needed learning opportunities that are otherwise unavailable to them, NCLB is treating vulnerable children as nonentities. As Ayers declares (chapter 12 of this volume), "Making students invisible is a singular accomplishment."

Also, what about parents whose children are fearful of the days of testing and who realize that their children may be held back in third or fifth grades? "As a parent, would you rather know that your child ranked in the 56th percentile of all students of the same age in the country—or that your child demonstrated two years' growth in a subject area during the previous school year?" (Yero, 2002, p. 9). Standardized testing provides quick numbers on where to further assess a child, but it should not be used as a basis for long-term decisions (Robinson, McKenna,

& Wedman, 2004). Accountability includes the overall progress of each student in the school, but it is illogical to demand that this progress be identical in content and rate for each student. Rather, parents want to know what the school is doing for their child and what the teacher expectations are for their child. As Ohanian emphasizes (chapter 13 of this volume), schools are not interchangable skill-delivery systems; rather, they are social institutions that are integral parts of the communities they serve.

Well-trained and caring teachers are the most resistant to federal mandates that they know from experience are ill-considered and potentially detrimental to student learning (Novinger, 2005). Ayers (chapter 12 of this volume) emphasizes that each teacher faces the task of developing an identity within the turmoil. He states that teachers are students of their students, and their stance is identification *with*, not identification *of*, their students. Teachers must begin by standing *with*, not above, their students. Yet teachers realize that if they do not help their schools achieve compliance with federal demands, there will be no money for the schools. "[T]he NCLB Act, with its high-sounding rhetoric and promise of millions of dollars for education, is like dangling a juicy chicken in front of a well-trained, but starving bird dog" (Yero, 2002, p. 8). If teachers speak out, they may be labeled as unwilling to help the education of children. If they try to work behind the scenes, "under the radar," or "between the cracks," they make it look as if NCLB is doing its job rather than their own professionalism. The tragedy is that teachers, isolated as they are in their work, often accept the corporate message of inadequacy and in so doing allow themselves to become deprofessionalized, notes Ohanian (chapter 13 of this volume). Finally, the atmosphere of mistrust in which they teach intensifies their personal dilemmas, and frustration causes more and more dedicated teachers to leave the profession (Bomer, 2005).

The atmosphere of mistrust also affects the children. Most dangerous is the betrayal of the relationship between student and teacher. Rather than trusted elders and guides, teachers now function as examiners. Katherine Bomer writes about cheerleading her way through tasks she found criminal:

> This is what my first graders thought reading meant—sitting at a table with an evaluator, unable to talk about what they were reading except in direct response to an authorized question, unable to predict the arc of the story or relate to the feelings and motivations of the characters. This was not reading, but rather playing an evil game, a game that can feel fun when you are winning, but that can devastate when you know you are losing (Bomer, 2005, p. 171).

Clearly, this experience does not qualify as anyone's definition of reading or an excellent reading teacher (International Reading Association, 2000).

Importantly, where are the colleges of teacher preparation in this muddle? Apparently, the New York City chancellor sees them as unnecessary. The Department of Education sees a need to extend some control over this facet of education as well. On February 1, 2005, Dr. Matthew Goldstein, chancellor of the City University of New York, which produces about a third of New York City teachers, announced the creation of a new undergraduate teacher academy that will run in partnership with the New York City Department of Education. The form the academy will take has yet to be announced, but the chancellor's remark, "I want to create a competitive environment for teacher education and have it run parallel, and let the market decide" (Arenson, 2005, B4), gives every assurance that, like the charter school experimentation currently under way, this endeavor will also be run along the lines of a business rather than an educational model. The new CUNY teacher academy will supply the "products" that the Department of Education buyer demands.

On August 22, 2005, the state of Connecticut filed its anticipated lawsuit against the U.S. Department of Education over the NCLB Act. The legal case rests largely on a provision in NCLB itself that states "nothing in this chapter shall be construed to authorize" the federal government to "mandate a state or any subdivision thereof to spend any funds or incur any costs not paid for under this chapter." The suit alleges that the law forces Connecticut to spend approximately $112.3 million to expand its testing program. Congress has appropriated only $70.6 million, leaving the state with the $41.6 million needed by 2008 compared to the $33.6 million the state is slated to receive from the federal government (Dillon, 2005, p. B1). However, legal scholars say that previous lawsuits brought against the federal government about underfunded mandates met with little success. Yet, Connecticut's suit could be successful because the NCLB law includes a passage, sponsored by Republicans during the Clinton administration, that forbids federal officials to require states to spend their own money to carry out the federal policies outlined in the laws (Dillon, 2005, p. B1). Moreover, the complaint also cites the spending clause in Article I of the Constitution, which has been construed by the courts as requiring Congress to make unambiguous any conditions attached to states' acceptance of federal money (Archer, 2005).

The Attorney General for the State of Connecticut, Richard Blumenthal, calls NCLB illegal and unconstitutional. He says, "There is burgeoning unhappiness among both Republicans and Democrats" (Dillon, 2005, p. B1). Ohanian emphasizes (chapter 13 of this volume) that some Democrats have said they would never have voted for NCLB if they had known the federal government would skimp on funding. At the 2004 Democratic National Convention, Pennsylvania's Democratic Governor Edward Rendell supported NCLB, as Spring notes (chapter 1 of this volume), because he believed that children need to be tested once a year but only if after testing there is money to remediate. "The dissatisfaction is felt across the country and across the board politically," Blumenthal states, "so, I can pretty much call any of my colleagues and get an earful" (Dillon, 2005, p. B1).

William Taylor, chairman of the Citizens' Commission on Civil Rights, questions the strategy of basing a lawsuit on claims of unfunded mandates. He feels that such a lawsuit may encourage other states to resist, and such resistance cannot help this major effort to help poor children. Mr. Blumenthal responds that Connecticut's quarrel with NCLB is not with its objectives but "with the failed implementation" (National School Boards Association, August 2005).

On August 24 at a press event in Atlanta, Secretary of Education Margaret Spellings called the unfunded mandate a red herring and asked why Connecticut was afraid to assess its performance. U.S. Department of Education spokeswoman Susan Aspey added that "nearly every state is on board and working with us to help their students" (Archer, 2005). The Civil Society Institute (Archer, 2005) countered that lawmakers in 21 states have considered bills critical of the federal education law and that 40 states have sought federal waivers or exemptions from some of its provisions. The institute is quietly cataloging recent state legislation, including Utah's passage of a measure that gives state education law precedence over federal rule, and a Colorado law offering financial protection to districts that opt out of the NCLB requirements. Also, Chuck Dow, a spokesman for the state attorney general's office in Maine, said that a lawsuit by his state challenging the NCLB law is "an open possibility" (Archer, 2005).

And so the education wars continue, always at the expense of America's children, the helpless victims of adult decisions.

REFERENCES

Archer, J. (2005, August 31). Connecticut files court challenge to NCLB. *Education Week* on-line. Available at http://ewdev.edweek.org.

Arenson, K. (2005, February 2). CUNY takes steps to draw better students to teaching. *The New York Times*, p. B4.

Bartlett, R., & von Zastrow, C. (2004, April 7). Commentary: Academic atrophy. *Education Week* online. Available at http://www.edweek.org.

Bomer, K. (2005). Missing the children: When politics and programs impede our teaching. *Language Arts, 82*, 168–176.

Bracey, G.W. (2004, October). *The seven deadly absurdities of No Child Left Behind.* http://nochildleft.com.

Coles, G. (2000). *Misreading reading: The bad science that hurts children.* Portsmouth, NH: Heinemann.

Coles, G. (2003). *Reading the naked truth: Literacy, legislation, and lies.* Portsmouth, NH: Heinemann.

Dillon, S. (2005, April 6). Connecticut to sue U.S. over cost of school testing law. *The New York Times*, pp. B1, B8.

Goodnough, A. (2003, January 22). City is converting reading and math to uniform course. *The New York Times*, p. A1.

International Reading Association (2000). Excellent reading teachers. Adopted position statement. *The Reading Teacher, 54*, 235–240.

Kohn, A. (2004, September). Feel-bad education. *Education Week* on-line. http://www.edweek.org.

Lazerson, M. (1987). *American education in the twentieth century: A documentary history.* New York: Teachers College Press.

Li, H. (2004, October 23). *But I thought I was a professional.* Transcript of opening panel, (2005, August) Queens College, Division of Education Conference.

Meier, D., & Wood, G. (Eds.). (2004). *Many children left behind: How the No Child Left Behind Act is damaging our children and our schools.* Boston: Beacon Press.

Murphy, S. (1998). *Fragile evidence: A critique of reading assessment.* Mahwah, NJ: Lawrence Erlbaum.

National School Boards Association (2005, August). *Legal clips.* http://www.nsba.org.

No Child Left (2004, October). *Research-based delusions.* http://nochildleft.com.

Novinger, S. (2005). Telling our stories: Speaking truth to power. *Language Arts, 82*, 195–203.

Robinson, R.D., McKenna, M.C., & Wedman, J.M. (2003). *Issues and trends in literacy education* (3rd ed.). Boston: Allyn & Bacon.

Saulny, S. (2005, April 4). A lucrative brand of tutoring grows unchecked. *The New York Times*, pp. A1, A18.

Smith, F. (2003). *Unspeakable acts, unnatural practices: Flaws and fallacies in "scientific" reading instruction.* Portsmouth NH: Heinemann.

U.S. Department of Education (2004). *No Child Left Behind: A toolkit for teachers.* Jessup, MD: Education Publications Center.

Yero, J.L. (2002). *Presuppositions of No Child Left Behind.* http://www.TeachersMind.com.

8

Whatever Happened to the Rest of the Curriculum?

MYRA ZARNOWSKI, AMIE BACKNER, AND LIBA ENGEL

One of the more startling results of the current New York City (NYC) curriculum mandates in reading and math has been the marginalization, and even squeezing out, of social studies and science. Teaching these subjects well requires providing students with hands-on experiences and in-depth inquiry. There simply is no time for this. Only when the threat of tests looms over a grade level do these subjects appear in full force—but then only in the form of test prep.

This serious lack of time is the result of mandated and strictly enforced curricular changes resulting from No Child Left Behind Legislation and local curriculum mandates which, as Joel Spring points out in chapter 1 of this volume, rest on unproven claims about long-term effects. As he explains, there are simply no longitudinal studies showing that standards-based instruction tied to high-stakes testing results in higher quality education—that is, students who are better able to compete in a global economy. Yet, teachers are expected to act as if this unsubstantiated knowledge does exist, and to ignore the substantiated knowledge they have acquired from professional training and classroom experience.

These were the conditions in New York City public schools in Queens as we ended 2004 and headed into 2005. This narrowing of the curriculum continued into 2006, as reported in the *New York Times* in March of that year (Dillon, 2006). In this chapter, we observe the elementary school curriculum from two perspectives—that of a college professor (Myra) and a classroom teacher (Amie). We begin first with Myra's experience at the college level as an instructor and a supervisor of student teachers and then situate her experiences within a national context. Then, we examine Amie's experiences as a New York City teacher compelled to make difficult decisions about the education of her students. Finally, we conclude by acknowledging that although there is currently a mismatch between the beliefs underlying our elementary education program at Queens College and the beliefs underlying current practices in schools, we can still see avenues for constructive change. We provide suggestions countering the marginalization of content subjects.

THE VANISHING CURRICULUM: THE PERSPECTIVE
OF A COLLEGE PROFESSOR

I (Myra) have been teaching at Queens College for 20 years. This is long enough for me to see my former undergraduate students become professional teachers and colleagues. In fact, many of the classrooms where I place student teachers are taught by former students. Our shared history has provided a firm foundation for continued professional growth.

Testing and lockstep teaching jolted and upset my professional world quite unexpectedly. It began with a phone call 2 years ago. The principal of the school where I have been supervising student teachers for more than a decade called to tell me the following startling news: Original teaching units based on grade-level curriculum topics prepared and taught by students teachers under my direction and the guidance of cooperating teachers could no longer be taught. Why? There was no time, and curriculum-based units no longer fit the goals of the school. Instead, everyone would be following the Balanced Literacy Curriculum and the materials distributed by the Teachers College Reading and Writing Project.

As a result, instead of guiding my students to teach social studies units, science units, or author studies, I observed students giving scripted lessons with scripted vocabulary and scripted procedures. Children were no longer called by their names; now they were addressed collectively as "good readers" or "good writers." Everyone wrote about small moments and made text-to-text connections. There were no whole-class conversations allowed; that is, students could "turn-and-talk" to each other, but not to the teacher. All lessons ended in an alarmingly monotonous sameness: "Good writers, today and every day when you are writing, remember to … ." do whatever the "teaching point" of the lesson happened to be. I had gone from a field-based program that was content-rich, creative, student-centered, and responsive into a world of sameness. A scary feature of this world is that teaching process trumped teaching content. "We do not teach books," I was told, "we teach process." In this new era, I am appalled to see that compelling content is vanishing.

At Queens College, we are, I have been told, the largest suppliers of teachers to the NYC public schools. Yet, we began the year ignorant and uninformed of these impending changes. Would I have assigned my students an impossible assignment if I had known what was to occur? In my case, I simply retracted the assignment, e-mailed the Chancellor of the New York City public schools, and asked for a copy of the curriculum. My e-mail was ignored. The director of student teaching at Queens College e-mailed the chancellor. Her e-mail was answered, but we did not receive the curriculum. The dean of the College of Education e-mailed the chancellor. You guessed it. We got no copy. Is there a message here? As an aside, the curriculum was provided to me by a school administrator and several teachers, but only on the condition that they remain anonymous. Why, I wonder, were we deliberately kept uninformed about curricular change?

A second event in the spring of 2003 provided me with another wake-up call. A graduate student in my Nonfiction Literature for Children class wrote me this alarming note at the beginning of an assignment that required her to use nonfiction literature and selected reading strategies with children:

> Before beginning, I seriously thought about how I wanted to approach this project. Being a fourth grade teacher I have a lot of pressure from my administration to focus on test prep all day long. I was torn between working with a group during my lunch period or working with the children in my literacy block.

Suddenly, my assignments, which were designed to raise the quality of teaching in school, were now out of bounds. These lessons were to be sneaked in during lunch or when no one was looking. My students and I became outlaws and conspirators.

I am very well aware that my anecdotes simply reflect my limited experience, so I began to look further. Specifically, I looked at what people were saying beyond my world. I looked at the impact of mandated curriculum on a content-rich subject like social studies in and beyond New York City.

THE VANISHING CURRICULUM: THE CASE OF THE SOCIAL STUDIES

The unavoidable conclusion is that we are not alone. Reports from different parts of the country mirror our experience in New York City. These reports point to an elementary school curriculum that is so out of balance that it has squeezed out social studies, the subject explicitly designed to teach the knowledge and skills students need to become effective citizens and make informed decisions about issues that affect their lives.

Academic Atrophy: The Waning of the Liberal Arts

A frequently cited report, *Academic Atrophy: The Condition of the Liberal Arts in America's Public Schools* (von Zastrow & Janc, 2004), published by the Council for Basic Education and funded by the Carnegie Corporation of New York, surveyed 956 elementary and secondary school principals in Illinois, Maryland, New York, and New Mexico in 2003. When asked about social studies, 29% of elementary school principals reported a decrease in time spent on that subject. Even worse, in high-minority schools, 47% of principals reported decreases in the time spent on social studies due to the impact the No Child Left Behind Act (see also District Administration, 2004; Manzo, 2004; Perkins-Gough, 2004; Toppo, 2004; *USA Today*, 2004).

This is serious. One commentator on this report described the results in terms of winners and losers. The winners were math, reading, and writing. The losers were all the other liberal arts subjects (Perkins-Gough, 2004). An article in *Education Week* quoted one of the authors of *Academic Atrophy*, Claus von Zastrow, as describing the report as indicating "evidence of curricular erosion" (von Zastrow, quoted in Manzo, 2004). A *USA Today* article reminded readers that as a result of No Child Left Behind legislation, elementary school students are getting less social studies, art, geography, history, and foreign languages (Toppo, 2004). In chapter 7 of this volume, Marcia Baghban and Harriet Li concur, noting that this pared-down curriculum imposes a kind of intellectual starvation on students.

Academic Atrophy: Teachers' Experience

Individual teachers and researchers are finding the same thing. In a report prepared by the staff of *Social Education* (2003), the journal of the National Council for the Social Studies, a sampling of teachers across the country who teach at different grade levels were asked about the impact of No Child Left Behind on their teaching. Their responses unanimously reaffirm the narrowing of the curriculum and the severe impact on the teaching of social studies.

Barbara Knighton, first-grade teacher from Lansing, Michigan, reported that teachers in her school were spending time on test-taking skills, using specially purchased test-taking materials, as early as grade two. Because of the time allotted to literacy and math, teachers were sacrificing social studies and science. Knighton went on to describe the negligible impact on learning when teachers attempted to teach the sacrificed subjects by integrating them into literacy instruction:

> The problem is that social studies, science, health and social skills are often put off to the side and forgotten. I have found that many teachers in the early grades (K-2) use literacy strategies as a way to try to meet the social studies goals. This often results, in my opinion, in surface learning and studying no topic in depth (*Social Education Staff*, 2003, p. 291).

The idea that social studies can somehow be taught through reading is a denial of the unique requirements of studying this subject. Reading about the past, as one researcher noted, has unique features that require content-specific forms of literacy (VanSledright, 2004). A generic approach to teaching reading contributes to what another researcher noted was students' mistaken idea that reading in all subjects was exactly the same (Bain, 2000).

A second crucial point that Knighton makes is that teaching social studies now and then—here a bit and there a bit—in no way enables teachers to do the in-depth teaching needed to build conceptual understanding. That is why when one administrator seriously suggested to me (Myra) that social studies could be accomplished during the time specifically set aside for reading aloud to children, I found that suggestion ridiculous. A subject that values the interpretation of information and is designed to promote informed decision making for the common good cannot be taught through "read alouds."

Carol Warren, third-grade teacher in Sacaton, Arizona, similarly wrote about the "surface learning" described by Barbara Knighton. She wrote about teaching less social studies:

> In these circumstances, teachers have to develop special strategies for social studies instruction. My strategies include integration with other subjects; preparing shorter lessons, for use in the *odd time slots* that often appear in elementary class schedules; and, the one I feel most comfortable with, using lessons that teach social studies while *practicing skills tested by No Child Left Behind.* (emphasis added; *Social Education Staff*, 2003, p. 292).

Although social studies is an integrative subject, it cannot be taught in "odd time slots" while practicing for high-stakes tests. Warren concluded by emphasizing the surface learning that has replaced the teaching she was accustomed to doing:

> As social studies instruction time has been cut, I have had to rely more on text material and do fewer extension activities … . Rather than cut whole subjects out, I teach less about each subject (*Social Education Staff*, p. 292).

This is a startling move backward, given what we know about the need for in-depth learning as a means of promoting understanding. If we are ever to reduce or eliminate the "paste-up" accounts of history—student writing that consists of random bits and pieces of facts lacking coherence, motivation, and organization (Beck & McKeown, 1994)—we need to do more, not less, to build understanding about our social world.

Rachel Sharpe, middle school social studies teacher in Gainesville, Florida, made this startling report: "At this time, social studies is not on the test, so social studies is seemingly not considered part of the core curriculum" (*Social Education Staff*, p. 292).

We all know what happens when a subject is considered unimportant. It gets pushed out. As these testimonials of teachers show, the marginalization of social studies is not a New York phenomenon. Phillip J. VanFossen (2003) of Purdue University found that "social studies instruction is not a high priority in many elementary classrooms across Indiana." In fact, he notes,

> Social studies is often referred to by elementary practitioners as the "bump" subject. This is because social studies is often bumped to the end of the day, bumped to the end of the week or, as is often the case, bumped right out of the curriculum (VanFossen, 2003, p. 1).

I am not unaware of the latest attempts by the Teachers College Reading and Writing Project to restore social studies. They have made an opening stab at examining the vast New York State curriculum and envisioning how it might be approached. Yet, they have not moved beyond deciding what is (to use the corporate phrase) nonnegotiable and what is negotiable to nail down actual books, materials, and discipline-specific strategies, and to give us the usual peek at exemplary lessons. They also flip-flop on whether teachers should convert the reading and writing workshop to a social studies endeavor or maintain a parallel reading and writing workshop dealing with a broad range of nonfiction literature at the same time; it is not recommended at the third-grade level but is by the end of the fourth grade. It seems hardly manageable to do both. In all honesty, Teachers College staff should be given some credit for stating the following: "Of course there is no one way (and even, perhaps, no way!) to translate New York State's standards into a manageable curriculum" (Teachers College Reading and Writing Project, 2004–2005). We owe them a debt of gratitude for acknowledging what all teachers already know: The curriculum—as interesting as it is—is too darn big. We need the freedom to pick and choose and some guidance for doing so.

The dilemma teachers face is that covering national, state, and local curriculum standards requires an allocation of time that teachers simply do not have. Referring to the standards documents in social studies (history, government, economics, and geography), researchers Boehm and Rutherford reported that "each discipline offered up what should be learned, not what was realistic given the length of the school day and year, the availability of qualified teachers, and already existing graduation requirements" (2004, p. 229).

Clearly, what we are experiencing in New York City is part of a larger national problem. Sometimes, the pressures defeat teachers and they give up. Katherine Bomer (2005) quit teaching because, as she put it, "a decade of fighting increased district, state, and federal intrusion into my classroom, and decreased trust in my ability and expertise as a teacher, had left me feeling like a used tube of toothpaste, squeezed and rolled up to that last sad, thin smear on the toothbrush" (p. 168). Other teachers continue to try to do their best to fulfill mandates from above while remaining true to their ideals. To get a sense of what "coping" teachers are up against, we now turn to Amie's description of her experience as a sixth-grade teacher responding to the impact of academic atrophy.

NO TIME FOR CURRICULUM: A TEACHER'S PERSPECTIVE

According to the New York City Department of Education, the mission of the Department of Social Studies is "that students become life-long learners who construct authentic inquiry, read critically, evaluate information and take action" (New York City Department of Education, 2004, p. 1). The plan they propose to accomplish this mission is to teach "in-depth inquiry based units of study." This sounds like a noble and educationally sound idea. Yet, in the New York City Public schools, social studies is a vanishing subject.

When I looked on the Department of Education's Web site for New York City Standards and Assessments in social studies, I found none. In fact, even under the No Child Left Behind Act signed by President Bush in 2002, there is little mention of social studies. At the Student Achievement and Accountability Conference for the No Child Left Behind Act in October of 2002, a timeline was created that says that by the 2005–2006 school year, states must have "academic standards and assessments in reading/language arts and math for each grade in grades 3–8 and high school." Further, [b]y 2005–2006, States must develop achievement levels and their descriptions in science." Finally, "beginning no later than 2007–2008 school year, a State must administer annual assessments in science … " (U.S. Department of Education, 2002, Standards and Assessments section). Taxpayers' dollars will only go to states that accomplish these mandates. There are no requirements for student academic achievement or assessments in social studies for any year in the No Child Left Behind Act. Taxpayers may continue to give money to schools that do not teach or assess social studies.

THE ISSUE OF TIME

Due to these mandates, a huge emphasis has been placed on literacy and math instruction, with science taking on some importance—after all, 2007–2008 is on the horizon. Social studies seems to be a nonissue at this point. New York City has contracted Columbia University's Teachers College to provide our literacy curriculum and has implemented new citywide math programs. This has meant an extended literacy and math block totaling 205 min as well as a mandated 20 min of instruction for at-risk students (those who scored 2 or lower on the citywide tests) out of a 360-min day. The remaining 135 min are taken up with lunch and a teacher preparation period, leaving 45 min for physical education, assembly, computer, library, social studies, and science (see Figure 1). In my school, every teacher in grades 3 to 6 has one preparation period covered by a science cluster. This eases some of the burden of "fitting in" science. However, New York State mandates three periods of science a week!

Obviously, the schedule does not work. Although teachers are required by their principals to complete a schedule showing how all the subjects in the curriculum are covered each week and to post it on their classroom doors, this is an impossible task. As you can see from the actual teaching schedules reproduced in Figure 2, teachers scramble to find time to include core curriculum into the day. Social studies is often slotted in for the end of the day and combined with afternoon homeroom, which includes packing up and copying homework.

Official New York City School Hours: 8:20 a.m.–2:40 p.m. = 390 minutes

390 = total minutes in a New York City school day
–20 = morning and afternoon homeroom (unpack/pack, bus, announcements,
        H.W., etc.)
370
–50 = lunch period
320
–45 = preparation period
275
–20 = mandated AIS instruction
255
–130 = mandated literacy instruction
125
–75 = mandated math instruction
  55 = **time left for social studies, science, gym, assembly, computer, library,
        art, etc.**

Figure 1   Allocation of time in typical NYC classroom day.

In other classrooms, there simply is no social studies. One teacher managed to leave one and a half periods a week for social studies. However, she was not complying with the requisite 130 min of literacy on those days.

SUGGESTIONS FROM TEACHERS COLLEGE

Because the fifth grade takes a social studies test in November, they were asked to stress social studies for the first months of school. Teachers College gave out a proposed fifth-grade social studies unit. It was a 4-week unit that was supposed to "teach" students geography, economics, government, and test-practice skills. This was to be done with documents following the literacy workshop model. Week 1 covers geography skills. Students are to learn about climate, landforms, products, and natural resources from studying maps. Week 2 encompasses economics, in which students are to learn about determining supply versus demand, wants versus needs, the connection between basic needs, natural resources, human resources, and the idea of dealing with scarcity. Week 3 is dedicated to government. On Monday students look at constitutions, rules, and laws that are made in democratic societies to maintain order, provide security, and protect individual rights. Tuesday is set aside for exploring how the rights of citizens in the United States are similar to and different from rights of citizens in other nations in the Western Hemisphere. Wednesday has students examining documents such as the Declaration of Independence, the Constitution, and the Bill of Rights. On

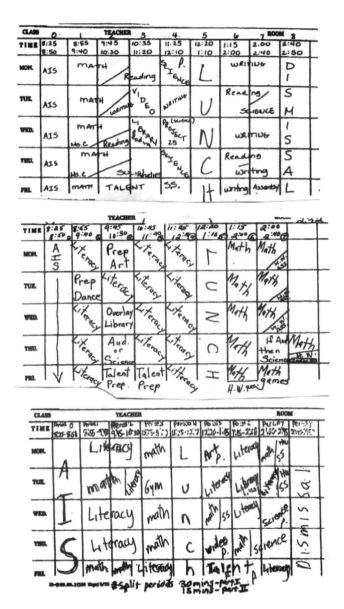

Figure 2   One school's attempt to "fit it all in"..

Thursday the structure of different governments in different countries are studied. Friday is the day set aside for review. Teachers are asked to go over test prep strategies with students during the last week of the unit. I had serious doubts as to the effectiveness of this program and could not see how students would be ready for a test that involved both historical knowledge as well as critical thinking ability after glossing over so many topics in such a short time period. I have since found out that the teachers in my region were asked to "lower their standards" when grading the tests so that more students would do well.

Teachers College has also addressed the problem of missing curriculum by suggesting teachers present one nonfiction unit in reading that centers on content-area ideas. This unit is to take approximately 4 weeks and emphasize examining the structure of nonfiction research books and how to read to gain facts about a topic. It is not an in-depth inquiry-based unit. More importantly, it is not social studies.

Reading is essential to social studies because researchers and historians must read to find answers to questions and to learn about the past. However, other skills are crucial as well, skills such as reasoning, questioning, reflecting, and debating. Social scientists and historians must be able to shift perspectives, combine pieces of information, make judgments, collect evidence, and form opinions. Social studies is also important to the continuation of a democratic society. Children need to be shown democracy in action and then be given chances to practice cooperative learning and decision making. None of this is addressed in the new curriculum.

SPEAKING OUT: SUGGESTIONS FOR CONSTRUCTIVE CHANGE

What can we do to restore the vanishing curriculum? What can we do to bring vibrant content into the classroom while still being true to mandated curricular changes? We begin with Amie's suggestions.

A TEACHER'S PERSPECTIVE

As a teacher who strongly believes in the importance of social studies, it has been a difficult 2 years. I have managed to allot some time to social studies, but certainly not the amount I feel the subject deserves. One of my solutions has been to do to the subjects of computer and library what has been done to social studies. I have collaborated with the computer teacher as well as the librarian in my school to create units that are partially done in their classrooms. Of course, this means they do not teach as much of their own curriculum.

We were able to incorporate parts of all our subjects. In computer class, the students learned how to do more efficient research on the Internet, create graphic organizers to manage their research notes and questions, and practice their keyboarding skills. In library, students were able to practice researching with multiple nonfiction sources. They also explored the idea of what to do when sources do not have the same information. We spent time considering authors' perspectives and changing theories in the social sciences. In my class, some time was spent thinking about and discussing actual content—in this case, the effects of geography on prehistoric humans. The rest of the time students worked on cooperative projects that incorporated all the research they did in the other classes.

It was not ideal, but when I asked my students to write an essay on what they had learned, I saw how worthwhile it was. Students wrote that they realized how important geography was to human evolution and how humans have changed to adapt to their environment. They stated that they now saw the influence of where people live on not only how they live, but what they look like. Many of them said they learned how to think about connections between ideas, how to use research materials, what to do if two texts have conflicting information, how to decide what was really important (how to look at big concepts rather than every detail or unrelated fact), how to ask questions to learn more about a subject, and how to organize and focus their thoughts. Even more significant was their enthusiasm about this project. They were very excited to learn new ideas. The content was interesting to them.

Reading and math are critical subjects. They are the cornerstone to a solid, basic education. However, they should not be the total educational package. I like the idea of teaching strategies. I agree with the mini-lesson structure. I want children to read and write independently every day. But surely, some of this independent time could include content-based thematic units. Surely, some of the guided-reading groups could focus on reading and interpreting social-studies-based work. Surely, part of the focus of the book clubs created by Teachers College could be on social studies content. One book club, in fact, is called "Social Issues." However, the proposed reading materials are fictional. Why not make them nonfiction and examine real social issues throughout history? Children are capable of looking beyond their own life experiences at times. And, if they are not—we better help them become able to. If students are to "become lifelong learners who construct authentic inquiry, read critically, evaluate information and take action," as advocated on the NYC Board of Education Web site, this is a crucial skill to have.

A COLLEGE PROFESSOR'S PERSPECTIVE

There is a serious mismatch between the principles that guide the elementary education program at Queens College and the principles at work in the schools in which our students teach. This mismatch raises serious questions about teaching and learning:

- Our faculty believes that students must learn to be reflective decision makers. They need to select from the array of instructional approaches those that will enhance the learning of the children they teach. How, then, can students become reflective decision makers if they are not allowed to make decisions?
- Our faculty believes that subjects such as social studies, science, physical education, and art are not frills. They are essential means of making sense of the world and caring for ourselves and others. How can our students apply what we teach them if there is no time for these subjects?
- Our faculty believes in preparing students to participate in a democratic society and to understand the ideals of social justice. A few teachers tell me that they do this, but that they "teach under the radar." That is, they do what they think is right for their students even though it is not allowed. "I close my door," they tell me. How can we condone "teaching under the radar," when we know better?

My experiences as a college professor and a student teaching supervisor have introduced me to some harsh realities. I believe in public education, and I will continue to work within the system. Here is what I suggest we should all be doing to respond to the vanishing curriculum.

- Speaking out: Presenting at conferences is one way, but there are others. All educators can share their observations and voice their opinions in conversations with parents, colleagues, and administrators.
- Staying informed: Reading about both educational theory and successful practice is essential. We need to know what constitutes effective classroom practice and why. We need to share our thinking with other educators.
- Critically observing educational practice: We need to carefully observe what is happening in classrooms and question how it can be improved. We need to ask ourselves: What is working? What is not?

I am convinced that teacher decision making based on watching, reflecting, and responding to the needs of actual children, combined with a rich liberal arts curriculum, are essential elements of good teaching and learning. So, too, are in-depth learning of subjects like social studies combined with frequent opportunity to engage in hands-on activity. Good teaching and learning, in essence, require that we halt the academic atrophy. What is at stake is the rigor of the educational experience and the professionalism of those entrusted to deliver it.

REFERENCES

Bain, R.B. (2000). Into the breach: Using research and theory to shape history instruction. In P.N. Stearns, P. Seixas, & S. Wineburg (Eds.). *Knowing, teaching, and learning history: National and international perspectives* (pp. 331–352). New York: New York University Press.

Beck, I.L., & McKeown, M.G. (1994). Outcomes of history instruction: Paste-up accounts. In M. Carretero & J.F. Voss (Eds.). *Cognitive and instructional processes in history and the social sciences* (pp. 237–256). Hillsdale, NJ: Erlbaum.

Boehm, R.G., & Rutherford, D.J. (2004). Implementation of national geography standards in the social studies: A ten-year retrospective. *The Social Studies, 95,* 228–230.

Bomer, K. (2005). Missing the children: When politics and programs impede our teaching. *Language Arts, 82,* 168–176.

Dillon, S. (2006, March 26). Schools cut back subjects to push reading and math. *New York Times,* pp. 1, 26.

District Administration. (2004). Sacrificing the arts and history. *District Administration, 40,* 23.

Manzo, K.K. (2004). Principals' poll shows erosion of liberal arts curriculum. *Education Week, 23,* 12.

New York City Department of Education. (2003). *Department of Social Studies.* Retrieved December 27, 2004, from http://www.nycenet.edu/teachlearn socialstudies/index. html.

Perkins-Gough, D. (2004). The eroding curriculum. *Educational Leadership, 62,* 84–85.

Social Education Staff. (2003). No Child Left Behind: The impact on social studies classrooms. *Social Education, 67,* 291–295.

Teachers College Reading and Writing Project (2004–2005). Draft of 3rd, 4th and 5th grade social studies curriculum 2004–2005. Teachers College Reading and Writing Project.

Toppo, G. (2004, March 8). Reform causes subject shift. *USA Today.* [http://www.usatoday. com/news/education/2004-03-08-social-studies-left-behind_x.htm].

U.S. Department of Education. (2002). *Standards and assessments.* Retrieved December 27, 2004, from http://www.ed.gov.

USA Today. (2004, March 9). Reform causes subject shift. *USA Today.* Life, p. 8.

VanFossen, P.J. (2003). *"Reading and math take so much of the time...": An overview of social studies instruction in elementary classrooms in Indiana.* Paper presented at the College and University Faculty Assembly of the National Council for Social Studies, Chicago, IL.

VanSledright, B. (2004). What does it mean to read history? *Reading Research Quarterly, 39,* 342–346.

von Zastrow, C., & Janc, H. (2004). *Academic atrophy: The condition of liberal arts in America's public schools.* Washington, DC: The Council for Basic Education.

9

The Campaign for
Fiscal Equity

Susan A. Kirch and Molly A. Hunter

INTRODUCTION

Although the quality of the opportunity provided varies dramatically, young people throughout the United States are provided with free, public education. This national commitment represents the historical consensus that every child has the right to an equal educational opportunity. Although this goal has never been fully realized, all states have education clauses in their constitutions that require them to establish and support a system of free public schools.

The states face the challenge of developing methods of funding public schools that ensure quality education to all students. Few states have been successful in devising and sustaining such methods. Success stories come from Kentucky and Vermont and are developing in New Jersey and Massachusetts, among others. In fact, nationwide, school-funding lawsuits have been filed in 45 of 50 states, usually on behalf of low-income and minority students. Two thirds of courts have ruled that state mechanisms for school funding are unconstitutional. The funding practices that are being challenged in these cases contradict America's egalitarian tradition and limit many young people's access to opportunity, justice, and democracy—this country's core democratic values (Sizer, 1997).

Many state education finance systems rely heavily on local property tax revenue. As a result, there are large differences in what is spent on children's education within and among states (Proefriedt, 2002). In 2003, the New York Court of Appeals, New York's highest court, found that New York State has consistently violated the "education article" of the state constitution by failing to provide the opportunity for a sound basic education to New York City public school students (Campaign for Fiscal Equity Inc. [CFE] v. State of New York [State], 2003 at 925–931). Now, over 2 years later, the state continues to delay; it has now appealed a follow-up compliance ruling that the trial court issued in March 2005 (Campaign for Fiscal Equity v. State, 2005). New York leaders are wasting time. In the equivalent span of time after a high court ruling, Kentucky, as one example, found itself well on its way to ensuring a brighter future for its children. In this chapter, we review the history of school-funding litigation in New York State, report recommendations from a New York costing-out study, and introduce the goals and activities of the National Access Network (Access), a CFE initiative established to promote the national quality education movement.

HISTORICAL OVERVIEW OF SCHOOL-FUNDING LITIGATION IN NEW YORK

New York State's constitution establishes a "positive right" to education:

> The legislature shall provide for the maintenance and support of a system of free common schools, wherein all the children of this state may be educated (Article XI, Section 1, the "education article").

In 1978, a group of property-poor Long Island school districts, joined by the "Big Five" New York school districts (Buffalo, New York City, Rochester, Syracuse, and Yonkers), filed a lawsuit challenging the state's education finance system (Levittown v. Nyquist, 1982). However, the Court of Appeals rejected plaintiffs' attempts to gain equal per-pupil funding. The court concluded that the New York State constitution does not require equal, or equitable, funding for education. Nonetheless, the court held, in this 1982 ruling, that the state constitution does entitle students to the opportunity to obtain "a sound basic education," thus establishing students' right to an "adequate" education (Levittown v. Nyquist, 1982). Plaintiffs in the Levittown case had not alleged that students were being denied the right to an adequate education, but the court's decision left the courthouse door open for a lawsuit claiming students were being denied this right. Levittown v. Nyquist (1982) was one of the cases in several states in the 1980s that contributed to an important shift in litigation strategy. Soon plaintiffs across the country began to emphasize education adequacy based on education clauses in state constitutions rather than equity based on constitutional equal protection clauses (Clune, 1994).

Another key to the shift in legal strategy was the development of student learning standards in almost all states. Standards-based reform provided "judicially manageable standards" for the courts hearing school-funding lawsuits. Consistent with their understanding of contemporary needs as articulated by the state learning standards, the state court adequacy rulings have defined "adequacy" as requiring education at "more than a minimum level."[1]

In 1993, a coalition of parent organizations, community school boards, concerned citizens, and advocacy groups, seeing the open door and seeking better opportunity for schoolchildren hurt by state-funding cuts, founded the not-for-profit corporation Campaign for Fiscal Equity, Inc. specifically to bring an education adequacy case on behalf of the 1.1 million students in New York City's public schools. The right to a sound basic education was at the heart of Campaign for Fiscal Equity v. State of New York. In a landmark decision, the Court of Appeals upheld CFE's right to pursue a constitutional challenge to the state's education finance system (Campaign for Fiscal Equity v. State, 1995 at 307). Based on its Levittown precedent, the court reiterated its interpretation of the education article of the state constitution, adopted in 1894. It said that the education article required the provision of "a sound basic education" and indicated that if CFE were able to prove that a substantial number of New York City students are being denied the opportunity to obtain a sound basic education, the state would have to act to remedy the situation (Campaign for Fiscal Equity v. State, 1995 at 316).

The court also presented a "template" definition of a sound basic education: Students must have the opportunity to acquire the "basic literacy, calculating and verbal skills necessary to enable them to function as civic participants capable of voting and serving as jurors" (Campaign for Fiscal Equity v. State, 1995 at 316). The court further declared that the state must ensure that certain essential resources are provided to public school students to support a sound basic education:

> Children are entitled to minimally adequate physical facilities and classrooms that provide enough light, space, heat, and air to permit children to learn. Children should have access to minimally adequate instrumentalities of learning such as desks, chairs, pencils, and reasonably current textbooks. Children are also entitled to minimally adequate teaching of reasonably up-to-date basic curricula such as reading, writing, mathematics, science, and social studies, by sufficient personnel adequately trained to teach those subject areas (Campaign for Fiscal Equity v. State, 1995 at 317).

Importantly, the court expected both the plaintiffs and the defendants to propose a definition for a sound basic education, including the essential resources to achieve it. Both parties, of course, were expected to present evidence to support their views during the trial.

The trial of Campaign for Fiscal Equity v. State of New York began on October 12, 1999, in the New York State Supreme Court and concluded on July 27, 2000. The court undertook a three-part inquiry to evaluate plaintiffs' claim that the State of New York was in violation of the education article in the state constitution. The issues before the court were, first, to define the opportunity to obtain a sound basic education based on presentations by both defendants and plaintiffs. Second, the court was to determine whether New York City schoolchildren were provided with that opportunity in the City's public schools, based on evidence presented at trial. And, third, if it was established that New York City schoolchildren did not have the opportunity to obtain a sound basic education, the court was to determine whether there was a "causal link" between that failure and the State's system for funding public schools (Campaign for Fiscal Equity v. State, 2001 at 482). Each of these steps is discussed in the following sections.

CFE V. STATE OF NEW YORK TRIAL AND TRIAL COURT RULING

What is "a Sound Basic Education"?

The definition of a "sound basic education" to be determined in Campaign for Fiscal Equity v. State (2001) would be pivotal to the case because it would articulate the constitutional obligation that the state has to all of its children. Rather than limit this definition to one only the organization deemed satisfactory, CFE felt it important to include the larger community in the formulation of the definition it would bring to the court. To do so, CFE researched similar efforts in other states and reviewed pertinent findings from other disciplines (Rebell, Hughes, & Grumet, 1995).

The community engagement with dialogic model that CFE developed and used in its public engagement forums was based on a combination of empirical sociological research findings and conflict resolution procedures proposed by Rebell and Hughes (1996). Using previously defined frameworks, Rebell and Hughes argued that if citizens were asked to engage in thinking about the purpose of education with their peers, then their commitment to the search for a common purpose would deepen (Bellah, Madsen, Tipton, Sullivan, & Swidler, 1991). Furthermore, consistent with findings of other litigators, they proposed that well-organized community dialogues would result in people finding that they agree on many more aspects of issues in education than they initially realized and that they would discover that competing doctrines often contain the same basic values (Rebell and Hughes, 1996).

Making decisions about the educational system in communities that include many stakeholders has never been easy. How do you persuade participants to put aside their self-interest and search for a common good? Rebell and Hughes (1996) suggested that implementing and sustaining a dialogue could be successful through the application of techniques used in alternative dispute resolution episodes. For example, to ensure equitable discussions, they proposed a simple set of rules. A neutral third-party convener should arrange meetings, moderate the discussions, assist in the exchange of information, and work to ensure an equitable process overall. Participants in the dialogue should be diverse and represent the views of individuals and groups in the community.

An integrative consensus process, however, is the key to reaching tentative agreement on a solution or set of solutions. Ratification, implementation, and evaluation or reconsideration of draft solutions are later stages in the problem-solving process and should be based on the initial agreement at the public forum. This dialogic approach to educational reform has proved to be a very successful model for generating solutions when considering local and regional educational policy issues (Berman & Dunphy, 1998; Cipollone, 1998; Hunter, 1998; Rebell & Metzler, 2000). Furthermore, the dialogic approach is intended to (a) establish public ownership of reform efforts, (b) build political capital to influence policy-makers and elected officials, and (c) enable coalition building.

CFE's public engagement efforts in New York State and similar approaches in other states have promoted important dialogues on education and school-funding reform.[2] After the 1995 Campaign for Fiscal Equity v. State decision by the Court of Appeals, CFE worked with state and local organizations to conduct public engagement campaigns. CFE partnered with the League of Women Voters, New York State School Boards Association, and many other organizations to include the public in developing the definition of a sound basic education. CFE structured these meetings as public engagement events, using the community dialogic model proposed by Rebell and Hughes (1996).

During a typical forum, participants were asked to brainstorm what they thought constituted a sound basic education. These ideas were recorded on chart paper and posted. After a period of discussion about the suggestions, the 1995 Appeals Court definition was shared, and participants were asked if, and how, they would like to see the court's version refined. This process was repeated in New York City and in numerous meetings across New York State. The resulting definition from the conversations at these public engagement forums, as it was proposed to the trial court, is shown in Table 1.

The first elaboration adopted by the litigation team in response to the public engagement discussions was to enumerate the knowledge and skills a New York State citizen capable of voting and serving on a jury must have, such as knowledge of the state and federal governmental system and its civic values, as well as the ability to evaluate courtroom evidence or information in a rational manner.

Interestingly, during the trial an expert witness for the defendants testified that "most media coverage of elections is pitched at an eighth- to ninth-grade level of reading comprehension and that therefore any student who passes the Regents Competency Tests (RCTs) is a productive citizen capable of voting or sitting on a jury" (Campaign for Fiscal Equity v. State, 2001 at 485). Although expert witnesses for both sides agreed that the RCTs measure eighth-grade reading and sixth-grade arithmetic skills, only the defendants argued that the RCTs serve as a reliable measure of the skills necessary for civic participation as a voter

Table 1   Comparison of "Sound Basic Education" Definitions from NYS Court of Appeals

Court of Appeals' 1995 "Template" Definition of a Sound Basic Education	Campaign for Fiscal Equity's Definition of a Sound Basic Education as Proposed to the Trial Court
1. A sound basic education should consist of the basic literacy, calculating, and verbal skills necessary to enable children to eventually function productively as civic participants capable of voting and serving on a jury 2. The state must also assure that the following essentials are provided: a. Minimally adequate physical facilities and classrooms b. Minimally adequate instrumentalities of learning, including supplies such as desks, chairs, and pencils, and reasonably current textbooks c. Minimally adequate teaching of reasonably up-to-date basic curricula such as reading, writing, mathematics, science, and social studies d. Minimally adequate teaching by sufficient personnel adequately trained to teach those subject areas	A sound basic education should consist of the skills students need to sustain competitive employment and function productively as civic participants capable of voting and serving on a jury. Development of those skills requires the provision of certain educational essentials, including: a. Teachers, principals, and other personnel who have appropriate skills, training, and professional supports b. Small classes c. Sufficient and up-to-date books, libraries, technology, and laboratories d. Appropriate support services for all students and supplemental aids, services, and suitable instructional programs for students with extraordinary needs e. Adequate and accessible facilities f. A safe, orderly environment g. Parent and community involvement

Note: From (a) Campaign for Fiscal Equity, Inc. vs. State of New York, (1995). 86 N.Y. 2d at 307 Court of Appeals [1995] and (b) Campaign for Fiscal Equity, Inc. vs. State of New York, (2001). 187 Misc. 2d 1. (S. Ct, N.Y. Co, 2001).

and juror (Campaign for Fiscal Equity v. State, 2001 at 485). The judge was not persuaded by the defendants' argument.

Participants in the public engagement forums also recognized that children should additionally be provided the skills necessary for competitive employment. CFE included this in the definition it presented to the court (see the CFE definition on Table 1), and expert witness testimony illustrated how preparing students for employment has traditionally been one of the rationales for public education. The defendants argued that the Court of Appeals' 1995 CFE v. State decision contains no explicit reference to public schools' duty to give students the foundational skills they need to obtain productive employment or pursue higher education. But the trial court disagreed and asserted that this duty is inherent in the 1995 decision that students must be prepared to become productive citizens. Furthermore, the court agreed with the plaintiffs, and concluded that any other interpretation of the decision would ignore one of the primary purposes of public education (Campaign for Fiscal Equity v. State, 2001 at 485).

Ultimately, the trial court adopted the CFE definition developed through public engagement activities, with little change, and found that a sound basic education "consists of the foundational skills that students need to become productive citizens capable of civic engagement and sustaining competitive employment" (Campaign for Fiscal Equity v. State, 2001 at 487).

Are New York City Schoolchildren Provided With the Opportunity to Obtain a Sound Basic Education in the City's Public Schools?

Do the educational "inputs" provide a sufficient opportunity? To ensure that students acquire the basic skills and knowledge bases outlined in the definition of a sound basic education, adequate facilities, supplies, equipment, and personnel should be provided to accomplish the task. In Campaign for Fiscal Equity v. State (2001) the court heard testimony, reviewed here, regarding the following "inputs": teacher quality, school facilities and classrooms, class size, and "instrumentalities of learning," such as desks, chairs, paper, books, pencils, and computers.

During the trial, several measures of teacher quality were discussed, including the number of uncertified teachers teaching in New York City public schools, teachers' scores on certification exams, teachers' experience on the job, and the quality of teachers' undergraduate education. Expert testimony for the plaintiffs showed that throughout the 1990s, approximately 10 to 14% of New York City's public school teachers lacked certification in any given school year. For example, in 1999, uncertified teachers taught 59,500 New York City students high school biology, 19,000 students high school chemistry, and 54,375 students high school mathematics. The plaintiffs also showed that these uncertified teachers tended to be concentrated in New York City's lowest performing schools (Campaign for Fiscal Equity v. State, 2001 at 493–494).

Expert witness testimony for the plaintiffs presented data that indicated New York City public school teachers had a much higher initial-failure rate on the state's certification examinations than did public school teachers in the rest of the state, and the court found that passage rates on certification examinations are predictive of teacher performance (Campaign for Fiscal Equity v. State, 2001 at 494).

The trial court also found that teaching experience of 2 years or less is correlated with poor teacher quality. New York City public school teachers tend to have fewer years' experience than teachers in the remainder of the state. Furthermore, just as for uncertified teachers, a disproportionate number of these inexperienced teachers are assigned to the lowest performing schools (Campaign for Fiscal Equity v. State, 2001 at 495).

Plaintiffs presented data indicating that New York City tends to hire its teachers from the less qualified graduates of any given undergraduate institution. The plaintiffs argued that New York City's lack of a sufficient number of qualified teachers is a function of its lack of competitiveness in the labor market. Witnesses showed that New York City schoolteachers worked under more difficult conditions than their suburban colleagues and their annual salaries were, on average, $17,000 less than those in the surrounding suburbs. It was further argued that crumbling school infrastructure, the perception of teachers that New York City public schools are unsafe, and the large class sizes found in most city schools also hinder New York City's ability to attract the most qualified teachers (Campaign for Fiscal Equity v. State, 2001 at 495–496, 498).

At the time of trial, the conditions of New York City public school facilities revealed a system in high need of remediation. Hundreds of New York City's approximately 1,100 public school buildings had serious structural deficiencies. Two hundred and thirty-one school buildings required complete exterior overhauls, 114 buildings had roofs that needed to be replaced, and many more had severe problems with their windows and external masonry. Inadequate wiring made it impossible for many schools to offer computer education, and only one fifth of classrooms had the climate control systems necessary to keep computers working properly during warmer months, if they worked at all. As cited at trial, schools were also plagued by malfunctioning lights and toilets, as well as peeling plaster and paint. The evidence presented in Campaign for Fiscal Equity v. State (2001) clearly illustrated that the physical condition of many New York City schools was extremely poor, and the Court found that those facilities deficits had a negative effect on the academic performance of the city's public school students (Campaign for Fiscal Equity v. State, 2001 at 501–508).

The plaintiffs argued that the overcrowding of New York City School facilities contributed to the deterioration and to the difficulty of conducting proper repairs. In addition to impacting the physical condition of the building, overcrowding had many more serious, negative consequences for students. Specialized spaces (e.g., gymnasiums, science laboratories, libraries, and art rooms) were often used as full-time classroom space. As a result the programs that should have used these rooms had been discontinued. In overcrowded schools where specialized spaces, temporary structures, and marginal spaces such as undersized offices, hallways, and storages spaces were already being used for general instruction, it was nearly impossible to reduce the number of students per class.

At the time of trial, New York City class sizes were consistently larger than the state averages at every level, including high school, for every year data are available in the previous 20 years, and this situation invariably hindered students' academic success. The court agreed with expert testimony for the plaintiffs that smaller class sizes have a positive impact on student outcomes and large class sizes have a negative effect on student performance. The defendants argued that class size in New York City was not due to insufficient classroom space, but to an inefficient deployment of teachers by the city's Board of Education. They argued that the city employs 1 teacher for every 14 students and that these teachers only spend approximately 3 hr, 45 min of their workday on classroom instruction. The court found that the student-to-teacher ratios reported by the defendants were misleading and agreed that the Board of Education might be able to improve some of its efficiency, but found teacher-to-student ratios to be only one element determining what is adequate, because without enough classroom space class size cannot actually be reduced (Campaign for Fiscal Equity v. State, 2001 at 508–513).

At the time of trial, New York City public school students were not only being denied the opportunity for a sound basic education because of inexperienced or uncertified teachers, large class sizes, and inadequate school facilities, but also from a lack of the "instrumentalities of learning." These included desks, chairs, pencils, paper, computers, books, and laboratories. For every one computer available to City students, two computers were available to students in districts outside New York City. Furthermore, computers in City schools usually had older platforms less capable of handling sophisticated software. City students interested in science were often disappointed with their facilities because, at the time of trial, many New York City public school buildings had obsolete science laboratories or none at all. A minimum of 31 high schools lacked a science laboratory, leaving 16,000 high school students without access to this resource. Schools that had laboratory space usually only had a single laboratory shared for biology, chemistry, and physics instruction. Many City students had no access to school libraries, whereas other students had to use libraries with fewer library books and books of lesser quality than their peers across the state. Finally, although City students had a quantity and quality of textbooks that satisfy the minimal adequacy standards for this resource, this phenomenon was very recent and it was shown by the plaintiffs that the current budget allocation was insufficient to maintain adequacy.

The evidence presented at trial demonstrated that this combination of inexperienced teachers, inadequate school facilities, and missing instrumentalities of learning had hampered the delivery of the "reasonably up-to-date curricula" listed as an essential resource by the Court of Appeals in its 1995 decision (Campaign for Fiscal Equity v. State, 1995 at 317). The court agreed (Campaign for Fiscal Equity v. State, 2001 at 551).

Are Educational "Outcomes" Satisfactory?

To determine whether the New York City schools provided a sound basic education, student performance (a form of educational output) was considered in addition to the educational inputs discussed in the preceding text. The court examined evidence concerning two measures of student performance—graduation and dropout rates, and standardized test scores—and found, by each outcome measure, that the New York City school system failed to provide the opportunity for a sound basic education to its students (Campaign for Fiscal Equity v. State, 2001 at 515–520).

In 1996 (the last class for which data were available at trial), approximately 30% of the students that entered ninth grade did not graduate, 47% of students earned a "local" diploma, 11% a "Regents" diploma, and 10% a general equivalency degree (GED). At the time of the trial, these percentages had not changed significantly. Plaintiffs' expert testified, "the job prospects and lifetime earning of the GED certificates is considerably less than the high school graduate; in fact, it is equal or close to that of high school dropouts" (Campaign for Fiscal Equity v. State, 2001 at 515–516). At the time of trial, a local diploma was one that was awarded to students who passed a series of Regents Competency Tests (RCTs), which represented the statewide requirements for graduation and required reading comprehension at a ninth-grade level and an understanding of sixth-grade level mathematics (i.e., no knowledge of algebra). Because of the low level of achievement measured by the RCTs, the New York State Education Department completely phased out the local diploma in 2004. A Regents diploma was only awarded to those who pass a series of standardized tests, or Regents exams. It was demonstrated at trial that a Regents diploma is the only diploma that demonstrates that students have received the sound basic education outlined in the New York State Learning Standards. At the time of trial, this diploma was typically awarded to the 10 to 12% of ninth graders who graduated from high school. In summary, 90% of students entering ninth grade in New York City ultimately did not receive a sound basic education, and therefore were not prepared to function as civic participants or gain the skills necessary for college or competitive employment (Campaign for Fiscal Equity v. State, 2001 at 516).

The state argued that it cannot be held responsible if students chose to drop out, and that the state is required only to provide the opportunity for a sound basic education. It claimed it was providing the opportunity and that students' failure to take it was a product of "various socio-economic deficits experienced by the large number of at-risk students in New York City public schools" (Campaign for Fiscal Equity v. State, 2001 at 517). The court agreed that the state is only required to provide the opportunity, but concluded that opportunity must be accessible by all students. The court concluded that when 30% of students drop out without even a GED, it is clear that the state is falling short of its obligation (Campaign for Fiscal Equity v. State, 2001 at 516–517).

In addition to graduation and dropout rates, the court also considered city students' performance on state and city standardized tests. Young students (kindergarteners, first graders) entering New York City public schools lacked important skills, such as knowledge of the alphabet, sound and symbol relationships, familiarity with counting and numbers, and vocabulary and concept development as shown by the diagnostic tool, ECLAS (Early Childhood Learning Assessment). Starting in third grade, New York State administers a series of two types of tests as part of its Pupil Evaluation Program: one that measures individual student achievement in reading and mathematics and the other meant to measure the general effectiveness of a school in teaching science and social studies. City students consistently lagged behind on all assessments in all grades tested. There was extensive testimony about the reliability and validity of the assessment results, but in the end the court agreed that the phenomenon (low test scores at all levels throughout the city) was real (Campaign for Fiscal Equity v. State, 2001 at 517–520).

Although the New York Campaign for Fiscal Equity v. State (2001) trial predated passage of NCLB, the federal statute bolsters school-funding cases, and its required testing regimen provides more data on student outcomes for plaintiffs to use in these cases. Cases filed since the law was enacted have generally included NCLB-based claims (Hoff, 2003; Hunter, 2003).

Is There a Causal Link Between the State's Public School Funding System and the Lack of Opportunity for a Sound Basic Education?

In the third part of the court's inquiry into the plaintiff's education article claim, it found that "the state's method of financing education is a substantial cause of the failure to provide the New York City public school students with the opportunity for a sound basic education" (Campaign for Fiscal Equity v. State, 2001 at 535). Justice Leland DeGrasse concluded that over the course of many years, New York State had consistently violated the education article of the state constitution by failing to provide the opportunity for a sound basic education to New York City public school students. He ordered the state to ensure that the following resources be provided to New York City's public school students:

1. Sufficient number of qualified teachers, principals, and other school personnel
2. Appropriate class sizes
3. Adequate and accessible school buildings with sufficient space to ensure appropriate class sizes and implementation of a sound curriculum
4. Sufficient and up-to-date books, supplies, libraries, educational technology, and laboratories
5. Suitable curricula, including an expanded platform of programs to help at-risk students by giving them "more time on task"

6. Adequate resources for students with extraordinary needs
7. A safe, orderly environment (Campaign for Fiscal Equity v. State, 2001 at 550)

Furthermore, Justice DeGrasse agreed with the plaintiffs that the state's public school financing system had "an unjustified disparate impact" (Campaign for Fiscal Equity v. State, 2001 at 448) on minority students and was in violation of the federal regulations implementing Title VI of the Civil Rights Act of 1964. He ordered that reforms to the current system of financing school funding should address the shortcomings of the current system by the following measures:

1. Ensuring that every school district has the resources necessary to provide the opportunity for a sound basic education
2. Taking into account variations in local costs
3. Providing sustained and stable funding to promote long-term planning by schools and school districts
4. Providing as much transparency as possible so that the public may understand how the state distributes school aid
5. Ensuring a system of accountability to measure whether the reforms implemented by the legislature actually provide the opportunity for a sound basic education and remedy the disparate impact of the current finance system (Campaign for Fiscal Equity v. State, 2001 at 550–551)

After a series of appeals, the New York State Court of Appeals affirmed the trial court's order in June 2003 and allowed New York State until July 30, 2004, to remedy the constitutional violation (Campaign for Fiscal Equity v. State, 2003 at 930).[3] During the appeals process, the CFE plaintiffs added NCLB to their court papers because they believed the new federal law (signed in January 2002) added more weight to their pursuit of adequate funding. CFE argued that NCLB requires the state to provide enough resources to help schools meet the federal goals.

The Court of Appeals June 2003 order provided guidance to the state without dictating any specifics of the remedy and set out a three-step plan of action. The court ordered the state to

1. Ascertain the actual cost of providing a sound basic education
2. Ensure that every school has the resources necessary for providing the opportunity for a sound basic education
3. Ensure a system of accountability to measure whether the reforms actually provide the opportunity for a sound basic education (Campaign for Fiscal Equity v. State, 2003 at 930)

FUNDING REFORM

Overview

Ever since states began to appropriate money to local communities to assist with the cost of education more than a century ago, state legislators have purported to provide an adequate amount for operations. In its first incarnation, such state funding took the form of a flat state grant for each schoolchild, theoretically an amount sufficient to provide a satisfactory education, but typically not including funding for school facilities. During the 1920s many states began adopting "foundation" programs because of insufficiencies in state funds and the inequity of providing the same amount of funding for students in both poor and wealthy districts. These programs required local school districts to levy taxes at a rate that was aimed at generating enough revenue to fund a minimum education, with the state supplementing the amount actually raised by poor districts when the designated tax rate did not yield the minimum "foundation level" (Strayer & Haig, 1923; Guthrie, Garms, & Pierce, 1988). No methodology was used to determine what the foundation should be, so legislatures typically established the foundation amount based on the amount of funding they were willing to allocate for educational services. These decisions were often made with little regard for actual needs (Campaign for Fiscal Equity, 2004, p. 7).

Currently, in New York State, over 50 separate, complex formulas and grants-in-aid are listed for distributing state aid for education (Campaign for Fiscal Equity, 2004, p. 4). One consequence of having over 50 separate funding streams available for distribution is that formulas have not been used to allocate school funds neutrally. In fact, evidence presented at the Campaign for Fiscal Equity v. State (2001) trial showed that these formulas are routinely manipulated to conform to annual budget agreements reached by three individuals in a room: the Governor, the Senate Majority Leader, and the Speaker of the State Assembly (Campaign for Fiscal Equity v. State, 2001 at 530). Although there is no legal reason why these leaders cannot make these agreements, their allocation decisions override the formulas themselves and can be challenged, especially when they appear to evidence little regard for actual needs or costs.

Several special New York commissions and task forces in the last 30 years have consistently concluded that the current system

- Involves numerous complex formulas that fail to meet any reasonable test of transparency and that sometimes operate at cross-purposes
- Contains too many categorical grant programs and other expenditure restrictions
- Is unfair to pupils and taxpayers in school districts with lower-than-average revenue-raising capacity or higher-than-average needs

- Includes some formulas that discourage cost efficiencies
- Fails to provide adequate consideration to students with special needs
- Does not recognize regional or local cost differences (Campaign for Fiscal Equity, 2004, pp. 4,5)

Ascertaining the Cost of Providing a Sound Basic Education in New York

The governor responded to the court order by establishing a commission to study education reform. The commission hired Standard and Poor's to perform some cost estimation work. Even before the Court of Appeals ordered the state to determine the cost of providing a sound basic education, however, charitable foundations had foreseen the need for a New York costing-out study and had initiated The New York Adequacy Study. This study was conducted by the American Institutes for Research and Management Analysis and Planning Inc., and financed by Atlantic Philanthropies, the Bill and Melinda Gates Foundation, and The Ford Foundation. The focus of the study was to answer the research question: "What is the cost of providing all New York public school students a full opportunity to meet the Regents Learning Standards?" (Chambers, et al., 2004, p.i). In 2001–2002, New York State spent $31.99 billion (excluding transportation, building aid, and capital construction costs) on education. The task of the New York Adequacy Study was to determine how much an "adequate" education actually costs in relation to this number (Chambers, et al., 2004).

The study determined that the cost of adequacy ranged from $6.21 billion to $8.40 billion in increases to 2001–2002 spending levels. The study outlined four options, depending on how comprehensive the plan was. Option 1 revealed that an additional $6.21 billion would be necessary to achieve adequacy in New York State without taking into account preschool and extended-time programs, resources for ELL, or district-level functions. In option 2 the estimate increased to $6.84 billion and reflected revised enrollments in preschool and extended-time programs. Option three ($7.20 billion) included the resources specified for ELL students and, finally, option 4 revealed that an additional $8.4 billion would be necessary to cover the costs in options 1 to 3, as well as spending on district-level functions. The study found that 517 districts across the state are not spending at "adequate" levels, whereas the remaining 162 districts met or exceeded adequate levels. To bring all districts to adequate spending levels, New York State needed to spend an additional $6.21 billion in 2001–2002, a 19.4% increase over the actual spending levels that year (bringing the total needed to $38.21 billion) (Chambers, et al., 2004).

In response to the findings of the New York Adequacy Study, CFE set up a task force of more than 100 individuals throughout the state who participated in deliberations to help develop proposals for school-funding reform in New York State. Members of the Sound Basic Education (SBE) Task Force included representatives from a variety of organizations, including but not limited to administrators (e.g., New York City Department of Education, New York State Education Department, and New York State Council of School Superintendents), educators (e.g., New York, United Federation of Teachers, National Education Association of New York), economists (e.g., Midstate School Finance Consortium) and citizens (e.g., New York Immigration Coalition, National Center for Schools and Communities, League of Women Voters; Campaign for Fiscal Equity, 2004). CFE's SBE Task Force and the Fiscal Policy Institute developed an Adequate Foundation for All Plan, which would implement the findings of the New York Adequacy Study through four actions: (a) establishing the comprehensive foundation amount, (b) making adjustments for student need and local cost factors, (c) dividing fiscal responsibility between local school districts and the state with mandatory contributions for each, and (d) instituting a 4-year phase-in plan and a 4-year stable funding period (Campaign for Fiscal Equity, 2004, pp. 1–3).

IMPLICATIONS OF CFE AND ITS NATIONAL ACCESS NETWORK

Based on the success of CFE's lawsuit and public engagement efforts and its extensive research, CFE developed a national knowledge base that other advocates turned to and used in support of similar advocacy in their own states. This base subsequently grew into the National Access Network (Access), with a mission to promote access to meaningful educational opportunities for all children, especially low-income and minority students currently being denied such opportunities. Together, the Campaign for Fiscal Equity and Access stand as models for promoting equitable educational opportunities for students through educational-funding reform. In pursuit of its mission, Access seeks to

- Expand and strengthen the national quality education movement, which fights for adequate funding for public education and improved public schools in all communities
- Promote school-funding reform by conducting research, developing effective strategies for litigation and remedies (including cost studies), and providing tools for public engagement
- Assist those seeking education and school-funding reform through an annual national conference, workshops, and other support services
- Provide up-to-date information and analysis of key education issues, including school funding, education policy, and the No Child Left Behind Act of 2001

Ongoing, state-level school-funding lawsuits, advocacy, and public outreach (with the support of extensive policy work) comprise the national quality education movement. Access has taken several steps to provide up-to-date information and analysis of key issues and trends for the network of attorneys and advocates involved in these efforts. After NCLB became law, Access analyzed this statute and provided an overview, comments, and analytical briefs on developments during the implementation of the legislation. Access focused on the weak implementation of the "highly qualified teacher" provisions and the need for true accountability, which must include capacity building at the state, district, and school levels (Rebell & Hunter, 2004). Access plans to issue a policy paper on NCLB in 2006.

At the time of this writing, the Access Web site provides the best source available on the litigations and the most complete compilation and fact sheets on the many cost studies (http://www.accessednetwork.org/). The section of the Access Web site on litigation provides a summary of all the school-funding cases, links to legal documents, recent litigation news, and other useful resources such as landmark publications and links to relevant studies. Access network members and visitors can find a state-by-state databank of information that includes recent events and links to the Web sites of relevant advocacy organizations, policy organizations, state government, as well as data on the finance system when available.

In addition to maintaining this service for the movement, Access provides speakers for national-, regional-, and state-level conferences and workshops, and works with other organizations to sponsor an annual Quality Education Conference open to plaintiff litigators, organizers, educators, and policymakers. The goal is to strengthen the quality-education movement and make it more visible as a major national voice for education reform.

Access links education advocacy and school-funding litigation with policy analysis and research. Access members are directed to publications that outline the most significant recent developments in policy analysis, including: (a) the use of costing-out studies, (b) greater emphasis on closing achievement gaps, (c) better understanding of programs that work for "at-risk" students, and (d) emerging critiques of NCLB. Because much of the research on education and school finance is conducted by faculty at schools of education and public administration, Access members are directed to research on critical issues such as: effective programs and school districts, quality teaching, class size, early childhood education, and rural education. Finally, to encourage involvement of the public in school-funding reform, network members are directed toward research on successful public engagement experiences.

CONCLUDING REMARKS

At the time of this writing, the state still has not complied with the Court of Appeals June 2003 order. Because the State of New York failed to meet the Court of Appeals' July 2004 deadline, on August 3, 2004, Justice DeGrasse appointed three referees to assess the state's noncompliance (Campaign for Fiscal Equity v. State, 2004a at 1–2). The referees held extensive hearings and issued their findings in a report to the court on November 30, 2004 (Campaign for Fiscal Equity v. State, 2004b). On March 16, 2005, Justice DeGrasse affirmed the referees' report and ordered that within 90 days the State shall: (a) take "all steps necessary to implement an operational funding plan" that will provide New York City with $1.41 billion in addition to current funding levels for the coming school year (7/1/2005–6/30/2006), and that these additional funds shall increase over the next 4 years from $1.41 billion in year 1 to $5.63 billion in year 4; (b) the State shall take all steps necessary to implement a capital-funding plan, to provide the New York City School District no less than $9.179 billion for capital improvements over the next 5 years; and (c) the State "shall take steps necessary to enhance the current system of educational accountability by requiring the New York City Department of Education to develop a comprehensive sound basic education plan that would set forth … the precise management reforms and instructional initiatives that the DOE will undertake … to improve student achievement" (Campaign for Fiscal Equity v. State, 2005 at 3–7). The court declined to determine how much of the funding should be provided from state and local sources.

Furthermore, the court ordered the State to perform costing-out studies every 4 years to determine the cost of providing a sound basic education to New York City schoolchildren and every 5 years to determine whether additional facilities funding is required to ensure that the city's school facilities are adequate to provide this opportunity (Campaign for Fiscal Equity v. State, 2005 at 3–8).

Unfortunately, rather than following the lead of other states and "promptly revamping the system from top to bottom within a year" (Rebell, 2005, p. A7), the State appealed, thereby gaining a stay of the court order. On March 23, 2006, the intermediate appeals court majority affirmed the lower court's order regarding $9.2 billion needed for the city schools' facilities and urged the governor and legislature to devise a plan to increase the city schools' annual operating funds by between $4.7 and $5.6 billion, but indicated that the courts could not mandate this. It was a ruling with "little bark, but no bite" (Medina, 2006). The court set an April 1, 2006, deadline for the State.

By April 1, the legislature and governor agreed to provide full facilities funding in compliance with the court's decision, but had made no progress on the operating funds. Plaintiffs filed an appeal on April 18 and asked the state's highest court for an expedited hearing and decision. As of this writing, the appeal is pending.

As of the writing of this chapter, the State of New York has complied with the courts' orders on facilities funding by enacting the capital funding package that will send $9.2 billion to New York City for school buildings over the next five years. Regarding operating funding, the governor and legislative leaders are negotiating in the face of an April 1 (2007) deadline for adoption of the state budget, an annual deadline that the state has seldom met over the last 20 years. The governor's education and budget proposals align well with the CFE court decisions and the policy recommendations developed by CFE in conjunction with 100 leaders from across the state. The Senate proposal, on the other hand, would provide more funding to well-to-do suburban school districts and less to low-wealth urban and rural districts.

Hundreds of thousands of children in New York City's public schools and thousands more in low-wealth districts across the state continue to be denied the opportunity for a sound basic education by the State. There is no recompense that can be offered these youngsters. Each year, more of them are cheated of a right granted to them by the Constitution of New York State. Moreover, the children enrolled when the case began have graduated—or dropped out—before a remedy was adopted and enacted. For many of these children, there is no way to compensate for the quality educational experiences denied to them. Justice delayed is ultimately justice denied.

This year for the first time since the CFE litigation began in 1993, a major breakthrough is possible, and some say likely, in Albany. If so, it will be an historic accomplishment and an important example for other states to follow.

REFERENCES

Bellah, R.N., Madsen, R., Tipton, S.M., Sullivan, W.M., & Swidler, A. (1991). *The good society*. New York: Knopf.

Berman, J.S., & Dunphy, D. (1998). Building plans for reform: Alabama's school finance litigation. *Studies in Judicial Remedies and Public Engagement, 1*, 1–32.

Campaign for Fiscal Equity (2004, May 11). Sound basic education task force: Ensuring educational opportunity for all. New York: CFE. Retrieved December 2004, from http://www.cfequity.org/.

Campaign for Fiscal Equity, Inc. v. State of New York, (1995). 86 N.Y. 2d 307. Court of Appeals [1995].

Campaign for Fiscal Equity, Inc. v. State of New York, (2001). 187 Misc. 2d 1. (S. Ct, N.Y. Co., 2001).

Campaign for Fiscal Equity, Inc. v. State of New York, (2002). 86 N.Y. 2d 307. Court of Appeals [2002, July 25].

Campaign for Fiscal Equity, Inc. v. State of New York, (2003). 100 N.Y. 2d 893. Court of Appeals [2003, June 26].

Campaign for Fiscal Equity, Inc. v. State of New York, (2004a). Court Order #111070/93 [2004, August 3].

Campaign for Fiscal Equity, Inc. v. State of New York, (2004b). Court Order #111070/93, Report and recommendations of the judicial referees. [2004, November 30]

Campaign for Fiscal Equity, Inc. v. State of New York, (2005). Court Order #111070/93 [2005, March 16].

Chambers, J.G., Parrish, T.B., Levin, J.D., Smith, J.R., Guthrie, J.W., Seder, R.C., & Taylor, L. (2004). *The New York Adequacy Study: Determining the cost of providing all children in New York an adequate education*. American Institutes for Research and Management Analysis and Planning, Inc.

Cipollone, D.W. (1998). Defining a "basic education": Equity and adequacy litigation in the State of Washington. *Studies in Judicial Remedies and Public Engagement, 1,* 1–30.

Civil Rights Act of 1964, Pub. L. No. 88-352, Title IV, Desegregation of Public Education.

Clune, W.H. (1994). The shift from equity to adequacy in school finance. *Educational Policy, 8,* 376–394.

Guthrie, J.W., Garms, W.I., & Pierce, L.C. (1988). *School finance and education policy: Enhancing educational efficiency, equality and choice* (2nd ed.). Englewood Cliffs, NJ: Prentice Hall.

Hoff, D.J. (2003, October 1). Federal law bolsters case for aid suits. *Education Week, 5*(1), 1, 20.

Hunter, M.A. (1998). All eyes forward: Public engagement and fiscal equity in Kentucky. *Journal of Law & Education, 28,* 485–516.

Hunter, M.A. (2000). Trying to bridge the gaps: Ohio's search for an education finance remedy. *Journal of Education Finance, 26,* 63–86.

Levittown v. Nyquist (1982), supra, 57 N.Y. 2d at 38 [1982].

Medina, J. (2006, March 25). Ruling with a little bark, but no bite. *New York Times,* p. B2.

Minorini, P.A., & Sugarman, S.D. (1999). Educational adequacy and the courts: The promise and the problems of moving to a new paradigm. In H.F. Ladd, R. Chalk, & J.S. Hansen (Eds.). *Equity and adequacy in education finance: Issues and perspectives* (pp. 175–208). Washington, DC: National Academy Press.

New York State Constitution, Article XI Education §1. Common Schools.

No Child Left Behind Act of 2001, Pub. L. No. 107-110.

Proefriedt, W.A. (2002, November 20). Other people's children. *Education Week, 22,* 33.

Rebell, M.A. (2005, March 26). Proposed budgets still ignore school kids. *Times Union,* p. A7.

Rebell, M.A., & Hughes, R.L. (1996). Schools, communities, and the courts: A dialogic approach to education reform. *Yale Law & Policy Review, 14,* 99–168.

Rebell, M.A., Hughes, R.L., & Grumet, L.F. (1995). *Fiscal equity in education: A proposal for a dialogic remedy.* New York: Campaign for Fiscal Equity.

Rebell, M.A., & Hunter, M.A. (2004, May). "Highly qualified" teachers: Pretense or legal requirement? *Phi Delta Kappan, 85*(9), 690–696.

Rebell, M.A., & Metzler, J. (2000). Rapid response, radical reform: The story of school finance litigation in Vermont. *Journal of Law & Education, 31,* 167–190.

Sizer, T.R. (1997). The meanings of "public education". In J.I. Goodlad & T.J. McMannon (Eds.). *The public purpose of education and schooling* (pp. 33–40). San Francisco: Jossey-Bass.

Strayer, G.D., & Haid, R.M. (1923). *Financing of education in the state of New York.* New York: Macmillan Company.

Yinger, J. (2004). State aid and the pursuit of educational equity: An overview. In J. Yinger (Ed.). *Helping children left behind* (pp. 3–57). Cambridge, MA: MIT Press.

NOTES

1. This "high-minimum" approach focuses on what would be necessary to ensure that all children have access to those educational opportunities that are necessary to gain a level of learning and skills that are now required, say, to obtain a decent job in our increasingly technologically complex society and to participate effectively in our ever-more complicated political process (Minorini & Sugarman, 1999). For a more detailed discussion of some of the adequacy and equity issues raised by the new approaches to foundation funding, see Yinger (2004).

2. For example, in Kentucky, a nonpartisan coalition conducted extensive statewide dialogues that eventually influenced the state to enact thorough and timely education and school-funding reforms in response to a state supreme court order in that state's school-funding adequacy case, Rose v. Council for Better Education. (Hunter, 1998). In Vermont public engagement proved to be essential in addressing the school-funding conflict that arose during litigation (Rebell & Metzler, 2000).

3. On January 10, 2001, Justice DeGrasse ordered the state to reform the school-funding system. On July 25, 2002, the intermediate Appellate Division court rejected the trial court's ruling and held that students in New York State are entitled only to an eight-grade level of education and preparation for low-level jobs (Campaign for Fiscal Equity v. State, 2002). After a series of appeals, the New York State Court of Appeals affirmed the trial court's order in June 2003 and allowed New York State until July 30, 2004, to remedy the constitutional violation. On June 26, 2003, the Court of Appeals reversed the Appellate Division and ruled in favor of the CFE plaintiffs, ordering the state to reform the funding system (Campaign for Fiscal Equity v. State, 2003). On July 30, 2004, the State of New York failed to meet the Court of Appeals' deadline. On August 3, 2004, Justice DeGrasse appointed three referees to assess the state's noncompliance (Campaign for Fiscal Equity v. State, 2004a).

10

The Impact of Community on Educational Reform

LISA J. SCOTT AND ANGELA LOVE

Educational institutions housed in urban communities are impacted by social situations such as high crime rates, physical and alcohol abuse, and illiteracy. Although educators and administrators attempt to promote change, the lack of support and resources makes change difficult, if not impossible. The results from feelings of despondency are high attrition and teacher turnover rates in schools in which consistency and mutual trust are especially vital to their sustainability. Instead of teachers working in isolation to address social issues affecting their classroom, educators and administrators need a practical methodology that promotes a vibrant social infrastructure and maintains a healthy community.

The term *healthy community* implies the presence of a vibrant social infrastructure consisting of numerous formal and informal organizations held together by the social fabric of the community. Social networks link organizations and individuals with each other and enable the community to function in a healthy way. In most urban communities, the weakening of the social fabric has exacerbated existing problems. What is necessary to rebuild the social fabric of the community is a strong social network characterized by trust, honest communication, and mutual support. This network allows a community of individuals to collectively address their problems through the development of a collective *sense of community*. When individuals communicate in a climate of trust and mutuality, they are able to influence the conditions of their lives in a positive way.

Typical educational reform movements look at the deficits of a community in an attempt to "fix" things that are wrong with our communities. But, in truth, we need to begin looking at the community and its *assets* first, before educational reform can begin. The most disparaged communities can find positive leadership: congregation members of a local church or synagogue, individuals working with already established grassroots organizations, and parents with social or political attachments to the community and its members. These assets or forms of social capital, available in even the most disparaged community, need the educational system and its administration's support. If educators focus on the community and its healthy sustainability, their influence on the lives of the community members and the students they teach can be fruitful.

In this chapter, we begin by outlining the history of community development and its foci on educational reformation; we further discuss the impact of community development on schools and how the mobilization of resources within a particular community benefits the school curriculum and its administrative policy. We discuss how parental involvement can mobilize resources for a school and its community. Finally, we conclude by providing concrete examples of successful community-based programs that focus on educational reform.

EDUCATIONAL REFORM BASED ON COMMUNITY DEVELOPMENT

Research has indicated that communities with scarce resources (e.g., financial assets; access to goods and services) tend to be characterized by ailing relationships between the educational systems and the members of the local community, which hurts the learning and development of the students (Warren, Thompson, & Saegert, 2001). Warren, Thompson, and Saegert further state that, by contrast, in higher socioeconomic communities, the collaborative relationships that schools have with the communities surrounding them facilitate the academic and social efforts of the students. This correlation indicates that the primary goals of educational reform should include the formation of healthy, sustainable communities in which community–school partnerships facilitate children's learning and development (Rothstein, 2004). However, such relationships are far from common; in fact, schools and community members rarely create interdependent relationships in which the development of one contributes to the development of the other (Cortes, 1993).

Education practitioners and researchers such as Boyd and Crowson (1991) indicate that community involvement promotes effective schooling. They state that schools must "reach out into the community in an attempt to strengthen the social capital available to children" (p. 36). Through social capital, students can obtain material and social resources and create networks vital to their academic success. They argue that community involvement in schools is critical primarily because "the problems of educational achievement and academic success demand resources beyond the scope of the school and most families" (Heath & McLaughlin, 1987). In Bronfenbrenner's (1973) theory of "overlapping spheres of influence," he identifies the community as one of the major environments that helps children develop cognitively, socially, and physically. He further contends that school, family, and community must all work collaboratively to ensure the academic success and socioemotional well-being of all students. It is hoped that through these collaborations, community fills in the missing gaps academically, by providing a nurturing constituency in which children find the social and emotional supports that contribute to their success.

Community as defined by Etienne Wenger (1998) is "a way of talking about the social configurations in which our enterprises are defined as worth pursuing and our participation is recognizable as competence" (p. 5). He continues by stating that we [as educators] need to value "the work of community building" so that the "participants [involved] have access to the resources necessary to learn what they need in order to take actions and make decisions that fully engage their knowledge-ability" (p. 10). If educators engage in meaningful discourse with the communities (as defined by Wenger) in which they reside and teach with deliberate thought and consideration, people in the community can become more self-reliant and empowered, and can "channel development to serve human and nonhuman interests both for the short and long term" (Kline, 1997, p. 17). Once empowered, community begins to take control of its own sustainability and engage its democracy. A community can potentially extend in such a way that it moves from an imagined state of being to a progressive and active state by which, as John Dewey states, "ideas and aspirations [are] used to organize the environment" (1915, p. 405). When this occurs, agency and accountability become intertwined within the framework of the community and transfer to the educational institutions and its members within that community, awakening what Paulo Freire calls *conscientization* (1970), a heightened social consciousness, a *wide-awakeness* (Greene, 2000), where marginalized communities are the change agents of educational reformation.

On this premise, the reciprocal relations among parents, community members, educators, and administrators become vital components of educational reformation and community development. Mobilizing broad-based community organizations with constituents who have an interest in community building and educational reformation rally the social and political capacity of federal and state administrations to make changes in policy initiatives and monetary distribution inclusive of community needs. This model of community building between community members and educators, although necessary at all socioeconomic levels, is especially critical in lower socioeconomic areas because impoverished communities face economic problems that are "unfixable" by teachers or the administration. As a result, teachers within those communities feel overwhelmed and helpless in promoting any form of success for their students (Kozol, 1991), which contributes to high attrition rates of teachers and administrators in such communities. A focus toward community development as outlined in this collaborative model would promote the collegiality necessary to increase teacher morale. Heightened morale among the teachers prompted by a sense of collegiality from community members can only benefit the students and, hopefully, reverse rising attrition rates.

Finally, impoverished schools lack many of the resources typically available in more affluent schools. They often have less qualified teachers, overcrowded classrooms, older buildings in need of serious repair, inadequate textbooks, and outdated facilities (such as computers or playground equipment; Kozol, 1991; Schrag, 2003, as cited in Warren, 2005). Parents involved in politically based community organizations can be the advocates for educational and civic reformation by voicing their concerns regarding the lack of resources in their schools in public forums locally and nationally, an essential voice that is critically missing in many citywide efforts regarding school reform (Stone, Henig, Jones, & Pierannunzi, 2001). Rather than acting simply as teachers' helpers, parents used substantively in community development can provide necessary resources to aid in their children's social and academic achievement. This active role negates the more passive stance of both parents and school administrators lacking collaboration and merely waiting for the federal and state officials to mobilize needed resources. Furthermore, organizing in collaboration helps low-income parents find their own voice and gain the self-confidence and power to influence decisions that affect their children. Contemporary school models limit parental involvement by restricting participation to PTA meetings or bake sales; however, with parental advocacy as an effective method of stimulating and sustaining education reformation, federal and state administrators become accountable as educators, and local administrators feel compelled to sustain improvements and develop new ways to improve systems and achieve results.

HISTORICAL OVERVIEW OF COMMUNITY BUILDING

The community-oriented approach to educational reformation has a historical past grounded in the theoretical framework of John Dewey (1915) and the community movements of the 1960s (Fantini, Gittell, & Magat, 1970); but educational reformation based in community building primarily stems from the "progressivists" of the 1920s and 1930s, who "emphasized that teaching students to be active participants in a democratic civic "community" would enable "to envision, articulate and act on conceptions of a better world" (Wertheimer, 1998). Progressivists believed that a community-centered curriculum molds students into constructive proponents of a "civic community." Therefore, the backbone of the philosophy was a focus on an educational curriculum that addresses critical contemporary issues that affect democracy. According to this vision, introduced by Theodore Brameld (1904–1987) and propounded by more current critical theorists such as Paulo Freire (1921–1997), systems must be changed for human conditions to improve for the benefit of individuals residing in such a democracy (Painter, 1995); and in order for such conditions to change, individuals residing within the democracy must first be informed of its social, political, and economic conditions.

The Progressive Movement advocated the idea that students should be encouraged to be independent thinkers, so they in turn can make informed decisions regarding our democracy. This philosophy was a sharp contrast to the prevalent educational approaches rooted in labor and industry in the early 1900s, particularly in the United States (Rippa, 1997). Such approaches did not foster the importance of individualism, creativity, and critical thinking, but instead emphasized classroom control, management, obedience to authority, and a structured curriculum that focused on memorization and repetition.

Advocates of the Progressive Movement included George Counts, Jane Addams, Margaret Naumburg, Ella Flagg Young, Francis W. Parker, Theodore Bramald, William H. Kilpatrick, Harold Rugg, and Marietta Johnson (Rippa, 1997). As educational theorists, many influenced by the philosophy of John Dewey, they felt there should be less authoritarianism in the schools, an elimination of set standards for school curriculum, and an emphasis on teaching what students needed to become democratic citizens. The Progressive Movement was at its peak in the 1930s, during the Great Depression. However, in the second half of the 20th century, critics in opposition to the Progressive Movement felt that education needed a foundation of basic skills and more discipline, and believed that progressive education was corrupting the minds of youth. During the 1940s and 1950s, in the context of the Cold War, the attacks on progressive education continued, and the movement lost its centrality in terms of influencing school practice. Although many principles of the Progressive Movement were partially adopted by educational systems and institutions in the second half of the 20th century, the movement would never recover the standing that it had during the first few decades, except for a short time during the 1960s when it rebounded under more radicalized forms, such as the free school movement, nongraded classrooms, the "deschooling" proposals posited by Ivan Illich (1971), and emancipatory adult education programs pioneered by Paulo Freire in São Paulo, Brazil, in the 1960s (Rippa, 1997).

This new educational model developed during the mid- to late 20th century in opposition to the Progressive Movement is a disquieting replica of the organizational structure evident in the business industries during the early 20th century, a model designed to promote efficiency, production, and compliance in its workers. The model developed and still prevalent in public education is due to an increase in industry and mass production resulting from the United States' involvement in World War II in 1939 (Adams, 1994). The industrial boom created by the war caused business owners to rely more on in-house administrators to facilitate growth of the industry by managing production, labor, and distribution (Illich, 1971). Therefore, a new form of public education was constructed to develop a compliant workforce; students enrolled in public schools would gain skills of print literacy and discipline that would enable them to function in a corporate economy based on accounting, commercial organization, and non-threatening communicative practices, supported by manual labor and service jobs (Illich, 1973). In other words, industry created schools and fueled many of the ideas behind public education. Students could be trained as future administrators and workers through the public educational systems in the hope that upon completion they would support the economic sustainability of the corporation.

Although this corporate model can meet some of the economic needs of a community and its school, it atrophies the intellectualism and leadership of its members, which are necessary components for a community moving toward a self-reliant and healthy sustainability. Ivan Illich in *Deschooling Society* (1971) points up the modern schooling practices of our current educational system and their promotion of conformity, bureaucracy, instrumental rationality, hierarchy, competition, and other features of existing social organization. Instead of such conformity and to promote community-school collaboration and reform efforts, education needs to provide the tools to free individuals from dependency and cultivate autonomy and sociality. If appropriated, these tools can create better modes of learning and social life that will benefit all of society. Illich further suggests a normative dimension to critique existing systems and construct alternative ones using values of "survival, justice, and self-defined work" as positive norms (1973, p. 13). These criteria could guide a reconstruction of education to serve the needs of the community, promote democracy and social justice, and redefine learning and work to promote creativity and a sense of community.

MODERN SCHOOLING PARADIGMS

Contemporary education initiatives often fail to link community development and school reform. Many educational initiatives, instead of looking at the community as a vital component of its educational systems and its development, focus more on administrative procedure and often marginalize the participants they are attempting to assist. The "top-down" approach of educational reformation, in which administrative power is centralized in local districts, has been the norm for many school administrations since the 1940s (Warren, Thompson, & Saegert, 2001). This approach, however, has not only led to the standardization of curriculum and administrative practices in our educational system, but has further marginalized the voice and contribution of parents, teachers, and students, moving farther away from the egalitarian model intended by the progressivists of the early 20th century to our present system of centralized administration.

For example, part of New York City Mayor Bloomberg's 2001 policy initiative regarding public school systems eradicated the community school by centralizing the school district system and adopting a uniform curriculum (Reid, 2003). The community school district and other district departments, which Bloomberg labeled as "Byzantine administrative fiefdoms" (p. 1), were replaced by one uni-fied chain of command and governed from the administrative offices located in Manhattan, distant from the remaining four boroughs of Queens, Brooklyn, The Bronx, and Staten Island.

At the heart of this new structure, under the supervision of a deputy chan-cellor for teaching and learning, are 10 instructional leadership divisions called *learning support centers*. Each such center is guided by one regional superinten-dent. These regional superintendents sit together at the Department of Educa-tion headquarters and devise policy initiatives from the top down. These learning support centers, physically spread throughout the city, each in turn house 10 local instructional supervisors, who directly oversee a dozen elementary, middle, and high schools through the on-site school principals. In other words, on the instructional side, accountability and responsibility go directly from 1 deputy chancellor to 10 regional superintendents to 100 local instructional supervisors to 1,200 principals, to 80,000 teachers, and to 1,100,000 students (Citizens Union Foundation, 2004).

The benefit of the previous "noncentralized" structure was that regional offices were located within the communities that they serviced, giving some connected-ness to community members, teachers, and administrators within their assigned schools. The new organizational structure requires that regional superintendents work from offices in the district's new headquarters in Manhattan. From a loca-tion behind City Hall, 10 instructional supervisors administrate up to 120 schools each (Citizens Union Foundation, 2004, p. 12). A concern among teachers and administrators alike is that rarely will instructional supervisors make an attempt to connect with their instructional staff and its community members, indicating that policy initiatives, including curriculum, will be based on test scores instead of the voices of the community members.

Furthermore, Mayor Bloomberg's initiatives reach into the classroom with a standardized reading, writing, and mathematics curriculum for approximately 1,000 of the city's 1,200 schools, while at the same time giving the top-performing 200 schools discretion in choosing their curricula, teacher training, and budget (Reid, 2003). The incentive for these exempted schools to adopt the standardized curriculum, however, is that the New York City Board of Education furnishes cur-riculum materials and manipulative learning materials for the standardized curric-ulum only. The remaining 1,000 schools are then left with "teacher-proof" material such as scripted lesson plans and retention policies based on test scores. Bloomberg's policy depletes the autonomy needed in these lower performing schools; instead, these schools become part of a "captured population" whereby they are trapped under the ever-watchful eye of administrative policy (Noguera, 2001).

Contemporary education theorists such as Diane Ravitch, Lydia Segal, and John E. Chubb have brought awareness to the academic community regarding the damage the centralization of administrative power inflicts on academic achievement, student and teacher morale, and community relationships. In response to these criticisms, superintendents and central office personnel point to their local school councils, staffed by parents, teachers, and school administrators, and claim that decision-making power has been given to the schools (Ouchi, 2003). However, *true* decentralization has not been achieved, much less attempted, which would require that power over the budget be given to each school and taken away from the central office. Instead, administrators engage in the proverbial "smoke and mirror" trick by moving *apparent* control over decisions up and down the system, between the central chancellor's office and the local superintendents, but never yielding a fraction of control to the schools (Ravitch, 1974). Yielding control to the local school districts and mobilizing funding sources would allow educators to exercise their professional judgment in organizing a capable and committed teaching force, in selecting and designing interesting and relevant texts and curricular materials, in tailoring instructional techniques to fit the needs of the students and families being served, and in orienting the school around a theme or mission that captures the imagination of teachers and students.

Decentralized structures, whereby teachers and administrators focus on the needs of the community that they serve, show that teachers in these schools "care," and have their interests at the forefront of their decision making. These actions created by teachers and local administrators can potentially create two significant effects among the school community: (a) a strong sense of affiliation with the school, leading many to liken such schools to a "family" and others to speak in terms more reminiscent of a membership one has enthusiastically assumed; and (b) a difference in the student's orientation toward school purposes and activities (Raywid, 1988). What these two effects demonstrate is a bonding to school-associated individuals and to the school's institutional norms. Such effects, quite pronounced in many alternative schools, make a substantial contribution to the quality of education as well as the quality of school life. Furthermore, as reciprocating relationships continue, such programs establish empathy and bonds to individuals and groups beyond the school, which in turn can simultaneously contribute to rebuilding the "democratic citizenry" (Raywid, 1988, p. 196).

THE MOBILIZATION OF RESOURCES AND ASSETS TO IMPROVE STUDENT ACHIEVEMENT AND COMMUNITY COLLABORATION

Community engagement between parents and teachers can play an essential role in making schools more responsive and accountable to the academic success of their students (Mediratta & Fruchter, 2003). The reality is that many schools can affect their students' academic success, but are limited because of the lack of resources available (Kozol, 1991). A social intersection among the adults (parents, teachers, and school personnel) can provide a form of *social closure* whereby all the children know that the adults are in a social connection, making each adult and child socially responsible for their actions (Coleman, 1988; Willis, 1995). The objective in this type of social network is for teachers, school personnel, and parents to build trust among one another and express their common vision for school reform and its maintenance (Bryk & Schneider, 2002). Through social practices that revolve around community building, such as the use of school space after hours, accommodations for working parents to attend teacher conferences, and the inclusion of parent voice, educators can transform the negative culture and practices of schools, and at the same time create a political constituency for public education as part of a broader agenda that addresses the needs of families and communities and provides a relational community on behalf of the school.

The strategy of social networking translates into the relational power absent from many community development programs. Relational power emphasizes the "power to get things done collectively." Unilateral power, however, is essentially the "power over others" (Cortes, 1993; Loomer, 1976; Putnam, 1995) whereby the "outsider," including researchers, administrators, and teachers who do not live in a particular community and who do not take the time to build relationships collectively, make administrative decisions regarding its members without their consultation. However necessary this unilateral method is at times, it is ultimately insufficient for improving schools, because, as evidenced in many community organizations, this method entails unreasonable demands and intrusions on the community and the school (Goldring, 1990). In opposition, a fundamental goal in the relational approach is collaboration, in which partnerships are created and mobilization of resources is based on the ideas and goals of the collective defined through the community itself and its needs.

Partnerships among community members can leverage power into the public arena by mobilizing key community members who are established in the community as leaders, or who evolved as leaders through social intersection. Marked leaders in the community can be parents, teachers, pastors, business owners, or even the students themselves; for all intents and purposes, a community leader can be anyone who shares the relational vision of the community and its development. Over time, as these key leaders develop their skills, they can mobilize others and become a catalyst for the transformation of the community and school culture.

In 1988 Mavis G. Sanders and Adia Harvey, two researchers from Johns Hopkins University, conducted a case study of an urban elementary school to investigate if a program of school, family, and community partnerships including connections with community businesses and organizations can make a positive impact on the school dynamic socially and academically; and what school systems if any, need to be in place to maintain such relationships. The case study revealed four factors as part of the school system that supported the school's ability to develop and maintain meaningful community partnerships. These factors are (a) a high commitment to learning, (b) principal support for community involvement, (c) a welcoming school climate, and (d) two-way communication about the level and kind of community involvement.

According to the results from the case study, these factors were linked to the principal's actions as school leader. The principal's ability to (a) maintain a school environment in which teachers and parents focused on students' academic success, (b) model for faculty and staff a genuine openness to community involvement and establish an expectation for emulation, (c) actively network with individuals in the community to inform them of the school's needs, and (d) support others in developing leadership in the area of family and community involvement, created fertile ground in which school–community partnerships flourished (Sanders & Harvey, 2002). As a result of these partnerships, the school had computers that students used, classrooms and a library full of books, an incentive program for honor-roll students, an after-school program, financial support for partnership activities and events, community speakers for parent workshops, and relationships with community businesses, organizations, and individuals that brought the school and its community partners a great deal of satisfaction. These partnerships thus supported the school's efforts to provide a challenging and nurturing learning environment for its students (p. 22).

This kind of sustainability is important for school improvement, especially for schools in high-risk, urban communities that are increasingly asked to improve students' academic and behavioral outcomes, often without the necessary increases in material and human resources. This case study suggests, then, that communities can play a vital role in the school improvement process. To attract useful and committed partners, however, schools need guidance and support from district and state leaders to create appropriate contexts for partnerships (Epstein, 1995).

Furthermore, principals need assistance in understanding (a) the benefits of effective school–community collaborations, (b) how to identify potential partners for collaboration and appropriate collaborative activities, and (c) how to create school environments that encourage and support such collaborations (Sanders & Harvey, 2002). School staff and faculty also need professional development and staff training to understand their role in attracting and maintaining community partnerships. This kind of guidance and support from district and state leaders can help all schools, especially those in high-risk urban communities, connect more effectively with families and communities to improve student outcomes.

Community development as discussed is a vital component of the culture of the school and its members; change starts through conversations among parents, teachers, and other staff about their concerns and goals for the school. Priorities are then created based on those conversations, but much of the initial work is concentrated around immediate and pressing community concerns, such as issues of safety or the mobilization of community resources. As understanding and capacities develop, the organizing effort turns toward more pedagogical concerns (Warren, 2005), such as after-school programming, increased tests scores, and instruction to develop critical thinking skills among students, all concerns of most parents and teachers in spite of socioeconomic status.

CONCLUSION

Many schools, especially in New York City, are in communities in which economic disparity hampers their academic potential. Children and parents in impoverished communities lack consistent health care, nutrition, adequate housing, and employment (hooks, 2000). Therefore, urban schools must work even harder at educating their children, but it is unreasonable and unrealistic to expect that the educational institutions alone can combat the effects of poverty and racism within that community (Rothstein, 2004, as cited by Warren, 2005). Community development organizations and policy initiatives must work directly in supporting the social and economic well-being of families and communities (Briggs & Mueller, 1997). By concentrating on the community and the maintenance of its economic well-being, the direct result is the health and sustainability of children within the schools of those communities.

The absence of policy initiatives inclusive of the community systems that directly affect a school's development creates a myopic view of the school and its community. Therefore, program initiatives are often based on outsider perspectives exclusive of its members and their development. "Such encompassing systems include the characteristics of the neighborhood, the relation between school and community and a host of other ecological circumstances and changes" (Bronfenbrenner, 1973, p. 45) existing in the community. If the ecological considerations are not factored into the determinations of policy initiatives, then policy initiatives and program changes are not authentic; instead, they promote an artificial sense of progress and community.

Community development programs achieve various outcomes, some more successful than others, but none of the aforementioned conceptualizations are quick fixes to the social, racial, or academic problems that plague our schools. In contemporary society the trend is to find a "one-size-fits-all" solution to our social ails. Yet, there is no program that can "fit all" sizes, and many programs fall short because they fail to take into account the considerations, interests, and support of the stakeholders at the local level (Payne & Kaba, n.d.).

Reform strategies mentioned in this paper incorporate experts and community stakeholders in and around the school. It is hoped that through an active dialogue, parents, principals, teachers, and community members can develop a paradigm that fits the values, interests, and social considerations of the community. This paradigm is the authentic educational reformation necessary, and often missing, from unilateral power structures ever-present in our current administrative models. As a final point, there must be a long-term commitment to the members of the community and the school, with a solid intent in building relational constructs inclusive of its members. It is hoped that with some failure and even more successes, the payoff will be life altering for our educational system and its practices in the classroom.

REFERENCES

Adams, M.C. (1994). *The best war ever: America and World War II.* Baltimore: Johns Hopkins University Press.

Boyd, R.L., & Crowson, W.L. 92001). The new role of community development in educational reform. *Peabody Journal of Education, 76,* 9–29.

Briggs, X.D.S., & Mueller, E.J., (1997). *From neighborhood to community: Evidence on the social effects of community development.* New York: New School for Social Research, Community Development Research Center.

Bronfenbrenner, U. (1973). *Interactions among theory, research and application in child development,* Paper presented at the President's Symposium, at the Annual Meeting of the Society for Research in Child Development, Philadelphia.

Bryk, A., & Schneider, B. (2002). *Trust in schools: A core resource for improvement.* New York: Russell Sage Foundation Press.

Citizens Union Foundation. (2004). *Gotham Gazette* @ www.GothamGazette.com.

Coleman, J.S. (1988). Social capital in the creation of human capital. *American Journal of Sociology, 94*(Suppl.), S95–S120.

Cortes, E. Jr. (1993). Reweaving the fabric: The iron rule and the IAF strategy for power and politics. In H.G. Cisneros (Ed.). *Interwoven destinies* (pp. 294–319). New York: W.W. Norton.

Dewey, J. (1915). The school and society. In *The child and the curriculum and the school and society.* Chicago: University of Chicago.

Epstein, J. (1995). School, family, community partnerships: Caring for the children we share. *Phi Delta Kappan, 76*(9), 701–712.

Famtini, M., Gittell, M., & Magat, R. (1970). *Community control and the urban school.* New York: Praeger.

Freire, P. (1970). *Pedagogy of the oppressed.* New York: Continuum.

Goldring, E.B. (1990). Elementary school principals as boundary spanners: Their engagement with parents. *Journal of Educational Administration, 28*(1), 53–62.

Greene, M. (2000). Imagining futures: The public school and possibility. *Curriculum Studies, 32,* 267–280.

Heath, S.B., & McLaughlin, M. (1991). Community organizations as family. *Phi Delta Kappan, 72,* 623.

hooks, B. (2000). *Where we stand: Class matters.* New York: Routledge Publishers.

Illich, I. (1971). *Deschooling society.* New York: Harper and Row.

Illich, I. (1973). *Tools for conviviality.* New York: Harper and Row.

Kline, E. (1997). *Eco-city dimensions: Healthy communities healthy planet.* San Francisco: New Society Publishers.

Knoblauch, C.H., & Brannon, L. (1993). *Critical teaching and the idea of literacy.* Portsmouth, N.H.: Heinemann.

Kozol, J. (1991). *Savage inequalities: Children in America's schools.* New York: Crown.

Loomer, B. (1976). Two conceptions of power. *Criterion, 15*(1), 11–29.

Mediratta, K. (2004). *Constituents of change: Community organizations and public education reform,* New York: New York University, Institute for Education and Social Policy.

Mediratta, K., & Fruchter, N., (2003). *From governance to accountability: Building relationships that make schools work.* New York: New York University, Institute for Education and Social Policy.

Noguera, P. (2001). Transforming urban schools through investments in the social capital of parents. In S. Saeger, J.P. Thompson, & M.R. Warren (Eds.). *Social capital and poor communities* (pp. 189–212). New York: Russell Sage Foundation Press.

Ouchi, W. (2003). Making schools work. *Education Week, 23,* 56–44.

Painter, M., & Durhan, W.H. (1995). *The social causes of environmental destruction in Latin America.* Ann Arbor, MI: University of Michigan.

Payne, C.M., & Kaba, M. (n.d.). *So much for reform, so little change: Building level obstacles to urban school reform.* Unpublished manuscript.

Putnam, R.D. (1995). Bowling alone: America's declining social capital. *Journal of Democracy, 6,* 65–78.

Ravitch, D. (1974). *The great school wars: New York City, 1805–1973.* New York: John Wiley Press.

Raywid, M.A. (1988). Community and schools: A prolegomenon. *Teachers College Record, 90*(2), 197–210.

Reid, K. (2003). Mayor outlines major overhaul of NYC System. *Education Week, 22*(19), 1.

Rippa, A. (1997). *Education in a free society: An American history.* New York: Longman.

Reese, W.J. (2002). *Power and the promise of urban school reform: Grassroots movements during the Progressive Era.* New York: Teachers' College Press.

Rothstein, R. (2004). *Class and schools: Using social, economic and educational reform to close the black-white achievement gap.* Washington, DC: Economic Policy Institute.

Sanders, M.G., & Harvey, A. (2002). Beyond the school wall: A case study for school leadership for school community collaboration. *Teachers College Record, 104,* 1345–1368.

Schrag, P. (2003). *Final test: The battle for adequacy in America's schools.* New York: New Press.

Stone, C.N., Hening, J.R., Jones, B.D., & Pierannunzi, C. (2001). *Building civic capacity: The politics of reforming urban schools.* Lawrence: University Press of Kansas.

The Progressive Education is Founded. http://fcis.oise.utoronto.ca/%7Edaniel_schugurensky/assignment1/1919pea.html (accessed December 17, 2005).

Warren, M.R., Thompson, J.P., & Saegert, S. (2001). The role of social capital in combating poverty. In S. Saegert, J.P. Thompson, & M.R. Warren (Eds.). *Social capital and poor communities* (pp. 1–28). New York: Russell Sage Foundation Press.

Warren, M.R. (2005). Communities and schools: A new view of urban education reform. *Harvard Educational Review, 65*(2).

Wenger, E. (1998). *Communities of practice: Learning, meaning and identity.* New York: Cambridge University Press.

Westheimer, J. (1998). *Among schoolteachers: Autonomy, community and ideology.* New York: Teachers College.

Willis, M.G. (1995). *We are family: Creating success in an African American public elementary school.* Unpublished dissertation, Georgia State University, Atlanta.

11

Equity in the Science Classroom

PENNY HAMMRICH AND MICHELLE MYERS

All students deserve equitable access to challenging and meaningful learning and achievement in science, regardless of race, ethnic group, gender, socioeconomic status, geographic location, age, language, disability, or prior science achievement. This concept has profound implications for teaching and learning science throughout the school community. It suggests that ensuring equity must be at the core of systemic reform efforts, not only in science, but in education as a whole.

Government actions such as Title IX of the Education Amendments Act, passed in 1972, were enacted to address the inequities in educational programs receiving federal dollars. Subsequently, in 1974, the Women's Educational Equity Act (WEEA) was passed. It expanded math, science, and technology programs for female students. In 1994, a package of gender equity provisions was included in the Elementary and Secondary Education Act. The provisions included the creation of teacher-training activities that worked to eliminate inequitable practices and to develop programs to increase girls' participation in science and mathematics. In turn, monies from these various forms of federal legislation have provided funding for reform in science, technology, engineering, and mathematics (STEM) education.

The current reform movement in science education has been under way since the 1960s. From the beginning of the reform movement in science education, there has been broad agreement that traditional modes of teaching and learning are obsolete, and that new curricula and modes of inquiry need to be "invented." The plethora of changes taking place in science has led to efforts by nearly all the developed countries to transform education in the sciences. Such changes include making existing courses more rigorous, teaching more science, reducing class size, increasing graduation rates, and focusing science teaching and learning on inquiry skills focused on standards. Although significant, such changes do not reflect a coherent view of influencing a culture of change in science education.

Instituting reform in science education is particularly urgent in urban schools because of the obstacles these schools face, including working conditions, limited science materials, limited time spent on science education, and inadequate accesses to resources. Equitable reform of science education involves a cohesive school and community clearly focused on science education reform, visionary and responsible leadership, effective teachers who have autonomy, equitable pedagogy, and a community that is involved.

Equity is central to the current reform movement in science education, especially when looking at the disparities between boys and girls as they progress from elementary school to middle school through high school. At the elementary level, boys and girls are equal in science achievement and interest, but as they progress through their education and science courses become optional, the participation of girls in science courses decreases, thereby leaving girls inadequately prepared to enter higher education in a field of science. Systemic science education reform requires three factors that contribute to success in science, including: (a) opportunities to learn science, (b) achievement in science, and (c) decisions to pursue science-related careers (Blosser, 2005). Although intervention strategies are needed, the focus must include careers in science as a vehicle to introduce the possibilities for girls to pursue careers in science-related fields.

Female students' academic achievements, perceptions, and attitudes toward mathematics and science are subjects that have received considerable attention from the educational research community for more than two decades (Tolley, 2003). Research from the National Science Foundation (NSF, 1990) and the Task Force on Women, Minorities, and Handicapped in Science and Technology (1989) noted that although efforts had been made to narrow the gap in achievement, little change had been realized. The consensus was that the methods for equitable practice must be embedded into the reform initiatives to ensure that all students were given the best possible chance for success. The national reform movement trickled down to state and local boards of education through the development of state and local science and mathematics curriculum standards, advocating specific content and equitable education. As schools searched for the best models of instruction to help teachers become effective, they incorporated the standards into their curricula. School administrators had little disagreement about the need for reform, but they differed on the specific modes to achieve reform. However, a commonly agreed upon theme for reform was the active involvement of learners. Government entities, colleges, universities, and K-12 systems have worked on many fronts to address the disparities between male and female students in science and mathematics achievement. Systematic efforts have been made to reverse the negative attitudes girls have about STEM. The negative attitudes that girls have about these areas are one reported source of the gender gap.

Subsequently, STEM-based educational programs have been implemented to adjust the often skewed perceptions girls possess about mathematicians, scientists, and careers in similar fields. A myriad of science and mathematics programs have been designed to meet the special needs of girls. Even more pronounced are the instructional materials, teachers' guides, checklists, and computer-based resources that have been created to change the face of instruction to close the achievement gap (AAUW, 2004). The WEEA Equity Resource Center is one such group that provides resources to the public. Similar to many other groups, the center has been working on the equity front for more than 20 years.

REASONS FOR INEQUITY

Decades of research on science education and gender equity suggests a number of reasons and remedies for gender inequity in STEM education. For many years, science education reforms focused on changing the curriculum, teaching, and assessment of K-12 education to make for a more equitable learning environment (Tolley, 2003). Science education classes and expectations have excluded girls, leading to lower participation and achievements. Teachers' beliefs about students' abilities were also found to affect the manner in which female students operated in the classroom. Studies suggested that within the same classrooms, male and female students received very different educations (Jones & Wheatley, 1990; Klein, 1991), with science education classes and expectations that simply excluded girls, leading to lower participation and achievements. In addition, it was noted that a female student's own perceptions of science also contributed to inequity in achievement (Jones and Wheately, 1990; Shakeshaft, 1995; Shepard-son & Pizzni, 1992; Tolley, 2003). Other avenues of inquiry demonstrated a lack of preservice and in-service teacher education curricula focused on equitable pedagogy in the STEM classroom.

Confounding the issue of gender inequity was the notion of culture. *Multiculturalism*, a term coined by James Banks, has been seen as a decisive factor in female students' success. Researchers who study the effects of cultural insensitivity in education suggest that much of the science education reform literature acknowledged the central importance of equity issues. However, the discussions centered around a color-blind point of view (Cochron-Smith, 1995; Ladson-Billings, 1995; Rodriguez, 1997) rather than acknowledging differences in students.

EQUITABLE INSTRUCTION

More recent science education reforms focused on changing the curriculum, teaching, and assessment of K-12 education to make for a more equitable classroom (National Research Council, 1996; Rutherford & Ahlgren, 1990). Specifically, the National Science Education Standards emphasized the "development of environments that enable [all] students to learn science that provide equitable opportunities" (National Research Council, 1996, pp. 4,7). Studies conducted suggest that in traditional and nontraditional STEM classroom environments, male and female students received very different educations (Hammrich, Richardson, & Livingston, 2000). Reformists believed that gender-sensitive classrooms were essential. These classrooms would include fostering a safe and nurturing environment, promoting problem-solving skills, building math confidence, displaying images depicting females in STEM-based careers, creating collaborative experiences, using hands-on learning, and allowing for open discussion about gender stereotypes. In addition, it would be important to acknowledge the contributions and barriers of women in science, and to use female-appropriate teaching strategies, showing careers in mathematics and science as interesting and relevant (Allen, 1995; Boland, 1995; Mann, 1994; Martin, 1996; Sanders, 2002). However, studies on equitable practices in the classroom told a different story of the educational climate (Eder, Evans, & Parker, 1995; Orenstein, 1994; Pipher, 1994). The Association for the Education of Teachers in Science (1996) indicated in its *Professional Knowledge Standards* that "unless prospective and practicing teachers can develop the knowledge, skills and beliefs called for in the reform documents little will change" (p. 1). Although the standards addressed the issue of equitable practice in the classroom, they failed to prepare teachers for issues of equity in the classroom. The consensus was that the methods for equitable practice must be embedded in the reform initiatives to ensure that all students were given the best possible chance for success.

Constructivist Pedagogy

Constructivism, an epistemological perspective of knowledge acquisition, served as the foundation for many of the noted suggestions regarding gender-sensitive science education. *Science for All Americans*, a groundbreaking report by the American Association for the Advancement of Science (AAAS), set new standards for science, mathematics, and technology education. Others suggested opportunities for students to express themselves in oral and written form, work in teams, solve problems, question, explore, discover concepts, use authentic tools, and learn about related professions and contributions to the field (Driver, 1995). Constructivist theory was also parlayed in the training of science educators. Accordingly, teachers were asked to model attitudes that fostered inquiry and knowledge and to seek ways to connect science learning to other disciplines (Richmond & Neureither, 1998).

GENDER EQUITY IN SCIENCE EDUCATION: THE CURRENT STATE

Presently, the U.S. Department of Education is launching a series of examinations in reading and mathematics to assess student achievement in an effort to improve the standing of American students in an ever-increasing global marketplace (U.S. Department of Education, 2004). At the same time, President George W. Bush's No Child Left Behind Act was passed, with the stated intent of assuring all students that they would have access to quality education. The federal government also committed to closing the achievement gap by improving teacher quality and implementing effective educational programs. Although funds have been made available for the professional development of preservice teachers (U.S. Department of Education, 2004), the No Child Left Behind Act in its implementation represents an underfunded, piecemeal approach to effecting educational reform.

Systemic reform must remain on the national agenda if this nation hopes to attain the goals posed by the federal government. It is important to recognize, therefore, that the conditions of many urban schools and the communities to which they belong are appalling (Kozol, 2000). Lifelong learning in science, mathematics, and technology is impossible when female students in urban school systems have no access to the World Wide Web and have fewer textbooks, manipulatives, and science equipment than suburban students. In particular, females, minority students, and students from low socioeconomic backgrounds face great structural challenges in choosing and performing well in the science, mathematics, and technology fields (Hammrich et al., 2000; Schnorr & Ware, 2001).

For students and teachers with limited access to science exploration, innovative programs must provide an opportunity to examine hands-on science with the newest and most advanced science, mathematics, and technology resources. An awareness of cultural differences, including learning style and relevance to real-world experiences, are essential to the format, organization, and content of an effective program (Nieto, 2003). A current view of how individuals receive and process information proposes several independent forms of information processing, including logical-mathematical, linguistic, musical, spatial, kinesthetic, interpersonal, and intrapersonal (Gardner, 2000). Based on this notion of multiple intelligences, effective education needs to be diverse in its offerings, both in terms of content and format of instruction.

Challenge: Barriers of the Mind

Although legal barriers to achieving gender equity in American society have been removed, many barriers still stymie females. Shirley Malcolm of the AAAS stated in her keynote address in 1997 to the American Association of University Women (AAUW) on Girls Succeeding in Science, Math, and Technology: Who Works and What Works:

> The effort to equalize educational opportunities for girls is far from complete .... Unlike some other nations, female students in the United States are legally guaranteed

access to math and science courses. While our legal barriers to this education have been removed, there are often still barriers we face; these are "barriers of the mind."

What are these "barriers of the mind" that prevent females from pursuing academic and professional careers in science, mathematics, technology, and engineering? They include the organizational structure of scientific and mathematics instruction, as well as females' perceptions of science and mathematics courses. Other barriers stem from societal influences such as parents' and teachers' lack of encouragement, authority figures' attitudes toward science, and the lack of support for females in science-based careers (Northrop, 2003). Researchers believe that fostering a safe and nurturing environment, promoting problem-solving skills, creating collaborative experiences, educating teachers, offering hands-on learning tools, and allowing open discussion of gender stereotypes are essential for encouraging female students' success in technological fields.

The organizational structure of current science instruction plays an important role in diminishing the success of females in science. Historically, science education has been taught as a competitive and individualistic discipline. Science instruction and science-based professions have been viewed as isolated enterprises that are objective in nature (Clewell & Campbell, 2002). The underlying discernment is that the barriers girls face in science often overshadow the very characteristics girls hold that promote their resilience in the actual practice of science, including seeking personal relevance, working collaboratively, and having keen observational, verbal, and writing skills (AAUW, 2000).

Challenge: Gender Gap and Science Education

Research studies have documented the wide gender gap in achievement scores between males and females in the areas of science and mathematics (NSF, 2000). The authors of this research assert that when girls are allowed to work in a manner intrinsic to their collective learning style, appropriate science and mathematics learning takes place. Such concerns have laid the groundwork for the Sisters in Science Equity Reform Project (SISERP) intervention programs, which specifically target females in order to increase their success in science and mathematics by providing access to gender-related teacher professional development, classroom materials, and curricula to maximize a gender-equitable approach to science education.

Researchers have reported that girls and boys have vastly different formal and informal science experiences, which contribute to the gender gap in science achievement (Linn, 1990). Indirect and direct experiences that contribute to such differences (Kahle & Meece, 1994) include the following:

- Entertainment choices, such as playing with science-based toys and games, and being exposed to science fiction movies and television shows
- Participation in science activities at home
- Taking science-related field trips
- Exposure to stimulating classroom instruction
- Stereotypical behavioral expectations held by authority figures, including teachers, parents, and others in the general public

Despite having preparatory experiences fairly dissimilar to boys, some girls succeed academically in science despite the obstacles they face (Richardson, Hammrich, & Livingston, 2003).

Challenge: Gender Bias and the Education of Urban Teachers

Another challenge female students must overcome is the effect of classroom teachers' perceptions of gender. Throughout world history, gender bias has been a problem that many women have strived to surmount. Although women work hard to conquer gender bias in all aspects of daily life, female students continue to struggle against considerable gender inequities within the educational system (Jones et al., 2000). Stereotypical practices concerning females and males are second nature to many members of our society. The notion that "girls do this" and "boys do that" is deeply entrenched in the American educational culture.

Unfortunately, very few in-service and preservice teacher education programs spend significant, if any, time on gender and the classroom. On average, preservice teachers participating in teacher education programs spend less than 2 hr per semester discussing issues surrounding gender equity in the classroom (Stiles, 2002). With this in mind, it is highly important that gender biases in the classroom are dispelled through heightened awareness and education in the "best practices" for gender equity. Current research on gender equity and the classroom has shown that the first step toward gender equity in classroom teaching practices is self-evaluation. In order for teachers and school administrators to promote gender equity in the classroom, educators must be conscious of their own gender biases (Jones, et al., 2000).

Females receive less attention from teachers, and this attention tends to be more often negative or contradictory. For instance, females may receive criticism for the content of work completed, yet praised for the neatness and the timeliness of the work. Males, on the other hand, are more frequently rewarded for intelligent answers and innate ability. Content is praised and appearance of work is criticized. This classroom practice leads female students to doubt themselves and their abilities, which leads to less participation in class and results in lowered self-confidence and underachievement (Sadker & Sadker, 1994).

If young Americans are to have options for their future education and multiple career choices in their adult lives, it is vital that veteran educators, school administrators, researchers, and academicians alike accept the challenge of ensuring that all students in the country have access to quality education. Furthermore, science educators must provide students with exceptional experiences that enable them to excel in the STEM areas. Undoubtedly, classroom preparation and the expertise of teachers correlate with the academic achievement of students.

As proposed by Tharp, Estrada, Dalton, and Yamauchi (2000), five standards are necessary to improve the achievement of students from culturally, ethnically, and economically diverse backgrounds. The Five Standards of Effective Pedagogy and Student Outcomes are:

- Teachers and students producing together
- Language and literacy development
- Making meaning by connecting schools to students' lives
- Teaching complex thinking
- Teaching through conversation

Research findings show a consistent, positive relationship between classroom implementation of the five standards and an increase in student test scores (Doherty, Hilberg, Pinal, & Tharp, 2003).

SISERP Programs: Meeting the Challenges

One of the many efforts to remedy the gender inequity is the Sisters in Science Equity Reform Project (SISERP). Funded by the NSF for over 10 years, the project focuses on the diversity inherent in learning through various tools by which scientific and mathematical principles can be explored, analyzed, and communicated. SISERP comprises six innovative science programs designed to foster gender equity and inclusion in STEM education: Sisters in Science™ (SIS), All Sisters in Science™ (ASIS), Sisters in Sports Science™ (SISS), Sisters in Science in the Community (SISCOM), Info-Sisters in Science Career Opportunities Matter (iSIS.com), and Sisters in Science Dissemination and Outreach Program™ (SISDO). The primary goal of the SISERP programs is to provide urban school-aged girls with access to meaningful STEM instruction in an environment unencumbered by the restrictions of stereotypical practices regarding gender.

Over the past 10 years, the SISERP has focused on two major obstacles preventing equity in science education. As evidenced by 10 years of research in the area of equity in science education, the gender gap and gender bias in the classroom tend to inhibit females from exploring careers, both academic and professional, in the sciences. SISERP was established in the interest of providing equitable avenues for all students to pursue academic success in STEM disciplines. Incorporated into the six components of SISERP are comprehensive science curricula based on national standards, through gender equity focused professional development for preservice and in-service teachers, family education programs, informal and formal science explorations, and educational components such as Saturday academies, summer camps, and after-school programs. The SISERP components are intended to reach underserved females in numerous capacities.

The premise for the SISERP lies in the continued underrepresentation of women and minorities in STEM fields. Over the past several decades, women have made considerable progress in narrowing the gender gap in STEM-related fields, but gaps persist. Statistics from the NSF (2000) revealed that in 1997 "[w]omen constituted 23% of the science and engineering labor force." Although females now account for half of all science and engineering bachelor's degrees earned, their share of bachelor's degrees in computer science has decreased from 37% in 1985 to 28% in 2001 (NSF, 2004). African Americans and Latinos are earning fewer science and engineering degrees relative to their population than are Whites (NSF, 2000).

Recent Program: The Sisters in Science in the Community Program

The most recent SISERP program is the Sisters in Science in the Community (SISCOM). The overall goal of the SISCOM program is to replicate the Sisters in Sport Science program, which is the most innovative and successful portion of the SISERP in area community-based organizations. Utilizing sports as a vehicle for learning, girls gain a better understanding of the underlying principles of science and mathematics embedded in the mechanics of participating in a sport. SISCOM is an informal science enrichment program that addresses the need for urban girls to gain equitable access to science education in a noncompetitive and academically nonthreatening community or family setting.

The SISCOM program is unique in many ways. Its inclusive target audience of middle school girls reaches students on multiple levels of intelligence, especially students with limited experiences or disability stereotypes. The hands-on curriculum is designed to meet national and local standards. Through the collaboration among the Division of Education and Equity Studies Research Center (Queens College), five community-based organizations, and the Black Women in Sport Foundation, SISCOM offers after-school programs at each community site, Saturday Sport Day events, summer science career camps, and bimonthly professional development sessions for staff and mentors.

The extended school-based program targets 6th- to 10th-grade girls. The intention is to reach a wider population of girls and to create a community approach to promoting science and mathematics literacy and career awareness. This approach also targets families that otherwise may not be involved in school-based initiatives. The project activities build upon the existing science and mathematics curriculum of the Sisters in Sport Science program through specific activities and learning methods shown to increase minority girls' interest and achievement in science and mathematics through the vehicle of sports.

The following objectives are being pursued: (a) to increase science and mathematics achievement of minority 6th- to 10th-grade girls, both with and without disabilities, through the vehicle of sport; (b) to enhance the self-identities of minority girls in the areas of self-esteem, physical fitness, skill development, goal setting, and problem solving through the vehicle of sport, science, and mathematics; (c) to increase families' and caregivers' knowledge of sports as an effective way to foster science and mathematics achievement; (d) to increase minority girls' career awareness of science, mathematics, and sport-related fields; and (e) to increase community-based organization youth workers' knowledge of, enthusiasm for, and expertise in teaching science and math to urban youth.

Unique Features of the Program

SISCOM addresses the need for urban girls to gain equitable access to science and mathematics education by using sports as a vehicle for learning. SISCOM addresses the diversity inherent in learning by using sports as the context through which scientific and mathematical principles can be explored. Through the vehicle of sports, girls not only learn the underlying principles of science and mathematics embedded in the mechanics of participating in a sport but also learn the scientific principles in an atmosphere that embraces the psycho-social-emotional connection to learning. For instance, each day, outside of the school setting, girls learn how to ride a bike, throw a ball, and jump rope. What they are not aware of are the scientific and mathematical principles inherent in performing these activities. In the classroom, girls learn these scientific and mathematical principles in a context that is foreign to their everyday experiences. They learn about the trajectory of a golf ball without connecting this principle with the actual practice of hitting a golf ball. Community–family settings provide an environment that is noncompetitive and nonthreatening academically. What is unique to the concept of SISCOM is that the academic and the everyday experiences of girls can be bridged in a community environment. To this end, the teaching and learning process embraces not only the academic principles of learning but also captures the psycho-social-emotional process of learning. In doing so, the context of learning science and mathematics is enriched for the girls. Additionally, girls begin to see and appreciate the relevance of science to their own lives.

Although programs that address the equitable achievement for all students in science and mathematics are not new, using sports as a vehicle for science and mathematics interest and achievement is unique and in the field of disabilities totally unprecedented. This approach bridges the application of concepts embedded in science and mathematics to the mechanics of participating in a sport. Sports provide a unique and innovative approach to reaching girls in a friendly atmosphere while they learn concepts usually too abstract for them to grasp, due to their limited experience or disability stereotypes. In doing so, SISCOM successfully reaches students on multiple levels of intelligence and strengthens the education of students in science and mathematics by creating a diverse and inclusive atmosphere. The AAUW (1998) publication *Gender Gaps: Where Schools Still Fail Our Children* suggests that "Sports participation in general is linked not just to higher academic achievement but also to better physical and mental health, and greater leadership capacity" (p. 74).

A second unique feature of this project is the focus on middle school science and mathematics. Middle school students often experience a drop in grades due to lack of organizational skills and difficulty in adjusting to the requirements of several teachers. Learning science and mathematics principles through participating in sports help girls through this transition phase and reduces the chances of "falling through the cracks." Girls and minority youth in the middle and high school years tend to struggle with self-esteem, physical fitness, skill development, goal setting, and problem solving. Sports is the one ideal mechanism to empower girls and minority youth during these uncertain years to explore their self-identities. Research links physical activity for girls to higher self-esteem, positive body image, and lifelong health (AAUW, 1998, p. 20), and " ... involvement in activities valued by school (athletics and the arts) leads to higher self-esteem, positive attitudes toward school, and less self-destructive behavior." (AAUW, 1998, p.77). By using sports as a vehicle for learning scientific principles, the SISCOM program responds to the national call for creating innovative programs that provide access to the latest strategies in promoting science literacy in urban communities.

A third unique SISCOM feature is its efforts on truly inclusive STEM education that transfers from the regular and special education classrooms into the community and beyond. Historically, two critical barriers have challenged children with disabilities: their lack of appropriate science and math education in their home classrooms, and their increasing sense of isolation and loneliness when leaving the protected school environment. Although families and teachers try to emphasize recreation and leisure for students with disabilities, these are the same children who are never asked to participate in neighborhood activities or chosen for after-school sports. In fact, the primary concern reported by adults who have grown up with disabilities is a pervading sense of isolation and loneliness. SISCOM is a proactive effort to change that, while also sparking academic achievement and future STEM careers.

Table 1   Modules/Units

Program/ Grade Level	Unit/Module	Unit/Module	Unit/Module	Unit/Module
Year 1	Geometry— Tennis	Forces—Fencing	Motion— Basketball	Mechanics— Golf
Year 2	Biomechanics— Track & Field	Anatomy & Physiology— Volleyball	Health— Soccer	
Year 3	Research	Research	Research	Research

Note: Year 3 experiences are not unit/modules

Modes of Inquiry

Through the utilization of minority athletes, university undergraduate and graduate students, and community-based staff, SISCOM provides a weekly after-school program, special Saturday sports events, and summer internships for sixth-grade girls; biweekly Saturday academies and career camps for seventh-grade girls; and academic research internships for eighth-grade girls. The sixth-grade curriculum features science activities linked to tennis, fencing, basketball, and golf. The seventh-grade units are centered around track and field, volleyball, and soccer. All sport science activities are matched to the AAAS Benchmarks and state-specific science and mathematics standards, and have an equity focus (see Table 1).

Program Results

Because the SISCOM program is relatively new, only baseline data are available at this time. However, the program is modeled after the successful Sisters in Sport Science (SISS) program, a 3-year intervention involving 529 girls from six middle schools, their teachers, college students, minority athletes, and mentors. It offers a second level of intervention in the middle schools for the elementary girls involved in the SIS program in the fourth and fifth grades. Findings over the past 3 years show that the girls in the program have increased their interest and achievement in science and mathematics and have noted the relevance of these subjects to the sports in which they have participated to date.

The sports science curriculum is standards based and has an equitable focus. The entire curriculum includes 40 activities driven by science and mathematics standards that feature a sport as the vehicle through which science or mathematics is learned.

For each of the after-school and Saturday academy activities, the middle school students took individually administered pre- and posttests addressing skills and concepts inherent to the science and mathematics concepts studied during the activity. The instruments were developed by the science faculty on staff, and the

Table 2   Sisters in Science Pre- and Posttest Mean Scores and Standard Deviations

Sport	Science	N	Pretest M	SD	Posttest M	SD	Gain
Basketball	Motion	32	27	16.5	77	23.3	50
Fencing	Forces	40	39	21.4	86	14.2	48
Golf	Mechanics	50	34	19.4	93	8.6	59
Soccer	Mechanics, engineering	35	28	19.0	88	12.2	60
Tennis	Geometry	52	29	22.1	84	17.3	55
Track (field)	Aerodynamics	33	36	22.3	90	12.5	54
Track (running)	Biomechanics	42	33	15.5	60	18.7	28
Volleyball	Aerodynamics	48	28	19.4	77	22.5	49

items were carefully matched with the content of the activity. Sample questions include: What does the word *velocity* mean? What is speed? What is a projectile? What is a trajectory?

Pretests were administered at the beginning of the day's activity, and posttests were administered at the conclusion of the day's activity. The pretests and posttests were identical instruments. Four questions were asked for each activity. The students' responses were open-ended, allowing the girls to express their understanding of the content. Each question was scored as correct or incorrect.

Gain scores were analyzed using a simple t test. Based on raw scores, the percentage of correct responses was used as the measure. The data consistently show statistically significant mean increases in content knowledge from pretest to posttest, ranging from 28 to 60 percentage points ($p < .01$ in each case). Looking at these gains in a different way, in every case the lower quartile on the posttest exceeded the upper quartile on the pretest. The results from the after-school program and Saturday academies are summarized in Table 2.

INTERVENTION PROGRAMS AND EDUCATIONAL REFORM

Persons interested in reforming science education are advocating measures that are beneficial to all students; therefore, such moves should help increase the number of women considering science-related careers. Reformers advocate the abolition of tracking because track placements in curriculum tend to be fixed and long-term, and tracking exacerbates differences among students by limiting opportunities to learn. Lower-track science courses may actually limit students' opportunities to learn the subject because of restricted content and diminished outcomes. Reformers are urging that science curricula focus on personal needs, create career awareness, and include the study of science–technology–society in terms of problems and issues found in the community or discussed through the media. Reformers also advocate that more hands-on activities be used in science, preferably in a cooperative learning situation. Girls benefit from such instructional tactics. If, as some research data imply, current teaching strategies have led to early gender differences in attitudes, which then lead to differences in participation, changing teaching methods as well as revising the curriculum should help counter this trend.

Klein (1990, pp. 5–11) has identified 10 "common ground science process goals" addressed in current science education reform reports:

1. Enabling all to experience success in science
2. Making the total science curriculum more unified and flexible
3. Establishing requirements and procedures so that students will take more mathematics, science, and technology courses
4. Making science curricula personally meaningful
5. Ensuring that tests and assessment procedures are unbiased and supportive of meaningful science instruction
6. Using heterogeneous and cooperative groups to promote a high level of participation for all students
7. Arranging for meaningful science role models
8. Supporting and enriching science education opportunities rather than ineffective remedial science education programs
9. Increasing cultural sensitivity in instructional materials and classroom interactions
10. Increasing support for science achievement from parents, peers, and the community

Such goals, Klein believes, will work toward equity as well as educational reform.

Although there is evidence that the gender gap in math and science achievement has been somewhat addressed, it is also important to note that these advances have occurred within the broader context of the nationwide gender equity reform movement. Today, the education standards for science, National Science Education Standards (NSES), and mathematics, National Council of Teachers of Mathematics (NCTM), address not only student learning but also content-area pedagogy, assessment, teacher training, and community development. Also of note is the fact that federal, state, and local initiatives continue to be designed and implemented to move not just female students but all Americans forward in mathematics and science. The authors of SISERP feel that the project stands as one of many gender equity reform initiatives that have had an impact on science and mathematics learning.

REFERENCES

Allen, D. (1995). Encouraging success in female students: Helping girls develop mathematics and science skills. *Gifted Child Today Magazine, 12*(2), 44–45.

American Association of University Women (AAUW) (1998). *Gender gaps: Where schools still fail our children*. Washington, DC: Author.

American Association of University Women. (2000). *Tech savvy: Educating girls in the new computer age*. Retrieved January 20, 2005, from http://www.aauw.org.

American Association of University Women. (2004). *Under the microscope: A decade of gender equity projects in the sciences*. Washington, DC: Author.

Association for the Education of Teachers in Science. (1996). *Professional knowledge standards for science teacher educators: Position statement*. Pittsburgh, PA: Author.

Blosser, P. (2005). *Procedures to increase the entry of women in science-related careers*. Retrieved December 8, 2005, from http://www.kidsource.com/kidsource/content2/girls_and_science.html.

Boland, P. (1995). *Gender-fair math*. Newton, MA: Education Development Center.

Braswell, J.S., Lutkus, A.D., Grigg, W.S., Santapau, S.L., Tay-Lim, & Johnson, M. (2001). *The nation's report card: Mathematics 2000*. Washington, DC: National Center for Education Statistics.

California State University Institute for Educational Reform. (1998). *Doing what matters most: Investing in quality teaching*. Retrieved April 21, 2004, from http://www.csus.edu/ier/reports/LDHRpt.pdf.

Clewell, B.C., & Campbell, P.B. (2002). Taking stock: Where we've been, where we are, where we're going. *Journal of Women and Minorities in Science and Engineering* (8), 255–284.

Cochron-Smith, M. (1995). Color blindness and basket making are not the answers: Confronting the dilemmas of race, culture, and language diversity in teacher education. *American Educational Research Journal, 32*(3), 493–522.

Doherty, R.W., Hilberg, R.S., Pinal, A., & Tharp, R.G. (2003). Five standards and student achievement. *National Association for Bilingual Education Journal of Research and Practice, 1*(1), 1–24.

Driver, R. (1995). Constructivist approaches to science teaching. In L.P. Steffe & J. Gale (Eds.), *Constructivism in education* (pp. 385–400). Hillsdale, NJ: Lawrence Erlbaum.

Eder, D., Evans, C., & Parker, S. (1995). *School talk: Gender and adolescent culture*. New Brunswick, NJ: Rutgers University Press.

Gardner, H. (2000). *Intelligence reframed: Multiple intelligences for the 21st century*. New York: Basic Books.

Hammrich, P., Richardson, G., & Livingston, B. (2000). Sisters in science: Confronting equity in science and mathematics. *Journal of Women and Minorities in Science and Engineering* (6), 207–220.

Jones, K., Evans, C., Byrd, R., & Campbel, K. (2000). Gender equity training and teaching behavior. *Journal of Instructional Psychology, 27*(3).

Jones, M.G., & Wheately, J. (1990). Gender differences in teacher-student interactions science classroom. *Journal of Research in Science Teaching, 27*(9), 861–874.

Kahle, J.B., & Meece, J. (1994). Research on gender issues in the classroom. In A.B. Champagne (Ed.). *Handbook of research on science teaching and learning*. New York: Macmillan.

Klein, C.A. (1991). What research says about girls and science. *Science and Children, 27*(2), 28–31.

Klein, S.S. (1990). *The role of research in identifying the "common ground" goals to promote sex equity in science and technology education.* Paper presented at the annual meeting of the American Educational Research Association, San Diego, CA.

Kozol, J. (2000) Still separate and unequal. *US Catholic, 65*(10), 18–21.

Ladson-Billings, G. (1995). Toward a theory of culturally relevant pedagogy. *Journal of Educational Research, 32*(3), 465–491.

Linn, M.C. (1990). *Gender, mathematics, and science: Trends and recommendations.* Paper prepared for the Council of Chief State Officers Summer Institute, Mystic, CT.

Malcolm, S.M. (1997). Girls succeeding in science, mathematics, and technology: Who works and what works. *American Association of University Women Conference Proceedings*, Philadelphia, PA.

Mann, J. (1994). Bridging the gender gap: How girls learn. *Streamlined Seminar, 12*(2).

Martin, M.V. (1996, April). *Inside a gender-sensitive classroom: An all girls physics class.* Paper presented at the annual meeting of the National Association for Research in Science Teaching, St. Louis, MO. ERIC Document Reproduction Service No. ED-398053.

McLaughlin, M.W., Irby, M.A., & and Langman, J. (1994). *Urban sanctuaries: Neighborhood organizations in the lives and futures of inner-city youth.* San Francisco: Jossey-Bass.

National Center for Education Statistics. (2002). *The nation's report card: Science highlights 2000.* Retrieved April 11, 2004, from http://nces.ed.gov/nationareportcard/pdf/main200/s002452.pdf.

National Research Council. (1996). *National science education standards.* Washington, DC: National Academy Press.

National Science Foundation (NSF). (1990). *Women and minorities in science and engineering* (NSF 90-301). Washington, DC: Author.

National Science Foundation. (2000). *Women, minorities, and persons with disabilities, 2000.* Retrieved April 22, 2004, from http://www.nsf.gov/sbe/srs/nsf00327/frames.htm.

Nieto, S. (2003). *Affirming diversity: The sociopolitical context of multicultural education.* Boston: Allyn & Bacon.

Northrop, D. (2003). Introducing equity in the classroom. [Electronic Version]. *Women's Educational Equity Resource Center Digest.* Retrieved from http://www2.edc.org.

Orenstein, P. (1994). *Schoolgirls: Young women, self-esteem, and the confidence gap.* New York: Doubleday.

Pipher, M. (1994). *Reviving Ophelia: Saving the selves of adolescent girls.* New York: Ballantine.

Richardson, G, Hammrich, P., & Livingston, B. (2003). Improving elementary school girls' attitudes, perceptions, and achievement in science and mathematics: Hindsights and new visions of the Sisters in Science program as an equity reform model. *Journal of Women and Minorities in Science and Engineering* (9), 333–348.

Richmond, G., & Neureither, B. (1998). Making a case for cases. *American Biology Teacher, 60*(5), 335–342.

Rodriguez, A.J. (1997). The dangerous discourse of invisibility: A critique of the National Research Council's national science education standards. *Journal of Research in Science Teaching, 34*, 19–38.

Rutherford, F.J., & Ahlgren, A. (1990). *Science for all Americans.* New York: Oxford University Press.

Sadker, M., & Sadker, D. (1994). *Failing at fairness: How America's schools shortchange girls.* New York: Touchstone.

Sanchez, K., Kellow, T., & Ye, R. (2000). *A comparison of Stanford 9 (SAT-9) achievement performance across grade, gender, ethnicity, and educational program placement.* Paper presented at the annual meeting of the American Education Research Association Conference, New Orleans, LA. (ERIC Document Reproduction Service No. ED-451284).

Sanders, J. (2002). Something is missing from teacher education: Attention to two genders. [Electronic Version]. *Phi Delta Kappa.* Retrieved from http://www.josanders. com/pdf/phidelta.pdf.

Schnorr, D., & Ware, H.W. (2001). Moving beyond a deficit model to describe and promote the career development of at-risk youth. *Journal of Career Development, 27,* 247–263.

Shakeshaft, C. (1995). Reforming science education to include girls. *Theory into Practice,* 34(1), 74–79.

Shepardson, D.P., & Pizzini, E.L. (1992). Gender bias in female elementary teachers' perceptions of the science ability of students. *Science Education, 76*(2), 147–153.

Stiles, L. (2002) *Gender equity in the classroom and the effect of conscious inhibition of gender bias.* Lyon College. Retrieved April 11, 2002, from http://www.lyoncollege. edu/webdata/groups/scarf/stiles%202002.htm.

Task Force on Women, Minorities, and Handicapped in Science and Technology. (1989). *Changing America: The new face of science and engineering.* Washington, DC: Author.

Tharp, R.G., Estrada, P., Dalton, S.S., & Yamauchi, L. (2000). *Teaching transformed: Achieving excellence, fairness, inclusion, and harmony.* Boulder, CO: Westview Press.

Tolley, K. (2003). *The science education of American girls: A historical perspective.* London: Routledge Falmer.

United States Department of Education. (2004, April). *Teachers to listen, learn, share. practices to improve student achievement.* Retrieved April 22, 2004, from http:// www.ed.gov/news/pressreleases/2004/04/04212004.html.

IV

WHAT IS TO BE DONE?

Public concern about the negative impact of current educational "reform" efforts is increasing. Too often, though, this concern focuses on the problems of implementation rather than the fundamental flaws in the vision of reform. Bill Ayers urges us to keep singing through these dark times, so that our songs can illuminate the path to more meaningful relationships between teachers, students, and communities. He brings us back to the potential of each classroom to uniquely represent "the intentional design of a particular intelligence" of a teacher and her vision for how she and the children in her classroom will engage with one another in the learning process. This teacher is an active, engaged professional, a planner, a decision maker, a curriculum designer, and a doer. The professional concerns of this teacher are focused on nurturing and challenging the students in her classroom.

This teacher's professional concerns are not addressed by the New York City Department of Education's policies on teacher support, which Susan Ohanian aptly sums up as "all you have to do is pay them on time and give them supplies." This teacher's professional concerns are also not acknowledged by the hodge-podge of standards and scripted curricula that constrain her ability to provide classroom experiences that take advantage of what the children in her class bring to school with them, which connect "school learning" to the price of asparagus in the local supermarket.

Bill Ayers and Susan Ohanian both see a lot of problems, and many missed opportunities, in the standards-based, depersonalized classrooms spawned by current educational policies. But Ayers and Ohanian also both offer us examples of how professional and caring teachers continue to find ways to personalize their response to the lives of their students and, in so doing, offer models for learning and teaching that represent authentic educational reform.

12

Educational Reform

WILLIAM AYERS

Bertolt Brecht asked in his poem "Motto": "In the dark times, will there also be singing?" And his answer was "Yes, there will be singing. / About the dark times."

Brecht knew something about the dark times—having been hounded and attacked and driven from the United States in the 1950s—and he wrote brilliantly about them in his play *Galileo.*

Galileo's breathtaking discoveries about the movement of the planets and the stars ignite in him the desire to pursue a particularly radical idealism: "The cities are narrow and so are brains," he declares boldly. "Superstition and plague. But now the word is: since it is so, it does not remain so. For everything moves, my friend." With this, Galileo launches a revolution—it is *his* idealism against the idealism of the church that must, in time, condemn the radical for challenging their privileged and dominant orthodoxy.

Galileo seems at first unstoppable. "It was always said that the stars were fastened to a crystal vault so they could not fall," he says. "Now we have taken heart and let them float in the air, without support, they are embarked on a great voyage—like us, who are also without support and embarked on a great voyage."

Here, Galileo ups the ante. He questions common sense, and he challenges the establishment in the realm of its own authority. For the church, after all, the great voyage we are on cannot be thought of as occurring without support. It is, in fact, the opposite: a sanctioned and planned voyage, the steps entirely mapped out with clockwork precision and mathematical certainty, and all the support we need in the institution of the church itself.

Clearly, more than theories of astronomy are in play here. The ideas, surely, but also the joy, the excitement, the reckless hope—all mark Galileo as a radical and an activist. After all, he could have just written a book, as Copernicus did, and let it go at that. But Galileo raised the stakes as high as he could. He wanted to teach the world. He wanted to make a revolution.

Galileo's struggle is punctuated with joy and grief, hope and despair, pain and torment, and pressure, but when he finally capitulates and denounces *what he knows to be true*, when he betrays his fire to learn and to teach, and is received by the church back "into the ranks of the faithful," he is exiled from humanity—by his own words. In the end, he is confronted by a former student, one of his crest-fallen disciples: "Many on all sides followed you with their eyes and ears," he says, "believing that you stood, not only for a particular view of the movement of the stars, but even more for the liberty of teaching—in all fields. Not then for any particular thoughts, but for the right to think at all. Which is in dispute." The right to think at all—a right that is in deep dispute now in our schools and in our society.

Martin Luther King Jr. famously said that the arc of the moral universe is long, but that it bends toward justice. This is not a scientific conclusion or an established fact, but rather an inspired expression of hope for a world that could be, but is not yet, a world that requires all of us to imagine and to act on behalf of freedom and enlightenment. It is a hope for humanity itself.

Our work here and now is to sing about the dark times, for the dark times are upon us. And in these times, it is essential to begin with a particularly precious ideal—the belief that education at its best is an enterprise geared to helping every human being reach the full measure of his or her humanity, inviting people on a journey to become more thoughtful and more capable, more powerful and courageous, more exquisitely human in their projects and their pursuits. That ideal—always revolutionary, and never more so than today—is central to achieving a democratic and open society. And like democracy itself, it is an ideal that is never quite finished, never easily or finally summed up; it is neither a commodity with readily recognized features nor a product for consumption. No. Rather, democracy, like education, is an aspiration to be continually nourished, engaged, and exercised, a dynamic, expansive experiment that must be achieved over and over again by every individual and each successive generation if it is to live at all. This is what makes teaching so exhilarating and so exhausting, so dazzling and so ordinary, and so lofty and so low at the same time.

The Chinese ideogram for *person* depicts a figure grounded in the earth and stretching toward heaven. What is she reaching for? What dream is she pursuing? Why so seemingly becalmed on one end, yet so relentlessly restless on the other? The character suggests the destiny of every human being: to be fated, but also to be free; to be both free and fated. Each of us is planted in the mud and the muck of daily existence, thrust into a world not of our choosing, and tethered then to hard-rock reality; each of us is also endowed with a mind able to reflect on that reality, to choose who to be in light of the cold facts and the merely given. We each have a spirit capable of joining that mind and soaring overhead, poised to transgress boundaries, destroy obstacles, and transform ourselves and our world.

Teachers live this tension with intense urgency—we meet our students as we are and as they are, right here and right now, finite but incomplete; we enlarge and expand in order to engage their minds and fire their hearts, to provoke their imaginations and our own. We jump into our work headfirst, and we toil in the common fields while we hold open the possibility of something more, something transcendent—enlightenment, perhaps, and liberation. Each morning, as we rise and venture toward a new day, and later, as we approach our classrooms, we might remind ourselves that a teacher's destination is always the same: that special spot between heaven and earth, that plain but spectacular space where we might once again try to teach toward freedom.

Each of us is born into a going world, thrust into an existing community, a society to step into that is up and running, filled with color and noise and texture, coming from somewhere in particular, and heading who knows where? We are creatures of that going world, and we are also, soon enough, creators of it.

We are born into company, intimate at first, and soon enough burst open into something larger, something pulling us forward. We press our faces against the glass, and then we open the door and step out.

Being thrust into the going world is to confront objective space, to face facts, all the givens I did not choose.

But soon, if we pay attention, we notice that there are choices to be made, decisions at hand. We decide who to be, how to act, what to do in light of the merely given. The experience of choice, of possibility, occurs against the hard edges of peril and pain, of hopelessness and despair.

This is what we know: Every human being is unfinished. Every one of us is in process, in motion, in medias res—moving from place to place, from here to there, migrating, sometimes in patterns and sometimes not, growing, sent into exile on a certain day and on another day returning, learning, changing, seeing old things in surprising new ways, entering strange rooms, coming out, taking right and wrong turns, lost and then found, and then lost again, meeting new people, passing through, riding on a bus, train, truck, plane, or—best of all, because we move at the speed of human reaction, unencumbered by steel and glass—a bicycle, drawing right and wrong conclusions, finding something, losing something else, practicing, reaching, missing, stretching, going, going, going. This is what we know of human beings: We are incomplete, and we are aware of our incompleteness. We are on a voyage, on the make and on the move.

The teacher who honors this defining incompleteness senses intuitively that to label a student is wrong in both senses of the word: it is immoral, and it is hopelessly stupid, wildly inaccurate. It is immoral to reduce a human being to an object. It is stupid to try to flatten a three-dimensional, darting, thrusting figure into a one-dimensional thing, because it creates a grotesque misrepresentation: to his community Harold may be a generous helper, but to the school he is a "reluctant reader"; among her friends Luz is known as an artist and a creative spirit, but at school she is reduced to an acronym, BD (behavior disordered); and all around the city Harp is an admired poet, but at school he is ADHD (attention deficit hyperactivity disordered). Something is out of focus, out of balance in these lopsided labels and judgments.

All of us are actors and subjects, stars of our own lives; each of us is our very own author and inventor, agent and manager, director, curator, coordinator, and chief of operations. Each human being is a project, and the human project is a project of inquiry conducted in the world and with one another, a project of restlessness and relentlessness, a ceaseless struggle to know and to be—the primal struggle that begins at birth and only ends with death. We seek the truth; we want to be free.

Students burst into classrooms with energy, desire, and intention. Each brings a voice, a set of experiences, knowledge and know-how, and a way of seeing, thinking, and being. Each, again, is an unruly spark of meaning-making energy on a voyage of discovery.

Right away the lessons of school try to assert themselves—lessons about obedience and conformity, about hierarchy and one's place in it, about the suppressing of desire and the delaying of satisfaction, about boredom, irrelevance, and meaninglessness. If the lessons begin to take, the life is being sucked out of students. The structure of school, the expectations, and the dull repetitiveness of regular routines, traditions, and assumptions will have accomplished something sinister. Students become arid, flat, and opaque. They arrived vivid and propulsive, full of color, noise, and life, but now they are still and lifeless, unseen, unheard, and invisible even to themselves. The late Lillian Weber, champion of children at the Workshop Center for Open Education at the City College of New York, once said: "They begin school an exclamation point and a question mark; too often they leave as a plain period." This is what teachers who teach toward freedom oppose.

Making students invisible is a singular accomplishment; it is aided by tests and grades that function more as autopsies than diagnostics, the well-meaning but entangling ideology of providing "services," the fragmentation of the curriculum, all manner of myths and half-truths, and received thinking about students and their communities.

A commitment to the visibility of students as persons requires a radical reversal. Teachers, whatever else they do, must become students of their students. The student becomes a source of knowledge, information, and energy; actor, speaker, creator, constructor, thinker, doer—a teacher as well as a learner. Together, students and teachers explore, inquire, investigate, search, ask questions, criticize, make connections, draw tentative conclusions, pose problems, act, seek the truth, name this and that phenomenon, circle back, plunge forward, reconsider, gather steam, pause, reflect, reimagine, wonder, build, assert themselves, listen carefully, speak, and so on.

This reversal, this dialectic, is recognized by any teacher who is paying attention. Plato saw it, and so did Rousseau. In *Democracy and Education*, John Dewey, speaking about shared activity, said: "The teacher is a learner, and the learner is, without knowing it, a teacher—and upon the whole, the less consciousness there is, on either side, of either giving or receiving instruction, the better."

Becoming a student of her students, the teacher opposes the manipulative reduction of their lives into neatly labeled packages. She resists both the easy embrace of oversimplified identities—a reliance on a single aspect of life to say it all—and the erosive gesture of fragmenting lives into conceptually crude categories. Her stance is identification *with*, not identification *of*, her students. Her approach is solidarity, not service.

This does not mean that the teacher busies herself with knowing everything about her students while avoiding knowing anything at all about herself. Hers is not the stance of surveillance; she is not the undercover cop wearing a wire. She is side by side, hand in hand, working in concert with her students to know the world and, if necessary, to change it. Teachers must commit to know themselves as they, too, change and grow.

The teacher takes a step out from behind the desk, away from the lectern, off the pedestal, and perhaps off the cliff. There is a feeling of vertigo as the teacher looks with new eyes, as the familiar is made strange. There is risk and there is fear—hard work, this never-ending attentiveness, this improvisation—but there is satisfaction, as well. She frees herself from the terror of teaching. She no longer has to pretend to be a God, all-knowing, all-powerful, beneficent one minute and punishing the next. She can shed the hypocrisy and phoniness of the teacher pose and begin to face herself as she really is. She can also discover her students as they really are, and recognize that there is always more to know in all directions. Who in the world are they?

In a lovely French documentary film called *To Be and to Have* (2003), we meet Georges Lopez, a middle-aged, one-room-schoolhouse teacher in rural France caring for a dozen or so youngsters who appear to range in age from 5 or 6 to about 12. The film opens with a long, still shot of the empty classroom—chairs on desks, brightly painted pictures everywhere, plants, photographs, pencils, and markers. It is the classroom at rest and one anticipates a sudden explosion of youthful energy as the day begins. But the camera lingers. And then, without fanfare, a turtle steps out from beneath a bookshelf, and then another. We watch the two plod slowly across the floor in a ponderous point, counterpoint.

The dance of the turtles is a metaphor for Lopez's teaching: things are slow, nothing is hurried. In a world of instant everything, of moving sidewalks and staircases, of fast food and processed words, Lopez acknowledges that the growth of a human being takes time. There is time to become deeply involved, time to pursue projects, time to make and correct mistakes, and time to resolve the little conflicts that will always erupt in a group. There is little evidence of the characteristic superficial encounter and the hurried plan—minutes here, minutes there—and the curriculum of "I know; you don't know." All five senses are engaged, big kids helping younger students, everyone with responsibilities, expectations, jobs, goals, and limits. There is a palpable feeling of growth and change, an exhilaration that our classroom now is not as it was yesterday, nor as it will be tomorrow, and neither are the students and the teacher. They are on a voyage with no clear beginning and no end in sight.

In a second-grade classroom I visited recently in Chicago, I saw a job chart, a cleanup chart, a free-time chart, and a chart of favorite books; a street map, a transit map, and several distinctly different world maps sharing space with student-made maps of the classroom, the neighborhood, and their own homes; a cooking area with a "juice bar" and colorful posters depicting "Noodles," "Chile," "Mushrooms," "Cheeses of the World," and "Natural Dyes"; each child's specific self-authored and handmade stamp, diary, dictionary, thesaurus, "tiny books," icon, math books, puzzles, and board games; puppets; blocks; a bowl of leaves; a sofa and a rug; two large tree stumps; and a bin of scrap wood. Like Lopez's classroom the environment felt rich and deep, inviting, and potentially engaging. I was dazzled by all the little things I had never seen or thought of before: The idea of a self-selected icon for each child, a symbol such as a sun or a toothbrush, which appeared next to the child's name on the board, the cubby, and books and papers, struck me as a smart addition to early reading; all the personalized handmade books extending even these very young students' sense of themselves as creators and authors. But what impressed me most about this collection of artifacts was not this or that piece in particular. Rather, I was struck by the sense that this learning space was the intentional design of a particular intelligence; that the architect of the environment had a purpose and a vision for her students and herself; and that her hopes, priorities, and commitments—moral, intellectual, social, individual—were evident in dazzling detail in her classroom.

As far as the education of children goes, rather than teach what Natalia Ginzberg, the Italian novelist, calls "the little virtues," we might aspire to teach the great ones. Not thrift, for example, but generosity, not caution but courage, not tact but love for our neighbors, and not a longing for success but a desire to know and to be. The great virtues come from some deep and hard-to-name place, an instinct, perhaps, but it is clear that with their development the little virtues will fall into their proportionate place.

Teachers must think about the environments they create; they must examine them, reflect upon them, and then rethink and reconstruct them. What would an environment built around the great virtues look like? The preschool wizard

Vivian Gussin Paley wrote a wise book called *You Can't Say You Can't Play* (1992) illuminating the central place of moral reflection and ethical action in the kindergarten. How would a teacher create a space where the great virtues were visible and available, modeled and rehearsed, enacted and demonstrated? Take the last great virtue in Ginzberg's list, a desire to know and to be. Surely a teacher with that in mind would recognize the importance of nourishing a sense of confidence and competence, feelings of self-love combined with compassion, and empathy for others; to be ethical is not to be perfect, but it is to strive for awareness, to choose, to try.

Each of us—each of you, each of your teachers, and each of your students—is born into a "going world," a dynamic site of action and interaction stretching back into deep history and forward toward infinity. Each of us encounters a historical flow, a social surround, and a cultural web. And each of us—each of you, each of your students—faces the task of developing an identity within the turmoil of multiplicity, of inventing and reinventing a self in a complex tangle of relationships and conflicting realities, of finding an "I" against a hard backdrop of "it," of facticity and "thingification."

All students, from preschool through adult education, bring two powerful, propulsive, and expansive questions with them each day into every classroom. Although largely unstated and implicit, even unconscious, these questions are nonetheless essential. Who in the world am I, or who am I in the world? What in the world are my choices and my chances? These are simple questions on the surface, but they roil with hidden and surprising meanings, always yeasty, unpredictable, and potentially volcanic. They are, in part, questions of identity in formation and, in part, questions of geography: of boundaries and of limits, but also of aspirations and of possibilities. Enrolling in a literacy class at the community center or an English language class at a local college, leaving home to attend a university, starting high school or kindergarten—these questions boom inside: Who in the world am I? What place is this? What will become of me here? What larger universe awaits me? What shall I make of what I have been made? What are my choices?

No teacher can ever answer these questions definitively, for there is too much going on; life is too vast, too complex. The wise teacher knows that the answers lie within the students' minds, hearts, and hands. Still, she acknowledges that the questions exist, and that they persevere. The wise teacher looks for opportunities to prod the questions, to agitate and awaken, and to pursue them across a range of boundaries, known as well as unknown.

Who in the world am I? Knowing that the question exists, that it abides, points to a compact between teacher and student, largely improvisational, often implied. Brought to light, made conscious, and articulated, it sounds something like this: I see you as a full human being, worthy of my effort and attention; I will do my best on your behalf; I will work hard and take you seriously on every appropriate level. In turn, you must, by your own lights, capture your education for yourself: seize it, take hold of it, and grasp it in your own hands, in your own way, and in your own time.

Committed and aware teachers, wrestling to engage this agreement, must endeavor to accomplish two crucial tasks: (a) to convince students, often against a background of having attended what we might call "obedience training school," that there is no such thing as receiving an education as a passive receptor or an inert vessel—in that direction lies nothing but subservience, indoctrination, and worse. All real education is and must always be self-education. (b) The second task is to demonstrate to students, and to oneself, through daily effort and interaction, that they are valued, that their humanity is honored, and that their growth, enlightenment, and liberation are of paramount concern. We take the side of the student.

Louisa Cruz-Acosta, a second-grade teacher at the Muscota School in New York City, develops a curricular theme each year. The theme in her 2003–2004 classroom was "Making Space." The children were learning to make space in their lives, their minds, and their hearts for one another, for their neighbors, for members of the larger community, for animals, and for different cultures and new ideas. One of the Latino kids referred fondly to "*this* America," meaning he knew more than one, and yet he embraced his new home, his classmates, as a unique "gathering of souls."

Louisa tries to create in her classroom an "island of decency," a safe harbor, where the most fraught issues can be talked about respectfully, candidly, and deeply. Louisa communicates a vital sense to each student: It matters that you are here. Stay awhile. Speak and listen. Come back tomorrow.

She posits rules for herself and others that can help to create these islands of decency: Listen. View everyone as an individual, not as a representative of a group. Respect silence. Learn to live with questions that have no easy answers. Ask first; speak later. Be conscious of the way you use the words "we," "they," and "you."

What and who do we see as we look out at our students? A sea of undifferentiated faces? A set of IQs and test scores, a collection of deficits? Are there any options at hand? And how do we position ourselves? As master and commander, potentate or patriarch? Do we rule our domain from a particular symbolic space, a throne, say, or a massive oak desk or a lectern? What are the alternatives?

The fundamental message of the teacher—the graduate school lecturer, the high school biology teacher, the preschool teacher, and everyone in between—is this: You can change your life. The good teacher provides recognition and holds out the possibility of growth and a change in direction, the possibility of a new and different outcome: Here's a sonnet, a formula, an equation, a way of seeing, figuring, or imagining. Take hold of your life, engage the world, and you must change.

We notice that our students are endowed with active minds, restless bodies, and dynamic hearts and spirits. They are on the go. And full of surprises. Each brings a unique set of experiences and capacities to class, and each is filled with his or her own hopes and aspirations. Do we know what they are? How can we find out?

We begin by standing *with*, not above, our students. We share their predicaments, and we do so in solidarity with them. We look beyond deficits to assets and capacities, strengths and abilities, something solid that we can build upon. We seek some common ground to pursue growth and development.

Just like us, each of our students contains some spit and snap, some fire. Can we sit? Can they? None of our students is fixed or motionless, none entirely quiet or still—and if they appear thus, it is an illusion—every one is churning and charging, packed with energy, a quality that physicists define as the potential for change. This is how we might see them: as unruly sparks of meaning-making energy on a voyage of discovery through life. They are poised to change. So are we.

13

In a Time of Universal Deceit, Telling the Truth Is a Revolutionary Act

SUSAN OHANIAN

When I became a teacher, I was stunned to read the union contract and learn that, by contractual obligation, the New York City Board of Education must provide adequate toilet paper supply in the teacher's restrooms. At the time, I wondered how a union of professionals could be so petty. A few years of teaching showed me that if an item is not grievable by contract stipulation, the teacher cannot depend on having it.

Take a look at the Education Plan for the City of New York School, Year 2004–2005, prepared for the Department of Education by the Education Committee of the New York City Council (Moskowitz, 2003). The Education Committee offers this plan for *Teacher and Principal Morale and Quality of Life:*

> **Needs and Goals:** Teachers must be treated as professionals and given the tools they need to do excellent work. To accomplish this, the Department should demonstrate improvement in the following areas:

> - Paying all teachers, including **new** hires, promptly. All employees must receive their first paychecks no later than one pay period after the start of the school year.
> - Providing benefits promptly. Health insurance and others benefits must be available for use as soon as the employee becomes eligible to receive them.
> - Providing enough school supplies for all classrooms. No teacher or principal should be forced to buy essential classroom supplies with his or her own money.

- Giving every teacher an e-mail address and access to a computer to use that e-mail address.
- Providing each school that needs new or upgraded copy machines with them.

There you have it: In the New York City Council's vision, to treat a teacher professionally, all you have to do is pay them on time and give them supplies.

Grateful for every paper clip they can wrest from the system, veteran teachers lose sight of what professionalism might be, and new teachers starting on their careers have no experience whatsoever of what professionalism should be. It suits plenty of corporate-politico interests that all they know is powerlessness.

- Professionals have power; they have control over decision making in their own classrooms.
- Professionals have power; they are not told what must appear on bulletin boards. Or when to sit on the carpet.

What is happening in New York City is an exaggeration of what is going on around the country. The media bombards us with constant and continual messages along similar themes:

- Corporate-politico functionaries trumpet a kindergarten crisis. Preschoolers are approaching the kindergarten door without the necessary phonetic talents for success in kindergarten. And these days success in kindergarten is declared as being able to read.
- Political fiat decrees that third graders cannot go to fourth grade if they do not demonstrate reading proficiency at an arbitrary level on a secret test, which professional educators are not allowed to examine for accuracy, fairness, or reliability.
- High schoolers are refused a high school diploma if they do not pass college-level exit exams that include higher math, which the Business Roundtable insists is necessary for jobs in the 21st century. They also have to write an essay responding to such literary luminaries as Roger Ascham, a 16th-century scholar known for his essays on archery.
- In such a system, it goes without saying that masses of teachers are also deemed inadequate. "Not highly qualified" is the federal term.
- Of late, we are hearing that college professors might not be so adequate either. In California, professors of reading at state universities must submit their course syllabi to a state department of education for approval of content.

These messages of schoolhouse inadequacy are nothing new. Remember *A Nation At Risk?* In that 1983 document, business leaders used their political clout to make a statement of doom and gloom: "If an unfriendly foreign power had attempted to impose on America the mediocre educational performance that exists today, we might well have viewed it as an act of war."

Corporate-politicos demanded more science, more mathematics, more computer science, more foreign language, more homework, more rigorous courses, more time on task, and more money for teachers. As noted researcher Gerald Bracey (2003) has observed, this is hardly the stuff of revolution. And even those mundane recommendations were based on a set of allegations of national risk that Peter Applebome of the *New York Times* later called "brilliant propaganda." Bracey summarizes the report as "a veritable treasury of slanted, spun, and distorted statistics." The global competitiveness of the United States tied to how well 13-years-olds bubbled in test answer sheets. And despite the dire predictions of national economic collapse without immediate education reform, the national productivity soared after the predictions were made. Did the schools get credit? Of course not. As Bracey documents, school bashing never stopped.

> [W]e must recognize that good news about public schools serves no one's reform agenda—even if it does make teachers, students, parents, and administrators feel a little better. Conservatives want vouchers and tuition tax credits; liberals want more resources for schools; free marketers want to privatize the schools and make money; fundamentalists want to teach religion and not worry about the First Amendment; Catholic schools want to stanch their student hemorrhage; home-schooling advocates want just that; and various groups no doubt just want to be with "their own kind." All groups believe that they will improve their chances of getting what they want if they pummel the public (Bracey, 2003, p. 616).

The tragedy of all this is that teachers, isolated as they are in their work, often accept the corporate message of inadequacy and, in so doing, allow themselves to become deprofessionalized. One way for teachers to break out of their isolation is to understand the meaning of the assault on public education and to become active in a struggle against corporate power. Particularly in the face of No Child Left Behind (NCLB), this is a mission we need now more than ever. We need it for our profession. We need it for our students.

EDUCATING KIDS FOR JOBS IN THE 21ST CENTURY

The Standardisto headlines screaming about the high skills needed for jobs in the 21st century are a scam. In reality, jobs of the 21st century are not different from those of the 20th century. All one has to do is to check the projections of the U.S. Bureau of Labor Statistics for 2010:

- 22% of jobs will require four years of college.
- 9% of jobs will require an AA degree—some technical training.

Our new economy creates many more unskilled than skilled jobs and, at the same time, it creates even more horrific income differences between the wealthy and the working classes. The shame of our nation is not that lots of young people choose to go to work instead of to college. The shame is that their honorable work, work that provides the glue holding our society together, does not pay them a living wage. As noted research associate of the Economic Policy Institute and visiting professor at Teachers College, Columbia University, Richard Rothstein, has pointed out, no matter how many fourth graders pass the test, it will not raise the minimum wage.

Speaking at Middlebury College in the spring of 2003, Richard Rothstein recounted renting a car at Enterprise Car Rental. Talking to the clerk who checks cars in and out, he learned that her position requires a college degree—for no good reason other than with a tight job market, employers can makes this demand. It did not take a souped-up global economy to put English majors in this bind. With a master's degree in medieval literature, I landed a job at a Madison Avenue address because I could type 85 WPM. That job paid a nickel above minimum wage. My boss, an egotistical luminary, liked bragging that his gofer had a master's degree from the University of California. The fact that I took the job did not make my degree necessary to do the job, any more than those pizza delivery persons with college degrees are using their education.

Sometimes you take a job because you need a job. In *A Working Stiff's Manifesto: A Memoir of Thirty Jobs I Quit, Nine That Fired Me, and Three I Can't Remember,* Iain Levison (2002) adds a footnote to the conventional wisdom that you are unemployable without a college degree: "That you are often unemployable with one is something a lot of people spend a lot of money to discover."

On Labor Day 2003, NPR's *The Connection* aired a program titled "The Democratization of Unemployment," documenting that the white-collar worker, the person with a college degree, is "every bit as vulnerable as others with less education." Writing in *Fortune* in June 2003, Nelson D. Schwartz noted, "Of the nine million Americans out of a job, 17.4% are managers or specialty workers … ." They should ask the Business Roundtable, Education Trust, Progressive Policy Institute, and all the other outfits pushing algebra as the gateway to success why their high-skill diplomas have not kept them employed. In information technology, to name just one area, we have lost 11% of the jobs that existed in February 2001.

Standardistos deliberately confuse technology with skill. In reality, technology deskills jobs as well as upgrades them. Take the clerk who passes your grocery items over the scanner so that they can tote up automatically in the cash register. I grew up hearing my Dad's stories of clerking at Piggy Wiggly. Every week he would walk through the store, memorizing price changes. He took great pride in knowing all the new prices as he rang up purchases. Today, Dad's job would be considered *unskilled*, but the clerk using the scanner would be classified as *skilled*.

The school reform model trumpeted by the Business Roundtable and its political cronies is based on a false economic model, and it cannot succeed. And it is not supposed to. When corporate moguls shop the world for cheap labor, we get an economy of meanness. If we had labor sections in our newspapers, the way we have business sections, the great global economy phenomenon—what corporate moguls call *outsourcing of jobs to foreign lands*—would be tagged as un-American. Certainly, a more honest descriptor would be *increase the company profits*. However, deceptive rhetoric goes unchallenged. At a press conference on July 20, 2003, when President Bush was asked about jobs being shipped overseas, he replied "As technology races through the country, workers' skills don't keep up … ." The name of the game is *blame the victim*. It marches along with *blame the schools*. The reason people are unemployed is because rotten schools have not provided kids with skills.

The 1990 report from the Commission on the Future of the American Workforce titled its report: *America's Choice: High Skills or Low Wages!* Robert Kuttner, cofounder and coeditor of *The American Prospect*, says a better title would have been: *America's Choice: High Skills and Low Wages!* In his book *Everything for Sale: The Virtues and Limits of Markets* (1998), Kuttner points out, "The skills gap is largely a mirage … millions of people who are literate and numerate and offer good work habits still receive dismal wages … except at the very top, workers are being compensated less generously for the skills they have." Iain Levison observes, "If you ask the rich why you're not capable of supporting yourself, they'll tell you it is your fault. The ones who make it to the lifeboats always think the ones in the water are to blame." Anyone who thinks the working poor are to blame for their condition should read Barbara Ehrenreich's (2001) *Nickel and Dimed*. It will change your life. This is the business plan for the schools: students and teachers should take the blame for an economy of greed. As Jeff Gates (no relation to Bill) points out in *Democracy at Risk: Rescuing Main Street from Wall Street* (2001), in 1998, the top-earning 1% of Americans had as much income as the lowest earning 100 million Americans. This is way beyond that adage "the rich get richer."

NCLB: HUBRIS ON SPEED

"The ESEA [renamed No Child Left Behind Act] is like a Russian novel. That's because it's long, it's complicated, and in the end, everybody gets killed" (Scott Howard, Superintendent of Public Schools, Perry, Ohio).

At the same time they are shipping jobs overseas, the Business Roundtable wants proof that all students are moving along a conveyor belt of skills toward a workforce for the global economy. And what the Business Roundtable wants, the U.S. Congress and the U.S. Department of Education deliver. The overwhelming Congressional endorsement of NCLB offers proof that the Business Roundtable gets a good bang for its lobbying buck—from January 1999 through December 2002, they tossed $51.3 million into Congressional briefcases.

If you ignore the increasing number of children living in poverty—without adequate healthcare, housing, or food—then the NCLB slogan, hijacked from the Children's Defense fund, sounds high-minded. The press and the public responded positively to the sentiment—until the devastating consequences of failure to measure up to Olympian imperatives started rolling in. Then the blame bandwagons swing into action. Across the country, schools well respected in their communities received scarlet letters. Hundreds of schools in Florida, highly rated by state guidelines, flunked the federal formula. Only 22% of the schools that earned A+ in Florida's ranking system escaped the NCLB criteria. Across Florida, only 13% of the schools measured up to NCLB criteria. Does anybody really believe that 87% of the schools are failing?

Of late, some Democrats have been saying that they would never have voted for NCLB if they had known that the feds were going to skimp on funding. That is a cheap and hollow sop to people who care about the future of public education. Even with full funding, NCLB, a fiat for perfection, dooms public schools to failure. A *Gotcha!* setup from the get-go; eventually, everybody will fail. Everybody. When schools are held responsible for 100% success, then no amount of money can prevent failure. Gerald Bracey terms NCLB a "weapon of mass destruction and its target is the public schools." Vermont Senator James Jeffers sees NCLB as "a backdoor to anything that will let the private sector take over public education."

Students with the lowest scores get first choice for moving out of a labeled school; so one can imagine a not-implausible scenario of the arrival of low-scoring students causing a receiving school's Adequate Yearly Progress (AYP) to tank, and the absence of those same students causing the sending school's AYP to move into positive territory. Then, the bus can reverse direction, with the sending school becoming the recipient. Just keep moving those low scorers around. Such a scheme looks at schools, not as social institutions that are integral parts of the communities they serve, but as interchangeable skill delivery systems.

A July press release from the Business Roundtable quotes Joseph Tucci, President and CEO of EMC Corporation and Chairman of The Business Round-table's Education and the Workface Task Force: "You can't manage what you don't measure. No executive can run a business without accurate, granular data that explains what's working and what's not. Our school systems should be no different. Better reporting of student performance will allow educators, parents and policymakers to see where we need to improve and by how much." Longtime teachers could tell Mr. Tucci to go soak his head in a bucket, that schools are a hell of a lot different from business, and vive la difference. Teachers can and must teach many things that cannot be measured, and granular data be damned. Note that in France it is illegal to make public the scores of individual schools.

If raising standardized test scores is the object, then schools should try two cheap and easy ways to get poor kids to perform better:

- Fix their teeth
- Reduce the lead levels in their homes

I have long been haunted by a Richard Rothstein column in the *New York Times*, in which he pointed out that the easiest and cheapest way to raise test scores is to provide breakfast at a cost of $1 a day. Poor kids suffer more than middle-class kids from anemia, which is known to cause cognitive difficulties, and therefore breakfast would alleviate the problem.

We do not hear the voices of concerned politicians calling out, "Leave no child unfed!"

Such solutions are ignored, because this whole corporate-politico operation is not about caring for children but about molding a workforce to be scared and compliant, about convincing tomorrow's workers for a global economy at an early age that they are not good enough, and that they do not measure up.

In Birmingham, Alabama, Steve Orel knows about blaming students. Steve discovered that between February 15, 2000 (40th day of the second semester when districts receive per capita funding for the rest of the semester), and April 15, 2000 (the first day that the SAT 9 was administered), 522 African American high schoolers were pushed out of Birmingham high schools with the official computer-printed reason: lack of interest. The students showed so much lack of interest that they were trying to sign up for an adult general equivalency degree (GED) program. Birmingham high schools were in danger of being taken over by the state if they did not raise their test scores. Obviously, when a district is anxious to raise scores, getting rid of low scorers seems easier than feeding them.

When Steve wrote a paper about his findings, the school district shut down the GED program where he worked. And the World of Opportunity (WOO) was born as a social justice and civil rights educational and job readiness program open to everybody who comes. When I sent Rothstein's column to Steve, he replied:

We've been trying to have dehydrated noodle soup around. Someone donated a microwave. Just add water, and you've got noodle soup. We haven't bothered to test folks before and after they eat. But, this much I can tell you. The students sit back, relaxed, carefully taking care of each noodle. One hand on a cup of noodles, the other with a pencil in it. Sure, our books have a few soup stains. It used to be that especially the young men would get up at 10:50 and disappear up to the neighborhood mom and pop store, and, on a good day, return 20 minutes later. Now, the students are engaged in their studies for the whole two hour session. They are engaged in their noodles too. About 30 cents a pack. We've been doing it for free but we are going to have to charge for them because the World of Opportunity funds have been closed out; temporarily, we hope.

It is difficult to articulate the outrage of the richest country on the entire planet allowing a significant number of its youth to go hungry—hungry for nutrition and hungry for an education. To feed our kids is a handout, but to pour millions into banking scams, the airline industry, and so on, is capitalistic free-for-all. How many packages of dried noodle soup could one buy with a $1.3 trillion tax rebate?

There is a whole lot more to the WOO than noodle soup. Run by a fellow who is living out a belief in civil rights, with financial and spiritual help of the local community, and dedicated volunteers from all walks of life, the WOO is pretty much ignored by the Birmingham press. Politics is not only local; it is also tricky, and the WOO's successes are a definite embarrassment to the school establishment and their political cronies. Guided and mentored by the WOO, a student shunned *for lack of interest* scored 100% on the GED and is now enrolled in the honors program at the University of Alabama. Many others are in college or in jobs for which they received skill training at the WOO.

When a group of activist resisters to high-stakes testing traveled to Birmingham to honor the WOO—with the Courage in Education award and a check representing donations from every state in the union—and to plan strategies of resistance, the CD *No Child Left Behind: Bring Back the Joy* was the result. The CD features 15 songs written by teachers and performed by musicians ranging from 12-year-old Lillie Kryzanek to Tom Chapin. One songwriter is an El Paso first-grade teacher afraid for her job if her identity becomes known.

This CD invites people across America to join hands and sing out loudly for kindergartners who have lost nap time, second graders who have lost recess, third graders terrified of not advancing to fourth grade, fifth graders who have lost science and social studies to test prep, and high schoolers denied a diploma because they flubbed one test. There is people power in these songs. Join hands and sing out against the destructive mandates of the federal government's NCLB Act. Sing out loud. Sing often. For more information, contact the author at: susano@gmavt.net or go to http://www.susaniohanian.org/bbtj.html. You can hear music excerpts and order online at http://www.cdbaby.com/cd/dhbdrake4.

Proceeds from this CD go to the WOO to help students still locked out of an education by a mania for high-stakes testing. But the message of this CD is for all teachers and children: Singing these songs will help us take back to our classrooms and our profession. Singing these songs will free the children.

LETTERS MINGLE SOULS[1]

When I told Michael's class we were going to exchange notes every day, they looked at me as though I was nuts. Why would they write me a note when I was standing right there? None complained louder than Michael, and yet he became the most avid note writer, even taking the spiral-bound notebook in which we exchanged notes on vacation, to write to me every day. Michael's notes were messy and horribly spelled, but they revealed a humor, wit, and compassion lovely to behold. When I complained about shoveling the sidewalk and driving on icy streets in my note, Michael advised, "I just take the months as they come."

As spring approached, I began to ask students for the first signs of spring, confessing that for me the asparagus ads in the paper are a sure sign that winter is loosening its strong grip. The kids, of course, thought that was a hoot, such a teacherly thing to say. But they began to watch the paper, competing for who could find the best asparagus bargain for Ms. O. They would tear out ads and leave them on my desk. Michael won the contest. One day he walked in and announced he was going to type his note:

Dear Mrs. O.

As you no I want to Boston firday. It was a lot a fun. Wen I first got to Boston we drov aron looking of a parking plas. We fon one and then we got out of the car. We walk to a fance market and had a bite to aet.

Then we went to the aquarium and that was eciting. There was a shoe with dolphins ands seals. Wan we got we want by a fruit markt. I thogt of you and chekt the pric of asprgus. It is $1.00 a lb in Boston and 3 heds of letis for $1.00. Boston is a long way to go for asprgus tho.

Your frend,

Michael

The week before his graduation from eighth grade, Michael's mother sent me a letter. "I was going to phone you," she wrote, "but Michael told me to write a letter. He says when you care about someone and you have something important to tell them, you write it in a letter … ."

I read Michael's asparagus letter every time I give a talk. I do this because it puts my professional values on display. Yes, despite all our hard work on spelling, Michael remains a rotten speller. But anyone who cannot look beyond this rotten spelling and see the humor and wit, the responsiveness to his audience (Imagine a seventh-grade rotten reader going to this trouble for a teacher! Michael told me his family thought he was nuts when he said he had an urgent need to go into a vegetable market for Ms. O.), should not be making decisions about the education of children. A teacher who is a professional must be erudite and smart; she must also be a model for treating children well. The scary thing about teaching is that every minute of every day we teach who we are. Every minute of every day.

I told Michael's story and read his letter one night at the State University of New York at Albany. Afterward, a teacher came up. She lives next door to Michael's parents, and she tells me Michael is now a big-time chef in an upscale restaurant in Connecticut. I wonder if our asparagus connection gives me the right to claim partial credit for Michael's success. In *Caught in the Middle: Non-standard Kids and a Killing Curriculum*, a book about Michael and his classmates (Ohanian, 2001), Michael gets a chapter of his own; where I recount his struggle to become an independent learner. I cannot tell you his standardized test scores, but I can tell you that Michael learned that he could find out about duck-billed platypuses on his own. He learned that words count, and that carefully chosen words give joy that will last. He even learned that the book is better than the TV show. When he visited class 3 years after his graduation to tell me this, he said, "I bet you never thought you'd hear me say such a thing."

And, of course, Michael learned that when you care about someone you write them a letter. I think these are far finer talents than the ability to circle *a, b, c,* or *d* on anybody's test. But the terrible thing is that if Michael were in New York State's schools today, he would not do well on Regents Exam essays by Roger Ascham or on algebra questions. Denied a high school diploma, he would not be able to get a job as an automobile mechanic; baker; broadcast technician; cardiology technologist; communications dispatcher; electroneurodiagnostic technologist; fingerprint classifier; forklift operator; graphics designer; heating, air-conditioning, and refrigeration mechanic; hotel desk clerk; land surveyor; legal secretary; medical transcriptionist; numerical control machinist; optometric technician; paramedic; plumber; robotics technician; sheet metal worker; short-hand reporter or court reporter; solar energy system installer; small appliance repairer; surgical technician; tool and die maker; translator or interpreter; veterinary technician; ward clerk (medical); Web page designer; and so on.

Without that high school diploma, Michael could not be a chef.

Read that list again. How many of these occupations would you like to eliminate as not necessary or useful in your life? How about carpenters, gardeners, stone wall builders? Poet Jane Hirschfield writes that she envies those who make something useful,

Or those who fix, perhaps
A leaking window:
Strip out the old cracked putty
Lay down cleanly the line of the new. (Hirschfield, 2001)

The Standardisto denigration of the jobs of people who know how to make things and fix things will wreak terrible havoc on us all.

SHOULD A MIAMI TEENAGER HAVE TO DECONSTRUCT A POETIC ACCOUNT OF TRACKING MOOSE IN ALASKA TO GET A HIGH SCHOOL DIPLOMA?

Test scores do not count for much in the real world. They do not predict success on the job. They do not predict wages. The do not even predict success in college beyond freshman year. And yet, we are letting these tests destroy our curriculum, destroy our very professional lives. Tests should come with a warning label. Parents should have to sign a statement that they have read this warning label before their children can be tested:

WARNING: Experts on child development have determined:

- This test may cause your child to vomit, have palpitations, nightmares, and school phobia.
- This test will make your child feel insecure, ignorant, and helpless.
- This test will distort your child's understanding of why people read.
- This test has no academic value. Nobody but $8-an-hour test correctors get to see your child's answers.
- By definition, 50% of the children who take this test must score below average.
- Because of this test, your child will no longer have recess.
- Because of this test, you will become the warden of homework mania.
- By taking this test, your child becomes the property of the state.

Teachers have been too silent about test questions for too long. I collect outrageous questions on my Web site (http://www.susanohanian.org) and urge teachers to send in more. An extremely significant result came from the unprecedented "copyright infringement" lawsuit brought by the Chicago School Board against George Schmidt and *Substance*, the education newspaper he publishes. Richard Posner, judge on the 7th Circuit Court of Appeals, ruled that Schmidt was in error for publishing whole tests, but that "the law recognizes as proper" for people to publish individual test questions when the intent is to make critical appraisal of the copyrighted work (www.ca7.uscourts.gov). In Posner's words: "Judges must not police criticism with a heavy hand." So send *Substance* loony test questions you encounter. (You may send them at the following address: *Substance*, 5132 Berteau Ave, Chicago, IL 60641-1440.) Include $16 for a subscription. We must support those who are fighting for students and teachers.

The following is a test item from Florida. (Note: This is what is known as a *sample* item. This actual item may or may not have ever been used on a Florida test. However, Florida authorities think it is good enough to post as an exemplar of the type of loony items that are found on their tests.) For starters, the test item writers cannot decide whether this piece of prose is a story or an essay, and things go downhill from there. Most objectionable is the fact that this type of questioning goes against everything we know about why people read or what they hope to get out of what they read.

I sent the questions to the author of the passage (who is a professor at the University of Alaska). Here is his response:

Dear Susan,

Thank you for the very weird pages from Florida education. I could hardly believe what I read, and then simply laughed. I gave copies to my students, and they laughed too! What is going on here? Education? I don't think so.

My regards,

John Haines

Here is the test item:

This story [sic] is a sample of the Florida Comprehensive Assessment Test reading exam for the 10th grade. After reading the story [sic], answer the six questions that follow. [What follows is billed as an adaptation of "Snow," from The *Stars, The Snow, The Fire: Twenty-Five Years in the Alaska Wilderness* by John Haines. www.firn.edu]

Snow

By John Haines

To one who lives in the snow and watches it day by day, it is a book to be read.

The pages turn as the winds blow; the characters shift and the images formed by their combinations change in meaning, but the language remains the same. It is a shadow language, spoken by things that have gone by and will come again. The same text has been written there for thousands of years, though I was not here, and will not be here in winters to come, to read it. These seemingly random ways, these paths, these beds, these footprints, these hard, round pellets in the snow: they all have meaning. Dark things may be written there, news of other lives, their sorties and excursions, their terrors and deaths.

I was walking home from Redmond Creek one morning late in January. On a divide between two watersheds, I came upon the scene of a battle between a moose and three wolves. The story was written plainly in the snow at my feet. The wolves had come in from the west, following an old trail from the Salcha River, and had found the moose feeding in an open stretch of the overgrown road I was walking.

The sign was fresh, it must have happened the night before .... [passage continues]

Questions. Base your answers on "Snow."

1. What does the author mean by this sentence from the essay?
   These seemingly random ways, these paths, these beds, these footprints, these hard, round pellets in the snow: they all have meaning.
   a.   Signs in the snow lead to different interpretations of the truth
   b.   Signs in the snow lead to different directions in the wilderness
   c.   Patterns in the snow can be connected to form a story of nature
   d.   Patterns in the snow can be connected to lead the observer to safety
   Objective: Student selects and uses strategies to understand words and text, and to make and confirm inferences from what is read.

2. According to the author, which word best describes the story of snow?
   a.   Frightening
   b.   Random
   c.   Timeless
   d.   Violent
   Objective: Student determines the main idea and identifies relevant details, methods of development, and their effectiveness in a variety of types of written material.

3. Which writing strategy does the author employ to express his views about snow?
   a.   Use of complex plot
   b.   Use of descriptive language
   c.   Development of varied structure
   d.   Development of believable characters
   Objective: Student determines the main idea and identifies relevant details, method of development, and their effectiveness in a variety of types of written material.

4. After examining the moose's tracks, the author concluded that the moose was
   a. Cold
   b. Confused
   c. Large
   d. Weak
   Objective: Student recognizes causes-and-effect relationships in literary texts.

5. How does the author create suspense in relating the story about the animals in the snow?
   a. By holding back information
   b. By constantly updating the plot
   c. Through detailed description
   d. Through frequent use of adjectives
   Objective: Student analyzes the effectiveness of complex elements of plot, such as setting, major events, problem, conflicts, and resolutions.

6. What is the mood of the opening and closing paragraphs?
   a. Chaotic
   b. Curious
   c. Forlorn
   d. Thoughtful
   Objective: Student analyzes the effectiveness of complex elements of plot, such as setting, major events, problems, conflicts, and resolutions.

Pardon me, but does the Florida State Department of Education really decree that essays have "plots" which include such "complex elements" as "setting, major events, problems, conflicts, and resolutions?" Is E.B. White rolling over in his grave? Do the people who write these test questions read anything besides state standards documents?

Clearly, students perform poorly because they are being asked to do the wrong things. A modest proposal: Let us camp out in offices of Standardistos—the politicos, corporate leaders, media, and educationists—and insist that they take the test, with prior warning that we are going to publicize the results. And we publicize the names of the refuseniks.

We also must make public the names of publishers and authors who allow their work to be distorted and dishonored by use on standardized tests that hurt children. Publishers from Cobblestone to the National Council of Teachers of English are guilty of allowing work appearing in their journals to be misused this way. Assuming they were paid by test publishers, surely it must be regarded as

Judas money. Test producers gobble up everything from Nathaniel Hawthorne's "Young Goodman Brown" to Paula Danziger's ever-popular *Amber Brown*. It is surprising how much adult work makes it into test—from Robert Hayden's poetry to Russell Baker's memoir. Ask yourself how appropriate it is that a Latino kid in Los Angeles taking the California Exit Exam is interrogated on the work of Gretel Ehrlich, known as the Whitman of Wyoming. Maya Angelou is an author favored by Standardistos, her work appearing in numerous state tests. As professionals, we need to document how badly used all this work is. We have always had the responsibility to do this. Now, thanks to George Schmidt, we also have the right.

RESIST MUCH, OBEY LITTLE[2]

I entered teaching without preparation (no student teaching) quite literally in the middle of someone else's lesson plan. In those days, New York City suffered a critical shortage of English teachers. I answered an ad in the *New York Times*, passed a test and an interview, and in mid-October found myself teaching 9th and 10th grades in a high school larger than my hometown. I was lucky enough to have a very helpful department chair, who visited my classroom once a week. He would watch the lesson, and then later give me a practical tip for reducing chaos.

I based my formal show-and-tell lesson, performed for official evaluation, on *Julius Caesar*, and my boss said everything went pretty well. He did add, however, that he was bothered by the presence of the girl in the back of the room who read a newspaper throughout the lesson. He said at one point he leaned across the aisle and asked, "Don't you think you should put down that paper and pay attention to what your teacher is saying?"

She replied, "Who the hell are you? If she wants me to put down the paper, let *her* tell me." And she continued reading.

I took a deep breath and said, "Well, when you think about it, who the hell *are* you? I made a mistake. I didn't introduce you. So, all these kids know is that some guy in a sports coat and carrying a briefcase is in the room writing furiously in a binder. More importantly, you don't know who they are. You don't know that Donna has been truant all year. She comes to class to read the *Daily News*, which I buy for her. This isn't where I plan to leave her—sitting back there reading the paper. But it's a beginning. She *is* coming to class."

As I look back over the years, I am very proud of that young teacher. I am proud that she had the guts to assert her professionalism, green though it was. After all, professionalism unnourished will wither and die. I look at that young green teacher, and I wonder why teachers today are so silent, so willing to be trampled on. I wonder why they are willing to see their very professional selves reduced to dust.

George Orwell insisted that "in a time of universal deceit, telling the truth is a revolutionary act." You cannot tell the truth while keeping your mouth shut. We must take back our profession. We must stand up and say, "Who the hell are you?"

REFERENCES

Bracey, G. (2003). April foolishness: The 20th anniversary of a nation at risk. *Phi Delta Kappan, 84*(8), 616–621.

Ehrenreich, B. (2001). *Nickel and dimed.* New York: Henry Holt.

Gates, J. (2001). *Democracy at risk: Rescuing Main Street from Wall Street.* Cambridge, MA: Perseus.

Hirschfield, J. (2001). Mathematics. In *Given sugar, given salt.* New York: Harper Collins.

Kuttner, R. (1998). *Everything for sale: The virtues and limits of markets.* New York: Knopf.

Levison, I. (2002). *A working stiff's manifesto.* New York: Random House.

Moskowitz, E. (2003). http://64.233.161.104/search?q=cache:ukRR1N1_4CUJ:www.evamoskowitz.com/docs/iep.pdf+%22teacher+and+principal+morale%22+New+York+City&hl=en.

Ohanian, S. (2001). *Caught in the middle: Nonstandard kids and a killing curriculum.* Portsmouth, NH: Heinemann.

Ohanian, S. http://www.susanohanian.org.

http://www.ca7.uscourts/op3.fwx?submit=showop&caseno=03-1479.pdf.

http://www.firn.edu/doe/sas/fcat/pdf/fc2005rb10.pdf.

NOTES

1. John Donne, verse letter to Sir Henry Wotton (1597–1598).
2. Walt Whitman,

Finding the Missing Child in NCLB: Pushing against the Compassionate Conservative Agenda

HELEN L. JOHNSON

The current controversy over conceptualizing reform in American education generally, and the No Child Left Behind (NCLB) legislation specifically, reflects fundamental political and social divides in this country. There is general consensus on the need for reform. Exactly what needs to be "reformed" or "made better," though, is viewed quite differently by various constituencies.

The compassionate conservative agenda seeks to improve American education by increasing its efficiency and cost-effectiveness through more fully imposing the business model first introduced during the 20th century (Nieto & Johnson, chapter 2 of this volume). From this perspective, the only outcomes worth considering are those that are easily defined and measured as discrete units or quantitative indicators (Scott & Love, chapter 10 of this volume). Decisions about educational programs and policy are driven by considerations of the "bottom line," and bookkeeping is more central to decision making than educational philosophy or theory. The repeated calls for "evidence-based practice" define "evidence" in a narrow, mechanistic way that discredits the experience of seasoned educators working with children. For whom does such restructuring make things better? Certainly not for teachers, who must disavow their professional judgment about what constitutes good practice for the children in their classrooms (Meyer, chapter 6 of this volume) and adhere to a regimen of scripted lessons and standardized assessments (Baghban & Li, chapter 7 of this volume) that does not permit the "reflective practice" emphasized in teacher education. And certainly not for children, whose educational experience has been narrowed to topics and activities covered by local and national tests (Zarnowski, Backner, & Engel, chapter 8 of this volume), and who must endure the pressures of high-stakes testing (P. Johnson, chapter 4 of this volume; Johnson & Johnson, 2002). Indeed, the experiences and perspectives of children are rarely considered in plans for school reform (Bishop & Pflaum, 2005). Discussing "the missing voice in school reform," Bishop and Pflaum suggest that little has changed since 1992, when Erickson and Shultz reported:

> Virtually no research has been done that places student experience at the center of attention. We do not see student interests and their known and unknown fears. (quoted in Bishop & Pflaum, 2005, p. 2)

Once we recognize that compassionate conservatives approach American education as fundamentally a business enterprise, it becomes easier to understand the policies that have been promulgated recently, deriving from two basic premises. First, standardization of process (curriculum) and outcomes (high-stakes testing) will result in economies of scale and fulfillment of the obligation to provide some "credible version" of equitable experience. In this way, while implementing policies that address the economic concerns underlying a business model, compassionate conservatives describe providing "the same" education for all students, regardless of their strengths or needs, as a matter of giving everyone an "equal chance." Second, by definition, attention to individual differences between children and groups is incompatible with the push for greater cost-effectiveness and efficiency of the system. Consequently, the argument for a "one-size-fits-all" approach to educational curriculum and assessment, although often couched in the language of equity, is essentially unresponsive to the varied needs of the diverse population of American schoolchildren. The idea that all children should be given "the same" opportunities is compelling. But the compassionate conservative response to this challenge simply requires all children to jump through the same hoops at the same time, with harsh penalties for children and their schools should they falter. There is no attention to the preparation that is required to make opportunities, or "hoops," accessible to all children. There is also no attention to the possibility that children might achieve and demonstrate equivalent competencies through alternative accomplishments. In this way, the insistence on standardization simply formalizes the longstanding devaluing of the talents and resources of children whose profiles, be it for economic, cultural, or idiosyncratic reasons, fall outside the boundaries of the socioeducational mainstream. And in this way, policies that are touted as ways to address inequities actually reinforce them.

The authors in this volume challenge the compassionate conservative agenda for education. They offer a different vision of what it means to provide an equitable educational experience for all children. After reviewing some keys aspects of these perspectives, this chapter will conclude with an exploration of educational reform that truly has the child at its center.

WHAT IS AUTHENTIC EDUCATIONAL REFORM?

Since the time of Horace Mann, public schools have been charged with preparing children to become good workers and good citizens, and with serving as the vehicle through which successive generations of immigrants could gain entry and mobility in American society. In the early 21st century, these goals have resulted in competing visions of the meaning of educational reform, of what schools should be teaching, and of how teachers should be prepared and evaluated in the classroom.

Salz (introduction to this volume) suggests that the competing visions of educational reform are best understood through Lakoff's bipolar construct of "nurturing" versus "authoritarian/strict father" approaches to public policy. This distinction captures an essential split in the current discourse regarding public policy issues across multiple domains, including health care, services for the elderly, as well as education. Hearkening back to Rousseau, nurturing approaches assert that human beings inherently want to be productive, constructive, and effective, and the mission of education is to "bring forth," or "educe," their essential capacities for competence and creativity. In contrast, authoritarian approaches counter that human beings must be trained to be productive, constructive and effective, and that the mission of education is to inculcate essential content knowledge as well as socially desirable cognitions and behaviors.

Not surprisingly, these contrasting views of human motivation and learning have spawned different, albeit sometimes overlapping, approaches to educational reform. As Imig and Imig (2006) note, "Today we are witnessing the almost paralyzing impact of the so-called teacher wars with sides pitted against sides in an ideological struggle for the future of teaching and teacher preparation" (p. 177). One of the difficulties in the current debates over educational policy and practice is that advocates for both nurturing and authoritarian approaches are using the same terminology, but with different meanings. Consequently, although both sides cite the need for "reform," there is a great variety of views on the scope and nature of what is to be done. The "strict father/essentialists," advocating a teacher-centered approach, focus reform efforts on the improvement of teacher effectiveness, defined in terms of "one who can raise student achievement scores on a variety of norm-referenced and commercially produced tests of student achievement" (Imig & Imig, 2006, p. 177). The "nurturing/progressivists," adopting a child-centered approach, focus reform efforts on providing constructivist education to support the functioning of democracy through public schools

(Scott & Love, chapter 10 of this volume). Clearly, there are many dimensions to the differences between these approaches to reform, ranging from financial and material resources to teacher preparation to assessment and curriculum design. In fact, the authors in this volume present a range of visions and varied perspectives on the nature of meaningful change in American education. Some advocate reform efforts directed toward the deleterious effects of standardized testing on classroom teaching and learning (Baghban & Li, chapter 7, P. Johnson, chapter 4, Malow-Iroff, Benhar, & Martin, chapter 5, Meyer, Chapter 6, Zarnowski, Backner, & Engel, chapter 8); others address enhancing the resources available to support public education (Kirch & Hunter, chapter 9, Samson & Belfield, chapter 3); some focus on instructional approaches within specific curriculum areas such as science (Hammrich & Myers, chapter 11); while still others envision broad systemic change in the teaching-learning community (Ayers, chapter 12, Nieto & H. Johnson, chapter 2, Ohanian, chapter 13, Scott & Love, chapter 10).

COMPASSIONATE CONSERVATISM: CURRENT MYTHS OF EDUCATIONAL REFORM

The current debate over educational reform reflects the highly polarized social and political climate in our country. The social and political contexts of schooling have been transformed by globalization and technology. Concern about the diminishing competitiveness of American students in the global economy has resulted in increasing focus on the preparation of teachers and students in math, science, and technology. Although this trend began with the launching of Sputnik, it has intensified as advances in technology have made outsourcing across international borders cost-efficient and commonplace. As Spring points out (chapter 1 of this volume), however, there is little evidence that the measures being implemented to ensure "good results" and "global competitiveness" actually predict long-term outcomes for student learning and achievement. Spring also cites the lack of longitudinal data indicating that specific educational strategies will produce workers "able to compete for the best paying jobs in the global economy." In line with Spring's argument, Krugman recently offered evidence to the contrary. Discussing the "80–20 fallacy" that suggests "that the 20 percent or so of American workers who have the skills to take advantage of new technology and globalization are pulling away from the 80 percent who don't," Krugman notes that far from supporting this, data actually show a decline of more than 5% in the real earnings of college graduates between 2000 and 2004 (*New York Times*, 2006). Ohanian (chapter 13 of this volume) points out that "our new economy creates many more unskilled than skilled jobs—at the same time that it creates even more horrific income differences between the wealthy and the working class." Ohanian's analysis is strongly supported by the data Krugman reports.

It is apparent, then, that although increasing the nation's global competitiveness may be an appealing goal, it is not a legitimate rationale for the current reform initiatives. The compassionate conservative agenda for educational reform must be examined from this perspective. The paradoxical effects of contemporary educational reform measures are epitomized in the NCLB legislation. Spring (chapter 1 of this volume) describes NCLB as "political fraud." The very title of the legislation misleads the audience about the content and thrust of NCLB. It suggests that the needs of all children will be met, and that the glaring inequalities in educational resources and opportunities will be eliminated. This is indeed a laudable goal for educational reform. As a slogan, it is guaranteed to attract support from those populations who have repeatedly received the short end of the stick in American education. As Nieto and Johnson point out (chapter 2 of this volume), poor and immigrant parents know that their children have not been fully included in the educational system. Too often, these parents have seen their children's academic potential and needs neglected by unresponsive teachers and dismissive administrators. The promises made by NCLB appeal to parents because they promise to hold schools accountable for their children's academic achievement. The deception in this promise is fourfold. First, NCLB reduces accountability to performance on standardized tests, which tap decontextualized and fragmented units of knowledge rather than critical thinking skills. These tests do not give students, especially those with differential preparation and experience, the opportunity to truly show what they know. Second, the negative consequences for poor accountability fall heavily on the students themselves. The impact of high-stakes testing on children's classroom experience (narrowed curriculum, less learner-centered instruction) as well as their academic progress (increased rates of retention and dropout) is profound. Third, the pressure to demonstrate achievement does not automatically translate into improved educational experiences; schools need resources to enhance practice. Johnson and Johnson (2002) quote Donald Anderson, the executive director of the National Community Development Organization:

> A plea for accountability is almost mocking. How can poor school districts achieve the same level of progress when they have no funds to upgrade staff, improve student/teacher ratios, upgrade their facilities or to provide such equipment as computers? (Johnson & Johnson, 2002, p. 190).

Finally, although presented to the public as legislation that would increase educational accountability, NCLB actually is an amalgam of provisions. Spring (chapter 1 of this volume) points out that some of these provisions address concerns of neoconservatives and religious conservatives, including "sections on privatization of school services, the use of faith-based organizations, phonics-based reading instruction, school prayer, English acquisition, traditional American history, and Boy Scout access to public schools." Several of these provisions have already produced significant changes in American public schooling, in directions that are not clearly related to ensuring that no child will be left behind.

IMPACT OF COMPASSIONATE CONSERVATISM ON EDUCATIONAL POLICIES AND PRACTICES

The Bush administration's success in selling this agenda to the public (although as Spring and P. Johnson note in chapters 1 and 4 of this volume, respectively, this has actually been a bipartisan effort over several decades) has been due in large part to the strategy of suggesting that standardization will increase achievement, and that high-stakes testing will ensure accountability of teachers and learners. Although no data are presented to support these principles, they have an intuitive appeal, and the lack of data has not prevented their implementation by an administration purportedly committed to "evidence-based practice."

High-stakes testing has been a critical element in the implementation of NCLB, as well as in the broader public discussion of accountability. This testing provides a cover of fairness and objectivity for educational policies that are fundamentally unfair and biased (Johnson & Johnson, 2002). The essentially punitive nature of such testing runs counter to the substantial body of research evidence on effective motivational strategies for learning (P. Johnson, chapter 4 of this volume). Indeed, the focus of current testing practices seems to be less on ensuring that children can learn successfully than on ensuring that they will suffer consequences when unsuccessful. Children are expected to strive to learn because of "fear of failure," but often, as P. Johnson indicates, they handle this fear by removing themselves, first psychologically and then physically, from the school environment. And so we can understand the increased retention and dropout rates that have been reported (Nieto & Johnson, chapter 2 of this volume)—clear, quantitative evidence of the negative impact of high-stakes testing.

High-stakes testing places great pressure on schools to maximize scoring gains. In response, schools have adopted a variety of practices that, although questionable on educational grounds, make sense financially. Such practices include targeting instruction at those students with the greatest likelihood of score improvement, rather than those with the greatest need (P. Johnson, chapter 4 of this volume). There are also instances in which low-performing students have been encouraged to remain out of school as noted by Ohanian (chapter 13).

One consequence of the high-stakes testing environment is that schools' view of special needs students has been altered. As Malow-Iroff and colleagues report (chapter 5 of this volume), NCLB requirements do not make clear allowances for the special provisions and individualized educational programs (IEPs) for children with special needs that had been mandated by Public Law 101-476 (IDEA). The push for standardization is particularly pernicious when applied in this context, and threatens to undermine the substantial progress that has been made in designing educational experiences to maximize the achievement of differentially prepared children (Malow-Iroff and colleagues, chapter 5 of this volume). Confronted with NCLB policies that fail to acknowledge the special educational challenges their children face, families of special needs children often seek alternatives to public education.

Indeed, NCLB has proved a major boost to efforts to privatize American public education. This point is at the heart of the political fraud Spring discussed (chapter 1 of this volume). For despite the purportedly inclusive educational vision of "leaving no child behind," the legislation in fact will further disadvantage children, schools, and families with the fewest resources. In their account of the invidious impact of high-stakes testing on education in the state of Louisiana, D. Johnson and B. Johnson state:

> Schools in America are unequally funded. If every child in a state is expected to take the same test, every school should have the same proportionate quantity and quality of certified teachers, the same quantity and quality of instructional material and resources, the same school environment in terms of building repair, cleanliness, absence of vermin, the same playground and recreational equipment, and the same support personnel such as counselors and school nurses. Children of poverty have so many strikes against them in their homes, neighborhoods, and daily lives that they must, at the least, have the same in-school advantages as children of the middle classes and the affluent if they are to be held to the same standards as measured by the same standardized tests (Johnson & Johnson, 2002, p. 204).

Yet efforts to achieve more equitable allocation of resources have been repeatedly rebuffed. A striking illustration of this has been the Campaign for Fiscal Equity (CFE; Kirch & Hunter, chapter 9 of this volume), directed at procuring an equitable share of New York State's education funding for the public schools of New York City. Even the court ruling in favor of CFE has not resulted in more equitable resource allocation for education in New York: In the absence of equal resources, what is achieved by insisting on "equal testing"?

Ironically, at the same time as it has insisted on "evidence-based practice," the Bush administration ignores the data that do not support its version of educational reform, such as the findings on academic achievement in charter schools (Samson & Belfield, chapter 3 of this volume). NCLB policies have in fact repeatedly been legitimized through the efforts of lobbyists rather than the data of evaluators or researchers (Samson & Belfield, chapter 3 of this volume). Moreover, at the same time as NCLB policies have pushed the privatization of public schools along, they have also generated a whole new education sector, comprising services related to test prep and remediation (Samson & Belfield, chapter 3 of this volume). Samson and Belfield offer a detailed account of the ways in which NCLB diverts resources from public education at the same time as it raises the standards that public schools must meet. They present a compelling case for viewing NCLB as a "stealth attack," whose ultimate goal is not educational equity but the dismantling of public education.

IMPACT OF COMPASSIONATE CONSERVATISM ON TEACHING AND LEARNING

The precarious condition of public education is reflected in the daily experiences of students and teachers. The push for national standards has been heralded as a way of ensuring more consistency in schools across the country in the content that children learn at different levels of schooling. The standards movement seeks to establish a national set of uniform grade-level standards for content learning for all children. The rationale is that setting the same expectations for all children will promote equitable educational experience, particularly for poor and minority children. But as Ronald A. Wolk, chairman of the board of Editorial Projects in Education, noted recently:

> Now driven by the federal No Child Left Behind legislation, standards-based reform is actually reinforcing the least desirable features of the traditional school: obsession with testing and test prep, inflexibility and inefficient use of time, overemphasis on coverage in curriculum and memorization and increased standardization that offers a one-size-fits-all education to students regardless of their differences (Wolk, 2006, p. 52).

Traditionally, teachers viewed themselves as professionals responsible for creating and implementing curriculum to maximize learning given the strengths and needs of their students. Now, however, their role has been reduced to being faithful implementers of prewritten and prescribed curricula, responsible for keeping the class on schedule (Meyer, chapter 6; Baghban & Li, chapter 7 of this volume). There is almost no opportunity for the extended exploration and elaboration that enables students to link their personal and academic worlds (Meyer, chapter 6 of this volume). Innovative curriculum programs operate outside the regular classroom day (Hammrich & Myers, chapter 11 of this volume). But within the regular classroom experience, there is no opportunity for coverage of subjects that are not part of the high-stakes testing schedule (Zarnowski, Backner, & Engel, chapter 8 of this volume). In fact, as Zarnowski and colleagues report, social studies has all but disappeared from many public schools, surely a puzzling approach to preparing an "educated citizenry."

AUTHENTIC EDUCATIONAL REFORM: WHAT IS TO BE DONE?

In a very real sense, defining authentic educational reform comes down to "the vision thing." Our view of the responsibilities and promise of the educational enterprise shapes the goals we set for reform and the criteria we use to judge its success. As Salz describes (introduction to this volume), the "strict father," authoritarian approach asserts that children learn in response to "sticks"—the threat of serious consequences should students fail to achieve specified outcomes within designated timeframes. "Education" is reduced to a matter of processing—children enter, are exposed to a specified set of predetermined activities, responses are measured, and children leave. This approach takes a similarly mechanistic view of teachers, requiring them to function as unquestioning implementers of curricula and assessments, with no discretion to adapt to the characteristics, interests, and circumstances of the children in their classrooms. The success of both children and teachers is ultimately measured by the children's test scores. This approach is well suited to business models of education—inputs and outcomes are clearly quantified; standardization of parts and processes reduces cost, and thereby maximizes profit. Absent from the "strict father" approach is any meaningful attention to the interests, needs, or experience of the child.

The experience of the child is central in the "nurturing father," or progressive model. The "nurturing father" approach asserts that children learn in response to "carrots"—interesting curricula and materials, inclusive and supportive classroom practices—that draw upon their innate curiosity and mastery motivation. This approach further asserts that teachers will be effective in the classroom when they are treated as professionals, and given autonomy and responsibility for designing effective educational strategies for the children in their classes. The rhetoric of NCLB and the Standardistos, to borrow Ohanian's term, discredits the nurturing approach. Child-centered education is dismissed as out of date and soft on learning. But Ohanian cuts through the rhetoric, pointing out that learning that children connect to their lives is learning that lasts beyond the test date (Ohanian, chapter 13 of this volume). Teachers need to see the individuality of their students to build these connections. One of the most devastating aspects of current high-stakes testing is the way that it constrains the teacher's view of the child. Teachers in my graduate education classes refer to children as "1's" or "2's" or "3's," using test scores instead of names. How do those numbers represent the complexity of characteristics of an individual learner? What does it mean when teachers do not use more than a score to describe a child? As Ayers points out (chapter 12 of this volume):

> To label a student is wrong in both senses of the word: it is immoral, and it is hopelessly stupid, wildly inaccurate. It is immoral to reduce a human being to an object.

It is stupid to try to flatten a three-dimensional, darting, thrusting figure into a one-dimensional thing, because it creates a grotesque misrepresentation ....

Upon closer examination, the current push for standardization is less about educational equity and more about educational control. This disturbing trend has now extended to the college level, where it is embodied in the pressure for accreditation of teacher education programs. D. Johnson and colleagues (2005) highlight the quest for control that underlies the credentialing and accreditation processes currently being foisted on higher education. Building on the seminal work of Illich, Johnson and colleagues (2005) assert that "schooling devoted to achieving standards perpetuates hopelessness" by establishing an elaborate system that controls access. Controlling access does not guarantee the quality of those who make it through. Rather, it limits the range of variability—uniformity of product to maximize efficiency of process. Once again, what is billed as a policy to benefit learners is actually designed to address concerns about productivity within a business model. Unmasked, the compassionate conservative agenda is revealed to be the new, 21st century version of the business model introduced to American education in the mid-1900s (Scott & Love, chapter 10 of this volume). Yes, it's been updated—there's talk now of equity, technology, standards, and, sometimes, multiculturalism, but at its core, this model strives to prepare workers, not thinkers or actively engaged citizens.

The primary educational mission is preparing the individual for a satisfying and productive life. To achieve this,

Children and youths need formative experiences that aid their growth and development along the physical, social-interactive, social-emotional, moral-ethical, linguistic, and cognitive pathways (Comer, 2006, p. 59).

NCLB and high-stakes testing, linchpins of the compassionate conservative agenda, ignore the needs of the individual learner. These policies have had a profoundly negative impact on children's classroom experience (narrowed curriculum and less learner-centered instruction) as well as their academic progress (increased rates of retention and dropout). As Scott and Love recount (chapter 10 of this volume), the model of preparing students to be thoughtful and effective participants in a democratic community has been replaced by one that emphasizes basic skills and compliance.

The push for standardization of learning has been described as an effort to promote equity for all learners by ignoring differences between learners and the resources that they bring to the learning environment. In other words, the playing field is leveled by requiring all students to finish at the same point, regardless of where they started. The appeal of this approach is its seemingly inclusive attitude—too often, schools have lowered expectations for children outside the mainstream culture, and then allocated fewer resources and less effort to their learning. But at a more fundamental level, ignoring what children "bring to school 'in their blood'" (Delpit, 1995) disadvantages children from outside the mainstream in two ways. First, it does not give them the opportunity to use what they *do* know from their experience to demonstrate and further their learning. Second, uniform standards make the repercussions of what children *don't* know more significant to their academic standing.

It is time for us to take back control of our schools. It is time for us to demand that our country, like others in the industrialized world, commit a significant portion of resources and attention to the needs of children, families, and communities. We must challenge the deceptive discourse swirling around education. We must insist that the evidence about what is happening to children in our schools be heard. It is time to shift the conversation about education away from numbers and assigning blame, and refocus on authentic assessment that documents children's progress. We need a discourse about possibility and hope. We also need to respond to the testing and statistics generated by NCLB with concrete evidence of the impact of effective teachers, families, and school–community collaborations.

There are a lot of dedicated teachers reaching out to the children and families in their school communities. Cynthia Carger (2004) documents her work with English language learners, using works of art to open up conversations that connect the languages of school and home. Sonia Nieto (2005, chapter 2 of this volume) quotes Bill Dunn, who is determined to continue teaching despite the pressures and threats of the current climate because he wants to give his students the opportunity know "that poverty does not equal stupidity, and that surviving a bleak, dismal childhood makes you strong and tough and beautiful in ways that only survivors of similar environments can appreciate and understand." Rick Meyer (chapter 6 of this volume) describes the classroom environment created by Kim, which "addressed children's literacy lives with depth, passion, and integrity." Meyer contrasts this with the classroom of Karen, who is forced by a mandated curriculum to ignore what she knows would work best with the children in her classroom. William Ayers (chapter 12 of this volume) describes how second-grade teacher Louisa Cruz-Acosta "tries to create in her classroom an 'island of decency,' a safe harbor where the most fraught issues can be talked about respectfully, candidly, deeply."

There is no shortage of examples of good practice. But somehow, these examples and the evidence of their impact on learning are not acknowledged in the discussion of academic achievement. We must reject the description of learner-centered education as soft and fuzzy. Focusing on the learner does not mean lowering standards. Focusing on the learner is the way to truly ensure that children are not left behind. We are living in a time when words and slogans too often obscure the intention of policy. It is incumbent on us to clear a path through the web of misrepresentations, and insist on an educational agenda that is truly compassionate, one that acknowledges the strengths and needs of all children and families, and reaches out to include them fully in educational opportunity and process.

REFERENCES

Bishop, P.A., & Pflaum, S.W. (2005). *Reaching and teaching middle school learners.* Thousand Oaks, CA: Corwin.

Carger, C.L. (2004). Art and literacy with bilingual children. *Language Arts, 81,* 282–292.

Comer, J.R. (2006, January 5). Our mission: It takes more than tests to prepare the young for success in life. *Education Week, 25*(17), 59–61.

Delpit, L. (1995). I just want to be myself: Discovering what students bring to school "in their blood." In W. Ayers (Ed.). *To become a teacher* (pp. 34–48). New York: Teachers College.

Dodge, K.A., Dishion, T.J., & Lansford, J.E. (2006). Deviant peer influences in intervention and public policy for youth. *Social Policy Report, 20*(1). Retrieved March 27, 2007, from http://www.srcd.org/spr.html.

Eisner, E.W. (2005). Opening a shuttered window: An introduction to a special section on the arts and the intellect. *Phi Delta Kappan, 87,* 8–10.

Imig, D.G., & Imig, S.R. (2006). The teacher effectiveness movement. *Journal of Teacher Education, 57,* 167–180.

Johnson, D.D., & Johnson, B. (2002). *High stakes: Children, testing, and failure in American schools.* Lanham, MD: Rowman & Littlefield.

Johnson, D.D., Johnson, B., Farenga, S.J., & Ness, D. (2005). *Trivializing teacher education: The accreditation squeeze.* Lanham, MD: Rowman & Littlefield.

Wolk, R.A. (2006, January 5). A second front: Betting everything on standards-based reform is neither wise nor necessary. *Education Week, 25*(17), 49–50, 52.

Index